Herbert Reed

The Bills of Sale Acts

Herbert Reed

The Bills of Sale Acts

ISBN/EAN: 9783337402167

Printed in Europe, USA, Canada, Australia, Japan

Cover: Foto ©Suzi / pixelio.de

More available books at **www.hansebooks.com**

THE

BILLS OF SALE ACTS,

WITH AN

EPITOME OF THE LAW

AS AFFECTED BY THE ACTS.

BY

HERBERT REED,

OF THE INNER TEMPLE, ONE OF HER MAJESTY'S COUNSEL.

TENTH EDITION.

LONDON:

WATERLOW BROS. & LAYTON, LIMITED,

24, BIRCHIN LANE, E.C.

1895.

LONDON :

WATERLOW BROS. & LAYTON, LIMITED, PRINTERS,
BIRCHIN LANE, AND BROKEN WHARF
12, UPPER THAMES STREET, E.C.

PREFACE TO THE TENTH EDITION.

It is the object of the following pages to present a short statement of the law of bills of sale, as affected by the Bills of Sale Acts, 1878, 1882, 1890 and 1891. The Acts will be found printed together, as they are to be so construed.

Under each section are collected such cases as involve points of practical importance, and in the interest of those at a distance from reports, a full extract of material facts has been given in dealing with recent decisions. A reference to contemporaneous reports will be found in the first citation of each authority.

In the Appendix will be found the Statutes, Orders, and Rules, relating to bills of sale, together with precedents. To these have been added extracts from bills of sale hitherto contested under section nine, shewing the present judicial views of accordance with the scheduled form.

The decisions throughout the work will be found noted to December, 1894.

H. R.

1, *Temple Gardens,*
    December, 1894.

CONTENTS.

CASES CITED.

THE

BILLS OF SALE ACTS, 1878, 1882, 1890 & 1891.

41 & 42 Vict. c. 31 ; 45 & 46 Vict. c. 43 ; 53 & 54 Vict. c. 53 ;
54 & 55 Vict. c. 35.

AN ACT

TO

CONSOLIDATE AND AMEND THE LAW FOR PREVENTING FRAUDS   **[1878.]**
UPON CREDITORS BY SECRET BILLS OF SALE
OF PERSONAL CHATTELS.

[*22nd July*, 1878.

AND

AN ACT

TO

AMEND THE BILLS OF SALE ACT, 1878.   **[1882.]**

[*18th August*, 1882.

AND

AN ACT

TO

EXEMPT CERTAIN LETTERS OF HYPOTHECATION FROM THE   **[1890.]**
OPERATION OF THE BILLS OF SALE ACT, 1882.

[*18th August*, 1890.

AND

AN ACT

TO

AMEND THE BILLS OF SALE ACT, 1890.   **[1891.]**

[*21st July*, 1891.

WHEREAS it is expedient to consolidate and *Preamble.*
amend the law relating to bills of sale of **[1878.]**
personal chattels :

Be it enacted by the Queen's most Excellent
Majesty, by and with the advice and consent of the
Lords Spiritual and Temporal, and Commons, in this
present Parliament assembled, and by the authority
of the same, as follows :

A

Preamble.

[1882.]

WHEREAS it is expedient to amend the Bills of Sale Act, 1878 :

Be it enacted by the Queen's most Excellent Majesty, by and with the advice and consent of the Lords Spiritual and Temporal, and Commons, in this present Parliament assembled, and by the authority of the same, as follows :

The preamble is said to be, as it were, a key to the understanding of a statute, [a] and the object of the Bills of Sale Acts has been to protect creditors, to give them a true idea of their debtor's position, and to prevent transactions by which a grantor is allowed to retain possession of property which the grantee may at any moment withdraw from the claims of creditors and dispose of as he thinks fit.[b]   The amendment Act, while continuing this protection, is also designed to define the rights of bill of sale holders and borrowers of money, and to protect the latter against inequitable claims.

[1890.]
[1891.]

Be it enacted by the Queen's most Excellent Majesty, by and with the advice and consent of the Lords Spiritual and Temporal, and Commons, in this present Parliament assembled, and by the authority of the same, as follows :—[c]

Short Title.

1. (1878.) This Act may be cited for all purposes as the Bills of Sale Act, 1878.

Short Title.

1. (1882.) This Act may be cited for all purposes as the Bills of Sale Act (1878) Amendment Act, 1882 ; and this Act and the Bills of Sale Act, 1878, may be cited together as the Bills of Sale Acts, 1878 and 1882.

Short Title.

3. (1890.) This Act may be cited as the Bills of Sale Act, 1890.

The Act was passed and came into operation on the 18th August, 1890. It has been amended by the Bills of Sale Act, 1891.

Short Title.

2. (1891.) This Act may be cited as the Bills of Sale Act, 1891.

(a) Co. Litt. 79a. (b) Exp. Sparrow, 2 De G. M. & G. 907. (c) Pages 240, 261 [1890] ; Pages 171, 262 [1891].

2. (1878.) This Act shall come into operation on   Sec. 2.
the first day of January one thousand eight hundred   [1882.]
and seventy-nine, which day is in this Act referred Commencement.
to as the commencement of this Act.

2. (1882.) This Act shall come into operation on Commencement.
the first day of November one thousand eight hundred
and eighty-two, which date is hereinafter referred to
as the commencement of this Act.

3. (1878.) This Act shall apply to every bill of sale Application of Act.
executed on or after the first day of January one
thousand eight hundred and seventy-nine (whether
the same be absolute, or subject or not subject to
any trust), whereby the holder or grantee has power,
either with or without notice, and either immediately
or at any future time, to seize or take possession of
any personal chattels comprised in or made subject
to such bill of sale.

By sec. 23 of the principal Act, any renewal, after the
commencement of the Act, of the registration of a bill of
sale, executed before its commencement, and registered under
the Acts thereby repealed, shall be made under the Act in
the same manner as the renewal of a registration made under
the Act; and the rule of construction enacted by sec. 7 of the
principal Act applies to all deeds or instruments, including
fixtures or growing crops, executed before the commencement
of the Act, and then subsisting and in force, in all questions
arising under any bankruptcy, liquidation, assignment for the
benefit of creditors, or execution of any process of any Court,
which shall take place or be issued after the commencement
of the Act.

The principal Act continues to apply to any bill of
sale duly registered before the 1st of November, 1882, so
long as its registration is not avoided by non-renewal or
otherwise, and to bills of sale executed more than seven days
before the commencement of the amendment Act, but
unregistered. *a*

The principal Act also applies to bills of sale given
otherwise than by way of security for the payment of
money, although executed and registered after the com-

(*a*) Sec. 3 [1882].   A 2

mencement of the amendment Act, for this class of bills of
sale is not affected by that Act.[a]

All bills of sale given on or after the 1st of November,
1882, by way of security for the payment of money, unless
within the exception of Bills of Sale Act, 1891, will be
governed by the amendment Act.

**Who may give
a bill of sale.** It may here be convenient to consider by whom a bill of
sale may be given. Any person with capacity to contract
may become the grantor of chattels personal, but cannot
transfer a right which he himself does not possess, although
if he has a qualified interest in goods, he can charge them to
the extent of that interest. [b]

If a person has obtained goods by fraud, under colour of a
contract intended to transfer to him the property in them,
though he himself could not detain the goods against the real
owner, a *bonâ fide* purchaser or mortgagee who has obtained
possession without notice of the fraud, and before the real
owner interferes to recover them, will have a good title to the
extent of his advances.[c] So by sec. 23, Sale of Goods Act,
1893, when the seller of goods has a voidable title thereto,
but his title has not been avoided at the time of the sale, the
buyer acquires a good title to the goods, provided he buys
them in good faith and without notice of the seller's defect of
title.

If the true owner stands by and allows another to deal with
goods as if he were the owner, and thereby induces a third
party to purchase or make advances upon them, he cannot
afterwards, though he acted under a mistake, claim them from
such third party; [d] although this estoppel would not prevent
seizure of the goods in the hands of the purchaser by an
execution creditor of the true owner,[e] unless the person
dealing with the goods was the true owner's agent.[f] So an
execution creditor may defeat a claimant's title, which the
execution debtor is estopped from denying.[g]

(a) Swift v. Pannell, 24 Ch. D. 210; 53 L. J. Ch. 341; 31 W. R. 543; 48 L. T.
351; Hickson v. Darlow, 31 W. R. 417; 48 L. T. 449; 23 Ch. D. 690; 52 L. J. Ch. 453.
(b) Coote on Mortgages, 5th Ed. 647; Exp. Barnett *re* Tamplin, 7 Mor. 70; 38
W. R. 351; 62 L. T. 264; 59 L. J. Q. B. 194.
(c) Cundy v. Lindsay, 3 App. Cases, 459; 47 L. J. Q. B. 481; 38 L. T. 573;
26 W. R. 406.
(d) Waller v. Drakeford, 1 E. & B. 749; 22 L. J. Q. B. 274; 17 Jur. 853;
Gregg v. Wells, 10 A. & E. 90.
(e) Richards v. Johnston, 4 H. & N. 660; 28 L. J. Ex. 322; 5 Jur. N. S. 520.
(f) Low v. McGill, 12 W. R. 826; 10 L. T. N. S. 495.
(g) Richards v. Jenkins, 18 Q. B. D. 451; 56 L. J. Q. B. 293; 56 L. T. 591;
53 W. R. 355.

By sec. 8, Factors Act, 1889,[a] where a person having sold
goods continues or is in possession of the goods or of the
documents of title to them, the delivery or transfer by that
person, or by a mercantile agent acting for him of the goods
or documents of title under any sale, pledge, or other disposition thereof, or under any agreement for sale, pledge, or
disposition thereof, to any person receiving the same in good
faith and without notice of the previous sale, shall have the
same effect as if the person making the delivery or transfer
were expressly authorized by the owner of the goods to make
the same.

And when a person having bought or agreed to buy *Who may give
a bill of sale.*
goods, obtains with the consent of the seller possession of the
goods or the documents of title to the goods, the delivery or
transfer, by that person or by a mercantile agent acting for
him, of the goods or documents of title, under any sale,
pledge, or other disposition thereof, or under any agreement
for sale, pledge, or other disposition thereof, to any person
receiving the same in good faith and without notice of any
lien or other right of the original seller in respect of the
goods, shall have the same effect as if the person making the
delivery or transfer were a mercantile agent in possession of
the goods or documents of title with the consent of the
owner.[b]

The expression "mercantile agent" is defined by sec. 1
(1), Factors Act, 1889, and his powers with respect to disposition of goods by sec. 2 (1).

Secs. 2, 9 of that Act have been held to protect a purchaser
in good faith, taking delivery of goods from a person in
possession under a hire agreement.[c]

Infants under the age of twenty-one years are clothed with
a qualified power of contracting, but are bound only by contracts which are necessary, and for their benefit and advantage. By ss. 1 and 2 of the Infants' Relief Act, 1874,[d] contracts
by infants to secure the payment of money lent or to be lent,
or goods supplied or to be supplied (other than contracts
for necessaries), are absolutely void, nor is a ratification after
full age, whether made for the same or a fresh consideration,
sufficient.

(a) 52 & 53 Vict. c. 45; see also sec. 25, Sale of Goods Act, 1893.
(b) Factors Act, 1889, sec. 9; Sale of Goods Act, 1893, sec. 25 (2).
(c) Lee v. Butler [1893], 2 Q. B. 318; 69 L. T. 370; 42 W. R. ss.
(d) 37 & 38 Vict. c. 62.

Deeds executed by an infant are voidable at his election,
nor can he be sued on any covenant therein contained; nor
will a mortgage deed be binding on an infant, unless executed
in pursuance of a legal obligation, or accessory to some other
act that the infant was bound to do; thus, a deed executed
by an infant to secure advances made to him for expenditure
for necessaries, whereby he covenanted to repay the same
with interest at the rate of ten per cent. per annum, and
granted and assigned his reversionary interest in certain
chattels to the plaintiff, subject to the usual proviso for
redemption on payment of the principal-money and interest,
was held voidable by him on attaining full age.[a]   However, in
equity, an infant who has by fraudulently misrepresenting his
estate or age obtained a loan upon mortgage, may be estopped
from disputing the mortgage; and as a general rule if an
infant be old enough to commit a fraud by inducing others by
his representations to think that he is of full age, if the Court
cannot restore the parties to their original position, the infant
will be bound as if he were an adult.[b]

Who may give
a bill of sale.   A married woman was incapable of binding herself by a
contract, unless made with reference to and on the faith of her
separate estate, as to which she might contract as freely as a
feme sole, and make it answerable for her engagements;
but it was said she could not give a bill of sale over property
in which she had merely an equitable interest, without
the concurrence of the person having the legal estate;[c]
although an assignment has been supported by a wife, without
her husband's concurrence, of goods to which by ante-nuptial
agreement she was entitled for her separate use.[d]   Now,
however, by the Married Women's Property Act, 1882, any
woman married after the 1st of January, 1883, the date of the
commencement of the Act, may dispose of her separate property
in the same manner as if she were a *feme sole*, without the inter-
vention of any trustee, or if married before the commencement of the Act, may so dispose of property her title to which
accrues after that date.

The contract of a lunatic or drunken person, made when
incapable of understanding its effect, is voidable at his option;

(a) Martin v. Gale, 46 L. J. Ch. 84; 4 Ch. D. 428; 25 W. R. 406; 36 L. T. 357.
(b) Nelson v. Stocker, 4 De G. & J. 458; 5 Jur. N. S. 751.
(c) Chapman v. Knight, 5 C. P. D. 308; 49 L. J. C. P. 425; 42 L. T. 538; 28
W. R. 907.
(d) Walrond v. Goldmann, 16 Q. B. D. 121; 34 W. R. 272; 53 L. T. 903; 55
L. J. Q. B. 323.

unless the other contracting party did not believe, and had
not reasonable cause to believe that he was drunk or of insane
mind; but every person is presumed to be of sound mind
and capable of making an agreement until the contrary
appears.[a]

An executor or administrator can confer a valid title to the Who may give
personalty of his testator by sale, mortgage or pledge, although a bill of sale.
the property may have been specifically bequeathed;[b] nor is it
incumbent on the purchaser or mortgagee to see the money
properly applied, although he knew that he was dealing with
a person acting in a representative capacity;[c] unless the
transaction affords intrinsic evidence that the person selling
or dealing with the property is not acting fairly in the execution of his duty, or unless collusion exists between him and
the purchaser or mortgagee: but it would seem that an
executor or administrator cannot make a valid sale or pledge
of the property of the testator in satisfaction of his own
debt.[c] An executor may make a valid assignment of all his
testator's property to trustees for the benefit of creditors[d]
and may, even before probate, take or give securities for
debts due to or from the deceased, acts so done being good
though he should die before the will has been proved. An
executor de son tort may set up a bill of sale given by the
deceased, although possession was not taken until after the
death.[f]

An execution against the goods of a debtor binds the
property in the goods as from the time when the writ is
delivered to the sheriff to be executed . . . . but shall
not prejudice the title to such goods acquired by any person
in good faith and for valuable consideration, unless such
person had, when he acquired his title, notice that such writ,
or any other writ by virtue of which such goods might be
seized or attached, had been delivered to and remained
unexecuted in the hands of the sheriff.[g] Notwithstanding
an execution, a debtor may sell his goods, but not so as to

(a) Leake on Contracts, 3rd Ed. 501.
(b) Mead v. Orrery, 3 Atk. 239; Scott v. Tyler, 2 Dick., 725.
(c) M'Leod v. Drummond, 17 Ves. 154.
(d) Wolverhampton Co. v. Marston, 7 H. & N. 148; 30 L. J. Ex. 492; 7 Jur.
N. S. 1040; 7 W. R. 700; 7 L. T. 524.
(e) Williams on Executors, 9th Ed. 250.
(f) Webster v. Blackman, 2 F. & F. 400.
(g) Sale of Goods Act, 1893, sec. 26; amending Mercantile Law Amendment
Act, 1856, sec. 1.

defeat the execution creditor's right, the execution constituting
a charge on the goods.[a]

Who may give a bill of sale. As property acquired by an undischarged bankrupt vests
in his trustee,[b] a bankrupt, before discharge, cannot as a rule
give a bill of sale; but all transactions entered into by an
undischarged bankrupt in respect of property acquired after
the bankruptcy, and before the trustee intervenes to claim
it, with a person who proves that he dealt with the bankrupt
in good faith and for value, whether with or without knowledge of the bankruptcy, are valid against the trustee.[c]
So if a bankrupt is permitted to trade and deal with
assets belonging to the estate, or to hold himself out as
the owner of property and raise money upon it, a purchaser
or transferee for value, without notice of the bankruptcy, will
be protected; but a trustee who leaves the bankrupt in possession of property is not by the mere fact of so doing estopped
from setting up his own title, unless the property is such as is
usually held for the purposes of sale.[d] An undischarged
bankrupt to whom furniture has been given by a resolution of
creditors can assign it by bill of sale.[e]

After a scheme of arrangement has been come to by which
an undischarged bankrupt is permitted to carry on his trade,
he may deal with or dispose of his property in the ordinary
course of business, and a bill of sale given to secure advances
made to assist his carrying out the arrangement will be
protected, even in cases where the mortgagee has notice of the
bankruptcy, and of the trustee's power to seize on default;[f]
and after a composition resolution has been approved, a compounding debtor may give a bill of sale over his property, which
will not be affected by fraud in obtaining the resolution.[g]

A bill of sale may be executed under a power of attorney,
and the grantee is not necessarily excluded from being
appointed as the attorney.[h] If the power of attorney is given

(a) Woodland v. Fuller, 11 A. & E. 850.

(b) Bankruptcy Act, 1883, sec. 44 (i).

(c) Cohen v. Mitchell, 25 Q. B. D. 262; 38 W. R. 551; 63 L. T. 206; 59 L. J. Q.
B. 409.

(d) Meggy v. Imperial Discount Co., 3 Q. B. D. 711; 47 L. J. Q. B. 119; 38
L. T. 300; 26 W. R. 342; Exp. Ford, re Caughey, 1 Ch. D. 521; 45 L. J. Bank.
96; 34 L. T. 634; 24 W. R. 590.

(e) Brown v. Hickinbotham, 50 L. J. Q. B. 426.

(f) Exp. Allard, re Simons, 16 Ch. D. 505; 44 L. T. 35; 29 W. R. 406.

(g) Seymour v. Coulson, 5 Q. B. D. 359; 49 L. J. Q. B. 604; 28 W. R. 664;
Exp. Burrell, re Robinson, 1 Ch. D. 537; 45 L. J. Bank, 68; 24 W. R. 353;
34 L. T. 198.

(h) Furnivall v. Hudson [1893], 1 Ch. 335; 41 W. R. 358; 68 L. T. 378; 62. L. J.
Ch. 178.

Sec. 3.
[1878.]

for value, and expressed to be irrevocable in the instrument
creating the power, it will not be revoked by anything done
by the donor of the power without the concurrence of the
donee, or by the death, marriage, lunacy, unsoundness of
mind or bankruptcy of the donor. [a] If a bill of sale is
executed by an agent authorized by parol only, it is said to
bind the principal so far as it is capable of operating otherwise
than as an instrument under seal. [b]

Sec. 3.
[1882.]

3. (1882.) The Bills of Sale Act, 1878, is hereinafter referred to as "the principal Act," and this
Act shall, so far as is consistent with the tenor
thereof, be construed as one with the principal Act;
but unless the context otherwise requires shall not
apply to any bill of sale duly registered before the
commencement of this Act so long as the registration thereof is not avoided by non-renewal or
otherwise.[1]

Construction
of Act.

The expression "bill of sale," and other expressions in this Act, have the same meaning as in the
principal Act, except as to bills of sale or other
documents mentioned in section four of the principal
Act, which may be given otherwise than by way of
security for the payment of money, to which last-
mentioned bills of sale and other documents this
Act shall not apply.[2]

(2) Page 38.

(1) The provisions of sec. 13 of the amendment Act apply to
all bills of sale, whether registered before or after the commencement of the Act; as also does sec. 7. so far as it em-
powers the Court to restrain removal or sale.[c]

Application
of Act.

The words of the section providing that, unless the context
otherwise requires, the Act shall not apply to any bill of sale
duly registered before the commencement of the Act, so long
as registration is not avoided by non-renewal or otherwise, are
by no means easy of construction. It may be that the words
of the section, being only negative, will be held not to apply to
any bill of sale which has been registered before the commence-

(a) Conveyancing Act, 1882, s. 8.
(b) Low c. McGill, 12 W. R. 820.
(c) Exp. Cotton, 11 Q. B. D. 301; 49 L. T. 52; 32 W. R. 58; 47 J. P. 599.

ment of the amendment Act, and that Act has been decided not to be retrospective so as to affect bills of sale executed more than seven days before its commencement;[a] nor does it avoid, as against the grantor, bills of sale duly registered under the Bills of Sale Act, 1854, of which no renewal of registration has been made.[b] It has not been decided which statute is to govern bills of sale executed within seven days before, and registered after, the commencement of the amendment Act.

(2) A definition of what is a bill of sale within the Acts will be found in sec. 4 of the principal Act, with which this section and sec. 3 of the principal Act must be read.

The effect of the exception will in most cases be to exclude from the operation of the amendment Act absolute bills of sale. Two classes of bills of sale would seem thus to be created, those given by way of security for the payment of money being within the scope of the amendment Act, while bills of sale given otherwise than by way of security will still be governed by the principal Act. This is the effect of a decision, by which the section is held to qualify the whole Act.[c]

A deed absolute in form, but in fact given to secure the payment of money, would seem to be within the amendment Act, and void under sec. 9 of that Act.

Absolute and conditional bills of sale.
A bill of sale may be absolute, the property in the articles assigned passing upon the execution of the deed, or conditional by way of mortgage to secure the payment of money at a future day; in which case the property in the goods passes to the grantee, the right of possession remaining in the grantor, who alone can maintain trover until default, when the estate vests in the grantee freed from the condition.[d]

By a bill of sale in the form scheduled to the amendment Act, the property in the chattels assigned passes to the grantee subject to the proviso, and on the happening of any of the events specified in section 7 of that Act, the grantor's right to the chattels ceases, unless an application for relief is made under the proviso to section 7, or proceedings are taken for redemption.[e] And if the mortgagee has a right to imme-

(a) Hickson v. Darlow, 23 Ch. D. 690.

(b) Cookson v. Swire, 9 App. Cases 653; 33 W. R. 181; 52 L. T. 30; 54 L. J. Q. B. 249.

(c) Swift v. Pannell, 24 Ch. D. 210.

(d) Bradley v. Copley, 1 C. B. 685; 14 L. J. C. P. 222; 9 Jur. 599; Wheeler v. Montefiore, 2 Q. B. 133; 6 Jur. 299; 1 G. & D. 493.

(e) Johnson v. Diprose [1893], 1 Q. B. 512; 41 W. R. 371; 62 L. J. Q. B. 291; 8 L. T. 455.

diate possession, though coupled with a trust to permit the
mortgagor to hold until demand, it will be sufficient to enable
him to support an action; thus where goods were assigned as
security for an advance, upon trust to permit the assignor
to remain in possession until default in payment at a stipulated
time, and upon further trust to sell them on such default being
made, the assignee, before any default, was held to have a sufficient right of possession to maintain trover.[a] The possession of
chattels by a *cestui que trust*, in accordance with the provisions
of the trust, being in law the possession of the trustee, the
latter can maintain an action against a wrong-doer for conversion of the chattels.[b]

It has been said that the fair criterion to determine *Absolute and conditional bills of sale.*
whether a transaction be a mortgage or not, is whether the
remedies are mutual and reciprocal; but in every case the
question is what, upon a fair construction, is the meaning of
the instrument; and the true nature and not the form of the
transaction is to be regarded;[c] thus a bill of sale, absolute in
form, will be within the amendment Act if the real intention
was that the property should be held as a security for the payment of money;[d] so, if there be evidence of the non-execution
or erasure, by mistake or fraud, of an intended defeasance,
or proviso for redemption; or if there be a separate defeasance
or agreement for a right of redemption, the transaction will
be treated as a mortgage. There may also be taken into consideration recitals in other instruments, payment of interest,
the inadequacy of the money paid to the value of the property,
the fact that the grantee has or has not taken immediate
possession under the assignment, payment by him or by the
grantor of the expenses, insurances, or other outgoings, and
other circumstances tending to shew that the assignment
was intended to be redeemable.[e]

Apart from any question under the Bills of Sale Acts, it
has been decided that if a mortgage has been fraudulently made to appear as an absolute conveyance, it will not
be rectified at the instance of those concerned in the fraud;[f]

(a) White v. Morris, 11 C. B. 1015; 16 Jur. 500; 21 L. J. C. P. 185.
(b) Barker v. Furlong [1891], 2 Ch. 172; 60 L. J. Ch. 636; 64 L. T. 411; 39 W. R.
621.
(c) *Re* Watson, 25 Q. B. D. 27; 38 W. R. 567; 59 L. J. Q. B. 394; 7 Mor. 155;
63 L. T. 209.
(d) Madell v. Thomas [1891], 1 Q. B. 230; 60 L. J. Q. B. 227; 64 L. T. 9; 9
W. R. 280.
(e) Fisher on Mortgages, 4th ed. 10.
(f) Baldwin v. Cawthorne, 19 Ves. 166.

Sec. 4.
[1878.]

and where there has been an absolute sale with a right of repurchase, such right must be exercised according to the strict
terms of the bargain between the parties, a right of repurchase being very different from an equity of redemption.[a]
For an absolute conveyance, containing nothing to show that
the relation of debtor and creditor is to exist between the
parties, does not cease to be an actual conveyance and become
a mortgage merely because the vendor stipulates that he
shall have a right to repurchase.[b]

It would appear that by the section post-nuptial settlements will, in most cases, be excluded from the operation of
the amendment Act. Post-nuptial settlements of chattels
were bills of sale within the repealed Acts, and required
registration; and now, when not given by way of security
for the payment of money, would seem to be governed by the
provisions of the principal Act. If given as security for the
payment of money they would appear within the amendment
Act, but having regard to sec. 9 great difficulty will be ex-
perienced in affording satisfactory protection.

Interpretation
of terms.

4. (1878.) In this Act the following words and
expressions shall have the meanings in this section
assigned to them respectively, unless there be something in the subject or context repugnant to such
construction; (that is to say),

The expression " bill of sale " shall include bills
of sale, assignments, transfers, declarations of
trust without transfer, inventories of goods
with receipt thereto attached, or receipts for
purchase moneys of goods, and other assurances of personal chattels,[1] and also powers
of attorney, authorities, or licences to take
possession of personal chattels as security for
any debt,[2] and also any agreement, whether
intended or not to be followed by the executon
of any other instrument, by which a right in
equity to any personal chattels, or to any
charge or security thereon shall be conferred,[3]

(1) Page 41.

2) Page 54.

(3) Page 56.

(a) Fisher on Mortgages, 4th ed. 8.

(b) Manchester, Sheffield and Lincolnshire Ry. v. North Central Wagon Co.,
13 App. Cases, 554; 58 L. J. Ch. 219; 37 W R. 305; 59 L. T. 730.

but shall not include the following documents :
that is to say, assignments for the benefit of the
creditors of the person making or giving the
same,[4] marriage settlements,[5] transfers or
assignments of any ship or vessel or any share
thereof,[6] transfers of goods in the ordinary
course of business of any trade or calling, bills
of sale of goods in foreign parts or at sea,[a]
bills of lading, India warrants, warehouse-
keepers' certificates, warrants or orders for
the delivery of goods, or any other documents
used in the ordinary course of business as
proof of the possession or control of goods, or
authorizing or purporting to authorize, either
by indorsement or by delivery, the possessor
of such document to transfer or receive goods
thereby represented.[b] (7)

(4) Page 6o.
(5) Page 61.
(6) Page 64.
(7) Page 65.

(1) The definition must be read with sec. 3 of the principal
Act, which applies the Act to instruments whereby the
holder has power to seize or take possession of personal
chattels, pointing to a bill of sale being a document on which
the right of the claimant to some extent depends, either as an
actual transfer, or as an agreement to transfer the property,
or as a muniment or document of title taken at the time, and
intended by the parties to be part of the bargain to pass the
property in the goods.

What is a bill of sale.

The definition must also be read subject to the qualification introduced by sec. 3, clause 2, of the amendment Act
by which bills of sale, or other documents given otherwise
than by way of security for the payment of money, are
excepted from the operation of that Act. Sec. 9 of the
amendment Act must also be considered, requiring every

(a) Scotland and Ireland are within the exception ; Cooter. Jeeks, L. R. 13 Eq.
507; 41 L. J. Cb. 599. A bill of sale, duly registered in England, over property,
part of which was in Ireland, has been held to protect such property against an
execution issued in Ireland by an English creditor on a judgment obtained in
England (Brookes r. Harrison, 6 L. R. Ir. 332).

(b) By sec. 17 of the amendment Act nothing in the Act shall apply to any
debentures issued by any mortgage, loan or other incorporated Company, and
secured upon the capital, stock or goods, chattels and effects of such Company.
By sec. 1, Bills of Sale Act, 1890, as amended by sec. 1, Bills of Sale Act, 1891,
an instrument charging or creating any security on or declaring trusts of
imported goods, as therein defined, shall not be deemed a bill of sale within
the principal or amendment Acts.

bill of sale within that Act to be in the prescribed form, and it would seem that inventories, receipts and other documents mentioned in the section not fulfilling this condition, will no longer be valid securities for the payment of money. But documents which by the principal Act are to be deemed bills of sale, as for example attornments under sec. 6, are not bills of sale for all purposes, though they are to be treated as bills of sale for the purposes of registration.[a] Bills of sale given by way of security for the payment of money are therefore subject to both Acts, must be in a particular form, and are in most cases absolutely void unless complying with the provisions of the amendment Act; while bills of sale given for purposes other than as security may be in any form the parties devise, and are void only in the events and as against the persons named in sec. 8 of the principal Act, and to this class of bill of sale the amendment Act has no application.

What is a bill of sale.

For the purposes of the section a bill of sale has been defined as a document transferring, or intended to transfer, or to be a record or evidence of the transfer of chattels personal, unless given in the ordinary course of business, or in other cases excluded from the operation of the Acts ;[b] and it seems that to be a bill of sale a document must be an assurance of personal chattels, or of the kind included by the subsequent words of the section, in the expression bill of sale.[c] But a document drawn up at the time when a transaction is being carried out, transferring goods from one party to another, is not necessarily a bill of sale; and in each case the circumstances must be looked at in order to see what is the transaction and what is the document; for it will be observed that the Acts deal only with documents and leave unaffected titles acquired independently of any writing; and the Bills of Sale Acts are not intended to interfere with dealings other than those expressly pointed out by the Acts.[d] If a document is intended by the parties to be part of the bargain passing the property in the goods, then whatever its form the Acts will apply; but if the document is not intended to be part of the bargain to pass the property in the goods, if the bargain

(a) Green v. Marsh [1892] 2 Q. B. 330; 40 W. R. 449; 66 L. T. 480; 61 L. J. Q. B. 442; 56 J. P. 839.

(b) Marsden v. Meadows, 7 Q. B. D. 80; 29 W. R. 816; 50 L. J. Ch. 536; 45 L. T. 301 ; Horsfall v. Key, 17 L. J. Ex. 266; 2 Ex. 778.

(c) Manchester, Sheffield and Lincolnshire Ry. v. North Central Wagon Co., 13 App. Cases, 554.

(d) Charlesworth v. Mills [1892], A. C. 231; 66 L. T. 690; 41 W. R. 129; 61 L. J. Q. B. 830.

is complete without it, so that the property passes independently, it is not to be deemed a bill of sale.[a]

A sale or mortgage of personal property, with certain
exceptions, may be effected by parol, [b] but to avoid the incon-
venience of proving complicated transactions by the uncertain
and often defective evidence of witnesses, the terms of the
contract are, in practice, generally reduced into writing
by which the rights and liabilities of the parties are clearly
defined. If the real agreement between the parties is
reduced into writing, there cannot be any question of an independent agreement, for the writing is the only evidence
of their bargain; but a document which is not intended
to, and does not, express the real agreement between the
parties will not, it seems, necessarily amount to an assurance within the Acts, or prevent the parties setting up a
title under an independent oral agreement[c]; the test being
whether it is necessary to put the document in evidence to prove
the transaction and support the title claimed;[d] unless the
writing, when produced, does not affect the rights of the
parties, or make them different from the rights they would
have before, or if no writing had been referred to.[e] Thus
where a deed purported to sell chattels to a person who afterwards repudiated the transaction as a purchase, but remained
in possession, claiming a lien for the money paid, to which the
grantor assented; it was held that as the document did not
represent the true transaction, possession taken under it did
not affect the lien obtained by verbal agreement.[f]

It has been observed that a person is at liberty to evade by
keeping outside of an Act of Parliament passed in derogation
or restriction of the legal rights and liberties of the subject; [g]
for an Act evaded is not an Act broken, and though an arrangement in contravention of the terms of an Act of Parliament would
be illegal, yet if its terms have been observed the arrangement will be effective, although the mischief aimed at by the
Act has not been prevented;[h] thus the Middlesex Registry

(a) Ramsay v. Margrett, 1894 , 2 Q. B. 18; 63 L. J. Q. B. 513; 70 L. T. 788.
(b) Flory v. Denny, 7 Exch. 581; 21 L. J. Exch. 223; Reeves v. Capper, 5 Bing.
N. C. 136; 6 Scott, 877, 2 Jur. 1067.
(c) Newlove v. Shrewsbury, 21 Q. B. D. 41; 36 W. R. 845; 57 L. J. Q. B. 176.
(d) Haydon v. Brown, 59 L. T. 810.
(e) Charlesworth v. Mills, 1892 , A. C. 231.
(f) Parker v. Lyon, 5 T. L. R. 10.
(g) Macbeth v. Ashley, 2 L. R. H. L. Sc. 359; 30 L. T. 110, per S. J. re., C.
(h) Ramshen v. Lee, L. R. 9 Q. B. 17, 44 L. J. Q. B. 7 22 W. R. 429, 29
L. T. 510.

Acts have been held not to apply to equitable mortgages by deposit, or to an unpaid vendor's lien, for there is no instrument to be registered;[a] nor do the Bills of Sale Acts apply to an unpaid vendor's lien existing independently of any writing,[b] and the same reasoning shews that a completed sale or mortgage of chattels unaccompanied by any writing will not be affected by the Acts, which avoid documents but not transactions.[c]

For these reasons, when a sale is followed by open delivery and taking of possession, the Acts do not apply; [d] nor do they apply to a pledge of goods, and a document accompanying a transaction by way of deposit or pledge of personal chattels, the object and effect of which is to transfer their immediate possession to the pledgee, is not a bill of sale, although recording the transaction and regulating the rights of the parties.[e] So a verbal charge, to secure a loan, on goods in a warehouse, which were transferred into the name of the lender, was held effectual, though accompanied by an unregistered delivery order on the warehouseman ; [f] and where furniture was warehoused as security for a debt, an agreement being drawn up recording the transaction and regulating the rights of the parties, the claimants having paid off the warehouse rent, and taken possession of the goods, the Acts were held not to apply.[g]

Pledge not within Acts.   And in order to give a security by pledge it is not necessary that actual possession should be contemporaneous with the pledge. There may be constructive possession, as where the borrower handed to the lender's agent the key of the place where the goods were stored, which was held to confer a valid security, though afterwards the transaction was recorded in an instrument which was void under the Acts.[h]

(a) Sumpter v. Cooper, 2. B. & Ad. 223 ; Kettlewell v. Watson, 26 Ch. D. 501 ; 53 J. Ch. 717 ; 51 L. T. 135 ; 32 W. R. 865.

(b) Re Vulcan Iron Works Co., W. N. 1888, 37.

(c) North Central Wagon Co. v. Manchester, Sheffield and Lincolnshire Ry., 35 Ch. D. 191 ; 35 W. R. 443 ; 56 L. J. Ch. 609 ; 56 L. T. 755.

(d) Shepherd v. Pulbrook, 59 L. T. 284 ; Marples v. Hartley, 1 B. & S. 1 ; 30 L. J. Q. B. 92 ; 7 Jur. N. S. 446 ; 9 W. R. 334 ; 3 L. T. 774.

(e) Exp. Hubbard, re Hardwick, 17 Q. B. D. 690 ; 55 L. J. Q. B. 490 ; 35 W. R. 2 ; Mor. 240 ; Exp. Close, re Hall, 14 Q. B. D. 386 ; 54 L. J. Q. B. 43 ; 33 W. R. 224; 51 L. T. 795.

(f) Grigg v. National Guardian Assurance Co. [1891], 3 Ch. 206 ; 39 W. R. 651 ; 64 L. T. 757 ; 61 L. J. Ch. 11.

(g) Wilkinson v. Giraud, 8 T. L. R. 266.

(h) Hilton v. Tucker, 36 W. R. 762 ; 59 L. T. 172 ; 39 C. D. 669 ; 57 L. J. Ch. 973.

But where goods are left in the possession of the seller, every
document on which the title to them depends should be treated
as a bill of sale and registered, and care should be taken that
such document are properly stamped, for being created bills of
sale by the section, it would seem that the ordinary appraise-
ment, receipt, or agreement stamp would not be sufficient.
Where the transaction is by way of security, regard also
should be had to sec. 9 of the amendment Act; for if the
arrangement between the parties cannot be in the form in the
schedule to that Act, it cannot be made at all. [a]

The expression "transfer" in the section means a document which, though not in form a bill of sale, assumes to
transfer the property in goods in the same way as a bill of
sale would. [b]

Declarations of trust in chattels are not required to be in   Declarations of
writing by sec. 7 of the Statute of Frauds; but if contained   trust.
in any document require registration under the Acts. Every
defeasance, condition, or declaration of trust is to be deemed
part of, and registered with, the bill of sale. [c]   By sec. 1,
Bills of Sale Act, 1890, as amended by the Bills of Sale Act,
1891, an instrument charging or creating any security on
or declaring trusts of imported goods, given or executed at
any time prior to their deposit in a warehouse, factory, or
store, or to their being reshipped for export, or delivered
to a purchaser not being the person giving or executing such
instrument, shall not be deemed a bill of sale within the
meaning of the principal or amendment Acts.

Declarations of trust in chattels personal might be created
by parol, upon the donor, by clear, unequivocal and
irrevocable words, declaring himself or some other person
a trustee. [d]   If a person expressly or impliedly constitutes
himself a trustee of personalty, that is a trust executed and
capable of being enforced, although without consideration, but
where the intention is to make an actual gift and not merely
to declare a trust, the settlor must have done everything which
according to the nature of the property is necessary to be done
in order to transfer it, for there is no equity to perfect an
imperfect gift. [e]

(a) *Exp.* Parsons, *re* Townsend, 16 Q. B. D. 532; 34 W. R. 320; 53 L. T. 597;
55 L. J. Q. B. 137.
(b) *Exp.* Hubbard, *re* Hardwick, 17 Q.B.D. 690.
(c) Sec. 10, sub-sec. 3 [1878].
(d) Peckham *r.* Taylor, 31 Beav. 254.
(e) Milroy *r.* Lord, 4 De G. F. & J. 264; 8 Jur. N. S. 806; Jones *r.* Lock, 3
L. J. Ch. 117; 14 W. R. 149; 11 Jur. N. S. 913; L. R. 1. Ch. 28.

B

An hypothecation note given on obtaining an advance from bankers, whereby the grantor undertook to hold goods in trust for his bankers, and to hand over the proceeds when received to the amount of the advance, has been held a declaration of trust without transfer within the section.[a]

Under the repealed statutes, the term "bill of sale" was held to include any assurance of chattels personal by which the property was intended to pass to the assignee, but did not include a document by which no property was intended to pass. Thus it was formerly decided that a mere memorandum or **receipt** for purchase-money of goods, not intended to operate as a record of a sale,[b] a receipt with an inventory,[c] or memorandum[d] attached, did not require registration, nor did a receipt and inventory given on an absolute sale by the sheriff.[e] It was, however, intimated that a receipt for goods might operate as an assurance of chattels; and a receipt appended to an inventory of furniture and effects, "for the purchase-money in respect of the goods mentioned in the foregoing inventory," was held to require registration, as within sec. 7 of the Bills of Sale Act, 1854.[f] It seems doubtful, however, whether an inventory and receipt, by separate documents, not intended to be operative in connection with each other, could be regarded as an inventory of goods with receipt thereto attached.[g]

Receipts.

But it is now settled that a receipt, or receipt and inventory, in order to be a bill of sale, must amount to an assurance of personal chattels at law or in equity, as altering the rights of the parties, either as regards the property in or possession of the goods : and where there is a complete contract of purchase and sale, independent of any document, the receipt being given merely as an acknowledgment of money paid, the Acts do not apply, for their effect is to invalidate documents, and not transactions, and to leave unimpeached any title acquired otherwise than by a bill of sale.[h]   But if the document or

(a) R. v. Townshend, 15 Cox C.C. 466.
(b) Byerley v. Prevost, L. R. 6 C. P. 144; Hale v. Met. Saloon Omnibus Company, 28 L. J. Ch. 777; 4 Drewry, 492; Thomson v. Barrett, 1 L. T. N. S. 268.
(c) Allsopp v. Day, 7 H. & N. 457; 31 L. J. Ex. 105; 5. L. T. 320; 10 W. R. 135; 8 Jur. N. S. 11.
(d) Graham v. Wilcockson, 46 L. J. Ex. 55; 35 L. T. 601.
(e) Woodgate v. Godfrey, 28 W. R. 88; 5 Ex. D. 24; 49 L. J. Ex. 1; 42 L. J. 34.
(f) Exp. Cooper, re Baum, 10 Ch. D. 313; 39 L. T. 521; 27 W. R. 298; 48 L. J. Bank, 40; Exp. Odell re Walden, 10 Ch. D. 76; 39 L. T. 333; 27 W. R. 274; 48 L. J. Bank. 1; Exp. Newport Co., re Bampfield, 20 W. R. 925.
(g) Manchester, &c., Ry., v. North Central Wagon Co., 13 App. Cases, 554.
(h) North Central Wagon Co. v. Manchester, Sheffield & Lincolnshire Ry., 35 C. D. 191; 35 W. R. 443; 56 L. J. Ch. 609; 56 L. T. 755.

documents form the whole contract on which title to the chattels rests, it seems that registration will still be necessary[a]; and the following cases, it is apprehended, depend, to a great extent, on this preliminary question of fact.

Goods in a defendant's possession were seized under a *fi. fa.*, Receipts. and on the same day sold by the sheriff to the execution creditor, who paid a deposit at the time of sale, whereupon the sheriff gave possession of the goods, the balance being paid the following day. The next day the sheriff sent a receipt, affixed by a pin to an inventory, enclosed in a letter referring to both, and thenceforth the creditor paid the rent of the premises, but allowed the defendant to remain in occupation and to use the furniture; nevertheless, it was decided that the inventory and receipt did not amount to a bill of sale, and that the purchaser was entitled to the goods as against a subsequent execution creditor.[b] And so the case was held not within the Acts where a sheriff's officer having seized goods under a *fi. fa.* issued against the execution debtor, sold them to the claimant, giving him a receipt for the purchase-money containing an inventory of the goods, the claimant, at the same time, by a written agreement bearing even date with the receipt, letting to the execution debtor the house where the goods had been seized, together with the goods, on a quarterly tenancy, and the execution debtor continued in possession as before.[c] And when a sheriff under an order for private sale sold to the execution creditor the goods seized, and by the judgment debtor's direction other goods, giving receipts and inventories on completion, it being arranged that the execution creditor should let the goods to the debtor's wife, which was done, the Court found that there was a complete contract of purchase independent of and previous to the writings, which were not a memorandum of the agreement, nor a record of the transaction, and were not therefore assurances within the Acts.[d] So where a wife agreed to buy certain furniture from her husband, stipulating that a receipt should be given, which her solicitor was to draw up; her title was held complete on payment of the purchase-money, though afterwards her husband signed a receipt in the form of an assurance of the goods.[e] Again, when the holder of a bill of

(a) Newlove v. Shrewsbury, 21 Q. B. D. 41.
(b) Marsden v. Meadows, 7 Q. B. D. 80.
(c) Woolgate v. Godfrey, 5 Ex. D. 24.
(d) Haydon v. Brown, 59 L. T. 510.
(e) Ramsey v. Margrett [1894], 2 Q. B. 18.

sale made an offer by letter to a bailiff who had seized the
goods in execution, to buy them by valuation, paying their
value in excess of his security, to which the bailiff verbally
assented, the goods then being valued and delivered to the
purchaser who paid the price; an inventory handed to him
by the bailiff, on which was a memorandum of the sale,
was held not to require registration.[a]

Receipts.

The grounds of the decisions would thus appear to
be that the sales were absolute, and the purchaser's title
did not depend upon the documents, which were not
the medium of transfer; and although a document may be
in form, a receipt given on the sale of goods, if such document
really is an embodiment of the contract made by the vendor
with the purchaser, and was so intended by the parties, it
amounts to an assurance, and must be registered as a bill of
sale.[b] Thus, where goods seized by a sheriff were, by leave of
the court, sold privately, a receipt given by the sheriff to the
purchaser. " Received from............ the sum............being
for the goods, chattels, and effects now in and upon the
premises............, which were seized by the sheriff of............
under and by virtue of a writ of *fi. fa.*, and hereby sold as far
as he lawfully can or may, without any warranty of title, and
with the consent of the defendant......... , under order of the
Master, dated &c.," was held to be a bill of sale within the Bills
of Sale Act, 1878, and void, being unregistered, as against an
execution creditor who seized the goods while in the
defendant's apparent possession.[c]   And a receipt reciting a
sale of chattels, and letting them to the vendor for a rent,
with a proviso entitling the purchaser to enter and take
possession if the rent should be unpaid, or if execution should
issue against the goods, was held to be merely a colourable bill
of sale.[d] But it would seem doubtful whether, in the case of
an actual sale, a receipt, coupled with an agreement for hire
or repurchase would be within the Acts.[e]

Again, where a person bought furniture of a judgment
debtor, taking at the same time a receipt for the purchase-
money, and shortly after removed the goods, which

(a) Grace *v.* Gard, 6 T. L. R. 74.
(b) Marsden *v.* Meadows, 7 Q. B. D. 80.
(c) *Exp.* Burgess, *re* Hood, 42 W. R. 23; 10 Mor. 231; 4 R. 502.
(d) Phillips *v.* Gibbons, 5 W. R. 527; 20 L. T. O. S. 91.
(e) Manchester, Sheffield & Lincolnshire Ry. *v.* North Central Wagon Co.,
13 App. Cases, 554.

were subsequently placed in another house taken by the purchaser, who let it furnished to the judgment debtor, it was held as against an execution creditor of the judgment debtor that the purchaser had acquired a good title apart from the receipt, which, therefore, was not affected by the principal Act.[a] And where there was a verbal agreement for the sale of goods, the price being paid and the goods delivered, the sale was held perfect and complete, and was not affected by an unregistered inventory and receipt given at the same time.[b]

The owners of a machine, in the possession of an intending purchaser under a hiring agreement, verbally made over the property in the machine and their interest in the agreement under which it was held, as security for the payment of money, indorsing on the agreement a receipt for what the lender paid, as on a sale, which receipt the Court found did not represent the real bargain, the transfer not being absolute but by way of security. The grantee having paid out a distress for which the machine had been seized, sold it, the grantors in the meantime having executed a deed of arrangement. It was held as against the assignees of the deed that the grantee was entitled to the machine under a title independent of the receipt, which therefore was not an assurance within the Act.[c]

Where, however, a receipt was given for the purchase-money of bricks, which remained in the seller's possession, the receipt was decided to require registration under the principal Act.[d]

Agreements under what is known as the hire system will not be within the operation of the Acts, for in such cases, when the agreement is in the ordinary form, no right of property at law or in equity passes to the hirer; and when by a written agreement a person hired furniture on the terms of payment by monthly instalments, depositing as collateral security, but without prejudice to the rights under the agreement, promissory notes for the whole amount, which were to become void on seizure, it being provided that in the event of non-payment of any instalment the bailor might, notwithstanding any payments, seize and remove the furniture which on payment of all instalments was to become the hirer's property, until which it was only let on hire and was to

Hiring agreements.

(a) Preece v. Gilling, 53 L. T. 763.
(b) Shepherd v. Pulbrook, 59 L. T. 289.
(c) Nowlove v. Shrewsbury, 21 Q. B. D. 41.
(d) Snell v. Heighton, 1 Cab. & E. 96.

remain the property of the bailor, the Court of Appeal held that as no property passed to the hirer until payment of the full amount of the instalments, neither the agreement nor the licence to seize amounted to a bill of sale, and that registration was unnecessary; [a] and a written agreement whereby a trader hired household furniture at a weekly rent, and the owner was empowered to repossess himself of the same upon the hirer becoming bankrupt, was held not to require registration. [b]

Hiring agreements.
But if an inventory and receipt, coupled with a hiring agreement, is given and taken as security for the payment of money, there being no title independent of the documents, it would seem the Acts would apply. [c] The Court will, however, decide each case according to the real truth and substance of the matter, and is not precluded from inquiry by the form the transaction takes; [d] the question being one of fact in each case, whether the transaction was an out and out sale of the chattels followed by a hiring, or a mere security for a loan under the cloak of an assignment and hiring agreement. [e] So where there purported to be a sale of chattels, followed by a hire-purchase agreement, under which, when a certain hire had been paid, the chattels were to revest in the vendor, the purchaser having power to take possession on default in payment, no real sale or hiring of the chattels being intended or effected, the object being merely to give and take a security for the loan, it was held that as the person letting to hire was never owner of the goods apart from the supposed hiring agreement, on which his title, if any, depended, the agreement was subject to the Acts as an assurance of chattels and as a licence to take possession as security for a debt. [d] And the same result followed where the alleged sale was effected by what purported to be an absolute assignment by deed; the Court holding that, notwithstanding the deed, the grantor was not estopped from proving the real nature of the transaction. [e] Also where persons applied to a money-lender for an advance on a bill

(a) *Exp.* Crawcour, *re* Robertson, 26 W. R. 733; 47 L. J. Bank, 94; 39 L. T. 2; 9 Ch. D. 419.
(b) *Exp.* Emerson, *re* Hawkins, 41 L. J. Bank. 20; 20 W. R. 110.
(c) French *v.* Bombernard, 60 L. T. 49; considered Jones *v.* Tower Furnishing Co., 61 L. T. 84; 6 Mor. 193.
(d) *Re* Watson, 25 Q. B. D. 27.
(e) Madell *v.* Thomas [1891], 1 Q. B. 230.

of sale of goods, which he refused to accept, but offered to buy
the goods, which thereupon were assigned to him by inventory
and receipt, which were registered, he taking a transfer of
an existing mortgage, and executing an agreement, which
was never registered, letting the goods to the grantors at a
rent, the Court of Appeal held that the transaction was really
a loan, and not a sale, and that the documents carrying it out
were void under the amendment Act.[a] So where a person
advanced £150 to a trader to pay out an execution, and the
trader gave a receipt, written at the foot of an inventory, for
£150 for the absolute sale of the "above-mentioned articles of
furniture," and on the same day both parties executed a
memorandum of agreement letting the goods to the trader
for two months for £170, with power to seize and sell on
default, and the usual clauses for disposing of the proceeds of
sale, but the receipt was not registered, it was held that the
two documents constituted a conditional bill of sale.[b]

Thus, though an actual and completed sale followed by   Hiring agreements.
a hiring agreement, if a separate and distinct dealing, does
not come within the Acts, even, it seems, if the effect of the
whole transaction is to secure the payment of money;[c] the
case will be otherwise if the sale, though actual, is only part
of one security intended to be completed by a hire agreement.

The plaintiff having applied for a loan secured on his furniture, it was arranged between the parties that the landlord
should distrain for rent in arrear, when the defendants
should buy the goods of him. Accordingly, at the plaintiff's
request, a distress was levied and the goods appraised, the
broker selling them to the defendants at the condemned
price. The next day the defendants produced an agreement
by which the goods were to be hired by the plaintiff's wife on
the terms that on payment of stipulated instalments they were
to become hers, a power to take possession on default being
reserved to the defendants. To this agreement the plaintiff
objected, but it was ultimately signed. Default having been
made the defendants seized, whereupon the plaintiff sued for
damages for trespass to the goods. Mr. Justice Cave found
that there was a sale to the defendants independently of the
hiring agreement, but the Court of Appeal reversed his
decision, holding that though the property in the goods

(a) Hooper v. Ker, 76 L. T. J. 307 ; Brown r. Blaine, 1 T. L. R. 158.
(b) Exp. Odell, re Walden, 10 Ch. D. 76.
(c) Exp. Collins, re Yarrow, 59 L. J. Q. B. 18 ; 38 W. R. 175 ; 61 L. T. 642.

passed to the defendants by the purchase, it did so subject to
a resulting trust in favour of the plaintiff until execution of
the hire agreement, and that as the beneficial interest in the
goods remained in the plaintiff until the agreement had been
executed giving the defendants a right to take possession, the
defendants had no title independently of the agreement,
which was consequently a bill of sale, and void, being unregistered.[a]

*Hiring agree-
ments.*
A different conclusion was come to in an earlier
case, which turned on particular facts, and does not
appear to establish any principle. An intending borrower
applied for a loan, but this being objected to, suggested
that the person applied to should purchase furniture
in the borrower's house and let it on a hiring agreement. Accordingly, a cheque for £100 was handed to the
borrower, no receipt being given, and by agreement in writing,
the furniture was let to hire for a month at a rent of £100, by
payments of £1 on signing the agreement, and two instalments
of £50, it being provided that on breach of any of the
stipulations the person letting the goods should be at liberty
to take possession, remove and sell them. The borrower
failed to pay the first instalment and died before the second
became due, whereupon the lender took possession and
removed part of the furniture. It was sought to recover the
proceeds which had been paid into Court, on the ground that
the agreement was within the Acts and void, but it was held
that the agreement for hire was unaffected by the Acts, which
did not avoid the transaction.[b]

An assignment to secure a debt by a person, who by
hiring agreement had let goods to hire, of all rights under the
agreement, with an authority to exercise all powers it conferred, not purporting to assign the goods themselves, is not
a bill of sale; being a chose in action, as an assignment of a
contract and the right to sue upon it.[c] But it has been held
that an unregistered memorandum, purporting to charge the
borrower's interest in trade machinery let by the borrower on
hire to third persons, was within the Acts, and conferred on
the lender no title either to the machinery or the money paid
for hire.[d]

(a) Beckett v. Tower Assets Co. [1891] 1 Q. B. 638; 60 L. J. Q. B. 493; 64
L. T. 497; 39 W. R. 438.

(b) Redhead v. Westwood, 59 L. T. J. 293.

(c) Exp. Rawlings, re Davis, 22 Q. B. D. 193; 37 W. R. 203; 60 L. T. 157.

(d) Jarvis v. Jarvis, 60 L. T. 412; 63 L. J. Ch. 10; 1 Mans. 199.

In an agreement for the hire of furniture, the word month means lunar month, although it is to be read calendar month in a mortgage.[a]

A power of distress on non-payment of the hire might have been inserted in such an agreement, and was not a fraud on the bankrupt laws;[b] and a demise of premises with the fixtures, machinery, and apparatus thereon, at a rent payable in advance, with a proviso that on non-payment of the rent or non-observance of the covenants the lessors might re-enter, but that if the lessees should punctually pay the rent and observe the covenants, they should, at the expiration of the term, be absolutely entitled to all fixtures and machinery thereby demised, was held not to require registration.[c]

Under a hiring agreement containing a proviso for retaking possession, and forfeiture of instalments paid on default in punctual payment, the owner was held entitled to take possession on the hirer's default, although the hirer tendered the instalment in arrear.[d]

A purchaser or pledgee of goods buying and taking delivery in good faith from a person in possession under a hire-purchase agreement, has been held to acquire a good title against the true owner, by virtue of section 9, Factors Act, 1889.[e]

The words assignments, transfers, and other assurances of *Assurances of* personal chattels, were to be found in the Bills of Sale Act, 1854, *personal* *chattels.* and were probably inserted in the present section to include documents or dealings of the same class, but not expressly within the words of the first part of the definition. They have been held to apply to an agreement for the sale of a business, of which the purchaser was given possession, providing for payment of the purchase-money by instalments with a lien or charge over the property sold in favour of the vendors for the balance of unpaid purchase-money.[f] So where at a sale of goods by auction, the auctioneer's clerk signed the purchaser's name in a book containing the conditions of sale, the auctioneer also signing for the vendor, but the requirements of sec. 17 of the Statute of Frauds were not

(*a*) Hutton *v.* Brown, 45 L. T. 343; 29 W. R., 928.

(*b*) Leman *v.* Yorks Wagon Co., 50 L. J. Ch. 293; 29 W. R. 896.

(*c*) *Exp.* Sergeant, *re* Gelder, W. N. 1891, 37.

(*d*) Cramer v. Giles, 1 Cab. & E. 151.

(*e*) Lee *v.* Butler [1893], 2 Q. B. 318; Helby *v.* Matthews, 42 W. R. 514; [1894] 2 Q. B. 262; 70 L. T. 837.

(*f*) Coburn *v.* Collins, 35 Ch.'D. 373; 56 L. J. Ch. 504; 35 W. R. 610; 56 L. T. 431

otherwise complied with, and the goods were left in the seller's possession, it was held that, as against an execution creditor, the memorandum in the auctioneer's book, without which the sale would have been invalid and incomplete, was an assurance of chattels and required registration. [a]

Powers of attorney.

(2) It has been decided that a bill of sale may be executed under a power of attorney, even though such attorney is the grantee. Two debtors covenanted in case of default in certain payments to execute such a bill of sale as their covenantee's solicitor might reasonably require, and in case of refusal irrevocably appointed the covenantee their attorney to make, execute, and deliver such bill of sale. The Court refused to restrain the covenantee from putting this power in force by executing a bill of sale in proper form, intimating that the power was no more than a contract to do what the Court would have ordered to be done in an action for specific performance. [b]

Licences to seize.

Having regard to the provisions of the amendment Act, licences to seize will seldom now be met with in practice, but some consideration of them is still necessary. A licence to take possession of chattels, as security for a debt, is a bill of sale within the amendment Act, and void unless in the statutory form; [c] but only such documents fall within the definition of licences to take possession as are consistent with possession of the goods remaining with the grantor, and if it was never intended that possession should remain with him, but that possession should at once be given to the grantee, the definition does not apply. [d] Thus, an auctioneer at an execution debtor's request agreed to pay out the sheriff, the man in possession to hold for the auctioneer, who was to sell the goods by auction, and after repaying his advance and expenses return any balance to the execution debtor. The auctioneer paid out the sheriff, and took his receipt, the execution debtor at the same time giving the auctioneer an authority to hold the goods, and sell on the agreed terms. The bailiff remained in possession for the auctioneer, and the next day the execution debtor gave a bill of sale over the goods to a third party, who on the auctioneer

(a) Evans v. Roberts, 36 Ch. D. 196; 56 L. J. Ch. 952; 35 W. R. 684; 57 L. T. 78.
(b) Furnivall v. Hudson [1893], 1 Ch. 335.
(c) Exp. Parsons, re Townsend, 16 Q. B. D 532; 34 W. R. 329; 53 L. T. 897; 55 L J. Q. B. 137.
(d) Exp. Hubbard re Hardwick, 17 Q. B. D. 690.

removing them, sued him in trover. The Court of Appeal held that the authority was within the Acts and void;[a] but the House of Lords reversed the decision, holding that as the written authority or mandate did not constitute the title, and was not intended to, and did not come into operation until possession had been actually transferred from the sheriff to the auctioneer, it was not a licence to take possession, or an assurance, or otherwise a bill of sale.[b]

As has been seen an agreement purporting to let goods on hire, but in fact given and taken to secure a loan, with power of seizure on default in payment of hire, may amount to a licence to seize within the section, where the person letting to hire was not owner of or entitled to the goods, apart from the supposed hiring agreement.[c]

The common law does not recognise the doctrine of hypothecation so as to permit a debtor to create a general lien upon all his goods, in the hands of whomsoever they may be, in favour of a particular creditor, but permits him to grant a right to seize and sell a specified chattel, or all his goods and chattels generally, on non-payment of a debt. Such a licence to seize gives the licensee no right to follow the goods into the hands of third parties, is available only so long as the goods remain in the debtor's possession and continue his property,[d] and unless coupled with a grant or interest, is revocable though under seal,[e] and is discharged by the grantor becoming bankrupt, or effecting a composition,[f] or by his death.[g] It confers no title to the goods until actual seizure, but when executed vests the property in the licensee;[h] and if the words specifically include property upon premises to be occupied by the mortgagor during the continuance of the security, might be extended to crops and other chattels on land or premises to be afterwards occupied or built.[i] A licence to seize cannot be assigned or granted to another so as to confer on him a right of seizure.[j]

Licences to seize.

(a) Mills v. Charlesworth, 25 Q. B. D. 421.

(b) Charlesworth v. Mills [1892], A.C. 231.

(c) Re Watson, 25 Q. B. D. 27.

(d) Addison on Contracts, 8th ed., 636; Howes v. Ball, 7 B. & C. 481; 1 M. & R. 288.

(e) Wood v. Manley, 11 A. & E. 34; 3 Per. & D. 5.

(f) Carr v. Acraman, 11 Exch. 566; 25 L. J. Exch. 90; Thompson v. Cohen, L. R. 7 Q. B. 527; 26 L. T. 693; 41 L. J. Q. B. 221.

(g) Campanari v. Woodburn, 15 C. B. 400; 24 L. J. C. P. 13; 1 Jur. N. S. 17.

(h) Hope v. Hayley, 5 E. & B. 830; 2 Jur. N. S. 488; 25 L. J. Q. B. 155.

(i) Chidell v. Galsworthy, 6 C. B. N. S. 471.

(j) Brown v. Metropolitan Counties Society, 28 L. J. Q. B. 286; 1 E. & E. 832; 5 Jur. 1028; Exp. Rawlings, re Davis, 22 Q. B. D. 193.

A stipulation in an agreement that in the event of bankruptcy a man's property shall go over to another. and be taken from his creditors, is void against his trustee; thus, where a building agreement provided that in case the tenant committed default in the building stipulations, or should become bankrupt, all improvements, materials and other effects on any part of the said land, not demised to him, should be forfeited to the landlord, who was to be at liberty to re-enter and take possession, it was held that as the landlord's claim rested on the bankruptcy. it could not be supported, and the tenant's trustee who had disclaimed the agreement was held justified in seizing the materials.[a]

Licences to seize.

If, however, the agreement conferred an immediate equitable interest in the chattels before bankruptcy was contemplated, it prevailed against an execution creditor or the trustee in the bankruptcy of the intended lessee; as where an agreement provided that all materials which should have been brought upon the premises for the purposes of building should be considered as immediately attached and belonging to the premises, and that no part thereof should be removed without the consent of the owner of the land, who in case of default was empowered to take possession of the land and materials : nor was such an agreement within the Bills of Sale Act, 1854, as an assurance of or licence to seize personal chattels;[b] inasmuch as, though a licence to take possession of personal chattels, the possession was not to be taken as security for any debt.[c]

So where a building agreement between a landowner and a builder contained a stipulation that the landowner, upon the default of the builder in fulfilling his part of the agreement, might re-enter upon the land and expel the builder, and that on such re-entry all the materials in and about the premises should be forfeited to and become the property of the landowner " as and for liquidated damages," it was held that, the interest of the builder in the materials being a defeasible one, the right of the landowner to seize was not defeated by the commission of an act of bankruptcy by the builder before the seizure was made, that the stipulation in the agreement, not being a licence to take possession of personal chattels as security for

(a) *Exp.* Jay, *re* Harrison, 14 Ch. D. 19; 28 W. R. 449; 42 L. T. 600; 49 L. J. Bank. 47; *exp.* Barter, *re* Walker, 26 Ch. D. 510; 32 W. R. 809; 53 L. J. Ch. 802.
(b) Blake *v.* Izard, 16 W. R. 108; Brown *v.* Bateman, L. R. 2 C. P. 272; 15 L. T. 658; 36 L. J. C. P. 134; 15 W. R. 350; *exp.* Dickin, *re* Waugh, 35 L. T. 769; 4 Ch. D. 524; 46 L. J. Bank. 26; 25 W. R. 258.
(c) *Exp.* Newitt, *re* Garrud, 16 Ch. D. 522; 29 W.R. 344; 44 L.T. 5; 51 L. J. Ch. 381.

a debt, did not amount to a bill of sale, and that the trustee
under the builder's bankruptcy took subject to the rights
of the landowner under the agreement.[a] Nor is a building agreement, providing that all building and other
materials brought upon the land by the builder, whether
affixed to the freehold or not, should become the property of the landlord, within the principal Act as an agreement by which a right in equity is conferred to chattels
personal; [b] and such a document, when not a security for the
payment of money, is excepted from the operation of the
amendment Act. [c]

But this exception will not apply to the mortgage of a   Licences to
building agreement, where neither mortgagor nor mortgagee   seize.
are owners of the land; thus, where a builder mortgaged a
building agreement, together with all plant and materials
then or thereafter on the premises, giving no express power of
sale, but empowering the mortgagee in certain events to take
possession of the premises and all plant and materials, and
complete the buildings, the mortgage was held to be a bill of
sale as regards plant and materials, void for want of registration as against an execution creditor. [d]

And where the lessee under a building lease assigned by
way of mortgage the demised premises and houses in course
of erection, together with all bricks, timber and other building materials then or thereafter on the premises, providing
that all such materials should when brought on the premises
be considered as immediately attaching to the land, and empowering the mortgagee in certain events to seize the building
materials and complete the buildings, and on default in payment to enter on the premises and sell them and any
materials thereon, either together or in parcels, the mortgage
was held a bill of sale as giving power to sell the personal
chattels apart from the land, and was so far void.[e]

A brewer's lease authorizing seizure of chattels on
default in payment of an account current has been held to
require registration;[f] and would be a bill of sale within

(a) Exp. Newitt, re Garrud, 16 Ch. D. 522 ; 29 W. R. 344 ; 44 L. T. 5 ; 51 L. J.
Ch. 381.
(b) Reeves r. Barlow, 12 Q. B. D. 436 ; 53 L. J. Q. B. 192 ; 32 W. R. 672 ; 50
L. T. 782.
(c) Sec. 3, clause 2 [1882].
(d) Church r. Sage, 67 L. T. 800 ; 41 W. R. 175.
(e) Climpson r. Coles, 23 Q. B. D. 465 ; 58 L. J. Q. B. 346 ; 61 L. T. 116 ; 38
W. R. 110.
(f) Exp. Hopcraft, re Flavell, 14 W. R. 168.

the Acts. So it has been decided is a tenancy agreement by which the landlords, brewers, on default in payment of money due for goods supplied, were empowered to enter the demised public-house and distrain for the amount so due; [a] and an agreement between a brewer and the tenant of a tied house, providing that the landlord should have the same rights, powers and remedies as landlords ordinarily possess in case of rent in arrear, for any amount due by the tenant for any liquors or other goods sold, or for any money advanced to the tenant, not exceeding a specified limit, and should be at liberty to seize and distrain any furniture, stock, or effects in respect of any such debts, and sell the same as by law landlords are empowered to do for rent, was held to be void under the Acts as a license to take possession of personal chattels as security for a debt, although no debt existed when the agreement was made.[b]

Licences to seize.

A mere licence to seize must not be confounded with a grant of future property, which, before the amendment Act, transferred to the mortgagee or purchaser the grantor's beneficial interest as soon as the property was acquired.

By sec. 6 of the principal Act, certain documents by which a power of distress is conferred by way of security for any debt, and whereby rent is payable as a mode of providing for the payment of interest on such debt, shall be deemed bills of sale of any personal chattels seized or taken under such power of distress. Such documents are not bills of sale for all purposes, but are to be treated as bills of sale for the purposes of registration. [c]

Agreements.

(3) The words "agreement by which a right in equity to any personal chattels or to any charge or security thereon shall be conferred" are intended to bring within the Acts documents which create a right in equity as distinguished from a right in law; and do not, it has been decided, apply to documents by which a right in law is given.[d] By an agreement appointing the plaintiff agent, the defendant agreed that advances by the plaintiff should be covered and secured by the stock of goods which should be in his hands. The agency having determined, the defendant sought to recover goods held

(a) Pulbrook v. Ashby, 35 W. R. 779; 56 L. J. Q. B. 376.
(b) Stevens v. Marston, 39 W. R. 129; 60 L. J. Q. B. 192; 64 L. T. 274; 55 J. P. 103.
(c) Green v. Marsh [1892] 2 Q. B. 330.
(d) Reeves v. Barlow, 12 Q. B. D. 436; exp. Hubbard, re Hardwick, 17 Q. B. D. 690.

by the plaintiff without satisfying a claim for expenses paid by
him as agent, contending that the agreement was a bill of sale
as conferring a right in equity to the goods. It was held that
as the plaintiff acquired no right to any specific goods until
they had been delivered to him, but was only entitled to retain
them when received, his right depended on possession, and
was a legal, and not an equitable right, and was not within the
section. [a]

An agreement for a bill of sale, if relied on as an equitable Agreements
assignment of property, required registration under the Bills
of Sale Act, 1854; [b] thus, a document undertaking to hold
goods at the disposal of third parties, and to transfer them
when required to do so, was held a bill of sale. [c] The words
of the section limit its application to cases where a
right in equity shall be conferred to personal chattels or to
any charge or security thereon; thus, a deed by which a debtor
covenanted that if the debt was not paid on a day named
certain chattels should be charged with it, and that he would,
when required, assign them to the creditor as security, was
held to require registration as a bill of sale. [d] Where a sum
of money is advanced on the faith of an absolute promise by
the debtor to give a bill of sale, the sum so advanced is to be
considered as advanced on the security of the bill of sale,
which stands on the same footing as if given at the time of
the advance, [e] but such promise or agreement, if in writing,
and relied upon as conferring an equitable right to a security
over chattels, would seem to be a bill of sale, requiring registration; [f] though under the provisions of sec. 9 such an
agreement would probably not be an effectual security. But an
agreement to give a bill of sale does not require registration
where the bill of sale has been given in pursuance of the
agreement, and duly registered, although the agreement is
relied on to support the *bona fides* of the transaction. [g]

(a) Morris v. Delobbel-Flipo [1892] 2 Ch. 352; 66 L. T. 320; 40 W. R. 492; 61
L. J. Ch. 518.

(b) *Exp.* Mackay, *re* Jeavons, L. R. 8 Ch. 643; 42 L. J. Bank, 68; 28 L. T. 828;
21 W. R. 664.

(c) *Exp.* Conning, *re* Steele, L. R. 16 Eq. 414; 21 W. R. 784; *exp.* Montague, *re*
O'Brien, 1 Ch. D. 554; 24 W. R. 309; 34 L. T. 197; Baghott v. Norman, 41 L. T.
787.

(d) Edwards v. Edwards, 45 L. J. Ch. 301; 24 W. R. 713; 2 Ch. D. 291; 34 L. T.
472.

(e) Harris v. Rickett, 4 H. & N. 1; 28 L. J. Ex. 197; Mercer v. Peterson, L. R.
3 Ex. 104; 37 L. J. Ex. 54; 16 W. R. 486; 18 L. T. 30; *exp.* King, 2 Ch. D. 256;
45 L. J. Bank, 109; 24 W. R. 550; 34 L. T. 466.

(f) Edwards v. Edwards, 2 Ch. D. 291.

(g) *Exp.* Hauxwell, *re* Hemmingway, 23 Ch. D. 626, 48 L. T. 742; 31 W. R.
711; 52 L. J. Ch. 737.

Although a mere contract to lend or borrow money on mortgage will not be enforced,[a] specific performance has been decreed of an agreement to execute a mortgage in consideration of a debt due, or of an advance actually made, unless the money be repaid.[b] It would seem doubtful how far an agreement to give a bill of sale would now confer any security, but it would be evidence of the good faith of a bill of sale afterwards given and registered. It has, however, been decided that the Court will not restrain the execution of a bill of sale in a form to which no valid objection can be taken, which a debtor has for valuable consideration covenanted to execute, appointing in case of refusal the proposed grantee his attorney for the purpose; for in the absence of a power of attorney the Court could order specific performance, and on the grantor's non-compliance could, under section 14, Judicature. Act, 1884, nominate a person to execute the bill of sale.[c]

Assignments for the benefit of creditors.

(4) By the Deeds of Arrangement Act, 1887 (50 & 51 Vict.. c. 57), deeds of arrangement, as defined by the Act, for the benefit of creditors generally, are declared void unless registered within the time and with the formalities prescribed by the Act.

An assignment for the benefit of creditors, to be within the exception of the Bills of Sale Acts, must be for the benefit of the creditors generally; but if it will include any creditor who chooses to accede to the arrangement and sign the deed, there being nothing on the face of it by which any creditor is excluded, it will be sufficient; thus, a deed in the form of a deed poll whereby the creditors, "whose names and seals were thereunto subscribed and set," agreed to accept a secured composition from their debtor, who assigned his property to the surety, was held within the exception of this section.[d]

And so was a deed whereby the debtor assigned all his property to a surety absolutely, the latter joining in promissory notes for the composition, and covenanting with the creditors to pay them;[e] and an assignment to trustees for "the parties hereto who shall execute these presents

(a) Rogers v. Challis, 27 Beav. 175; 29 L. J. Ch. 240.

(b) Ashton v. Corrigan. 13 Eq. 76; 41 L. J. Ch. 96; Hermann v. Hodges, 16 Eq. 18; 43 L. J. Ch. 192.

(c) Furnivall v. Hudson [1893], 1 Ch. 335.

(d) General Furnishing Company v. Venn. 2 H. & C. 153; 32 L. J. Ex. 220; 11 W. R. 756; 8 L. T. 432; 9 Jur. N. S. 550; Johnson v. Osenton L. R. 4 Ex. 108; 38 L. J. Ex. 76; 19 L. T. 793.

(e) Beevor v. Savage, 16 L. T. 359.

within one calendar month from the date hereof," was held to be for the benefit of all the creditors; [a] as also was an assignment for the benefit of all such creditors as should elect to execute the same.[b]

But a deed expressed to be made for certain creditors named **Assignments for the benefit of creditors.** therein, with a resulting trust for the grantor, was held to require registration; [c] and a similar deed has been held void under the Statute 13 Eliz. cap. 5; [d] the decision depending, however, on the special circumstances of the case; [e] so an instrument authorizing a creditor to take possession of a debtor's goods and sell them, paying out of the proceeds the debts due to himself and other creditors, was decided to be a bill of sale requiring registration.[f]

Before the passing of the Bills of Sale Acts, where a debtor, pending suit and before execution, being then insolvent, assigned all his effects to trustees for the benefit of his creditors, and possession was immediately taken, the assignment was held valid against an execution creditor; [g] for if a deed is executed for the benefit of one or more creditors, and is not meant as a cloak for retaining a benefit to the grantor, it is not void within the Statute of Elizabeth, although it may operate to the prejudice of some particular creditor.[h]

A conveyance or assignment by deed of all a debtor's property for the benefit of creditors is an act of bankruptcy, [i] but cannot be relied on to ground a petition by parties acquiescing in the arrangement.

(5) The object of this exception is to exclude from the **Marriage settlements.** operation of the Acts instruments the intention and effect of which is, not merely assign goods from one person to another, but to create a trust for the purpose of carrying out a provision for a marriage. The exception in the section will therefore include a memorandum of agreement for a

(a) Ashford v. Tuite, 7 Ir. C. L. Rep. 91.

(b) Paine v. Matthews, 53 L. T. 572.

(c) R. v. Creese, 2 C. C. R. 105; 43 L. J. M. C. 51; 29 L. T. 897　22 W. R. 375.

(d) Spencer v. Slater, 4. Q. B. D. 13; 48 L. J. Q. B. 204; 27 W. R. 134; 40 L. T.) 124.

(e) Boldero v. London & Westminster Discount Co., 5 Ex. D. 47, 28 W. R. 154; 42 L. T. 56.

(f) Exp. Parsons, re Townsend, 34 W. R. 329.

(g) Pickstock v. Lyster, 3 M. & S. 371.

(h) Alton v. Harrison, L. R. 4 Ch. 622; 38 L. J. Ch. 669, 21 L. T. 282; 17 W. R. 1034.

(i) See Exp. May, re Spackman, 24 Q. B. D. 728; 38 W. R. 197, 59 L. J. Q. B. 306; 62 L. T. 849.

(j) Exp. Stray, 30 L. J. Bank. 7; L. R. 2 Ch. 374; 16 L. T. 250; 15 W. R. 600.

marriage settlement, although informal, and not under seal;
thus, where an agreement provided that if the intended
marriage should take place all real and leasehold property,
and all personal estate and effects, of or to which the settlor
was then possessed or entitled, should be assigned to a
trustee upon the trusts thereby declared; and that at any
time after solemnization of the marriage the settlor would,
on request, execute a proper settlement for carrying the
trusts into effect, it was held that goods agreed to be settled
were protected from execution creditors, though the
agreement was unregistered, and no settlement was ever
executed.[a]

Marriage
settlements.

But post-nuptial settlements are not within this exception,[b]
though it would seem that the effect of clause 2 of sec. 3 of the
amendment Act will in most cases be to exclude them from the
operation of that Act, the section excepting from the definition
of bills of sale documents given otherwise than by way of security for the payment of money. Registration and attestation
with the formalities prescribed by the principal Act is still
necessary,[c] and if the object of the settlement is to secure payment of money, the amendment Act it seems will also apply.

A duly registered bill of sale, given for valuable consideration, by which a husband assigned to his wife for her
separate use furniture which remained in the joint possession
of the husband and wife at the time of the former's
liquidation was upheld against his creditors; [d] and furniture
purchased by a married woman, out of the savings of her
separate estate, in renewal or substitution for that included
in a marriage settlement, was protected against an execution
creditor of her husband;[e] and so where furniture contracted
to be purchased was settled upon the intended wife of the
settlor, with power to trustees to renew or substitute other
furniture, but the purchase was never completed, the settlor
buying other furniture, a memorandum of its substitution
being indorsed on the deed, the Court of Appeal held the case
within the exception.[f]

(a) Wenman v. Lyon [1891], 2 Q. B. 193; 39 W. R. 519; 65 L. T. 136; 60 L. J.
Q. B. 663.

(b) Fowler v. Foster, 28 L. J. Q. B. 210; 5 Jur. N. S. 99; Ashton v. Blackshaw,
39 L. J. Ch. 205; 9 Eq. 510; 18 W. R. 307; 22 L. T. 197.

(c) Casson v. Churchley, 53 L. J. Q. B. 335; 50 L. T. 568.

(d) Exp. Cox, re Reed, 1 Ch. D. 302; 24 W. R. 302; 34 L. T. 757.

(e) Duncan v. Cashin, L. R. 10 C. P. 554; 44 L. J. C. P. 225; 23 W. R. 561;
32 L. T. 497.

(f) Courcier v. Bardili, 27 S. J. 276.

But where a trader executed a settlement upon his marriage by which he settled certain specific chattels upon trust for the benefit of his wife and the issue of the marriage, covenanting that all future real or personal estate which he should at any time during the coverture be possessed of or entitled to should be assigned to the trustees upon the tru ts thereby declared, it was held that property obtained by the trader while solvent, but subsequent to the marriage, could not be withdrawn from the claims of creditors, and passed to the trustee under his liquidation.[a]

A settlement on an intended wife, before and in considera- Marriage settlements. tion of marriage, is not a bill of sale, and will be supported against the husband's creditors, although, to the knowledge of the wife, he was in embarrassed circumstances at the time of making it; [b] unless, perhaps, the settlement is on the face of it so extravagant, and so grossly out of proportion to the station of the parties, that it ought to awaken inquiry.[c] But if the wife takes the settlement with notice of an available act of bankruptcy committed by the husband, she cannot hold the property against his trustee.[d] When the marriage itself is a contrivance between the husband and wife to defraud creditors, the settlement will be invalid against them;[e] and the result will be the same where there is no intention by either husband or wife to make or accept a real settlement, but only by means of a marriage and a sham settlement to defraud the husband's creditors.[f]

Although a marriage settlement may not be within the section, regard should be had to sec. 47 of the Bankruptcy Act, 1883, by which (1) any settlement, which includes any conveyance or transfer of property, not being a settlement made before and in consideration of marriage, or made in favour of a purchaser[g] or incumbrancer in good faith and for valuable consideration, or a settlement made on or for the

(a) *Exp.* Bolland, *re* Clint, 43 L. J. Bank. 10; 17 Eq. 115; 29 L. T. 543 ; 22 W. R. 152.

(b) Campion *c.* Cotton, 17 Ves. 264 ; Fraser *c.* Thompson, 1 Giff. 65.

(c) *Exp.* McBurnie, 1 De G. M. & G. 441.

(d) Fraser *c.* Thompson, 4 De G. & J. 659.

(e) *Exp.* Pennington 5 Mor. 268; Colombine *c.* Penhall, 1 Sm. & Giff. 228 Bulmer *c.* Hunter, 8 Eq. 46; 20 L. T. 942 ; 38 L. J. Ch. 543.

(f) Parnell *c.* Steadman, 1 Cab. & E. 153.

(g) Purchaser in this section includes a person who gives valuable consideration for the settlement, not being limited to one who buys by contract of purchase and sale (Hance *c.* Harding, 20 Q. B. D. 732; 57 L. J. Q. B. 403; 59 L. T. 659 ; 36 W. R. 629) ; but will not include a person who gives to valuable consideration, though he may be a purchaser in the legal sense of the word *Exp.* Hillman, *re* Pumfrey, 10 Ch. D. 622 ; 40 L. T. 178).

wife or children of the settlor of property which has accrued
to the settlor after marriage in right of his wife, shall
if the settlor becomes bankrupt within two years after the
date of the settlement, be void against the trustee in the
bankruptcy, and shall, if the settlor becomes bankrupt at any
subsequent time within ten years after the date of the settlement be void against the trustee in the bankruptcy, unless the
parties claiming under the settlement can prove that the
settlor was at the time of making the settlement able to pay
all his debts without the aid of the property comprised in the
settlement, and that the interest of the settlor in such property had passed to the trustee of such settlement on the
execution thereof; (2) any covenant or contract made in
consideration of marriage, for the future settlement on, or for
the settlor's wife or children, of any money or property wherein
he had not, at the date of his marriage, any estate or interest,
whether vested or contingent, in possession or remainder, and
not being money or property of or in right of his wife, shall,
on his becoming bankrupt before the property or money has
been actually transferred or paid pursuant to the contract
or covenant, be void against the trustee in his bankruptcy.[a]

The expression " void" in this section must be construed as
voidable, and a purchaser, in good faith and for value, before
avoidance, whether buying with or without notice of the
voluntary settlement, has a good title against the settlor's
trustee in bankruptcy.[b] But a purchaser will not be compelled
to complete a purchase from trustees of a settlement subject
to avoidance under section 47, Bankruptcy Act, 1883, even
though the settlor offers to concur.[c]

Shipping transfers. (6) The expression " ship or vessel" in the section does
not mean what is technically so called, but includes whatever
in popular language is a ship or vessel; and it seems that
anything ordinarily called a vessel, beyond a mere boat, is
within the exception; thus it was held that a dumb barge
propelled by oars, carrying goods but not passengers, was
protected.[d]

(a) The operation of the corresponding sec. 91, Bankruptcy Act, 1869, was
confined to traders; and sec. 47 of the Act of 1883 does not apply to settlements
executed by non-traders before the commencement of the Act (exp. Todd, re
Ashcroft, 19 Q. B. D. 186; 56 L. J. Q. B. 431; 57 L. T. 835; 35 W. R. 676).

(b) Exp. Norton, re Brall [1893], 2 Q. B. 381; 62 L. J. Q. B. 457; 69 L. T. 323;
41 W. R. 623; 10 Mor. 166; exp. Brown, re Vansittart [1893], 2 Q. B. 377; 62 L. J.
Q. B. 279; 68 L. T. 233; 41 W. R. 286.

(c) Re Briggs & Spicer [1891] 2 Ch. 127; 39 W. R. 377; 64 L.T. 187; 60 L. J. Ch. 514.
(d) Gapp v. Bond, 19 Q. B. D. 200; 35 W. R. 683; 56 L. J. Q. B. 438; 57 L. T.
437.

The exception has been held to apply, although the ship is unfinished; and when a shipbuilder, at a creditor's request, lodged with him as security for a debt the builder's certificate, which, describing the ship and her engines, stated that she had been built for the creditor, but in fact she was not completed, nor were her engines in position, it was held that the creditor had obtained an equitable mortgage of the debtor's interest in the ship, which did not require registration.[a]

By the Merchant Shipping Act transfers or mortgages of ships, or any share therein, are required to be by bill of sale in a prescribed form, and take priority according to date of registration, but although the transfer or assignment is not in the form given by that Act, and is not registered, it will not be within the Bills of Sale Acts.[b] Under the word "ship" in the mortgage of a ship with its appurtenances, in the statutory form under the Merchant Shipping Act, all articles and materials, whether stored or in use, necessary for the accomplishment of the ship's voyage, and on board at the date of the mortgage, will pass; and all articles and materials of the like kind substituted subsequently to the mortgage will also pass; such articles and materials will therefore be protected by the mortgage without registration under the Bills of Sale Acts.[c] And by sec. 36, Merchant Shipping Act, 1894, a registered mortgage of a ship or share shall not be affected by any act of bankruptcy committed by the mortgagor after the date of the record of the mortgage, notwithstanding that the mortgagor at the time of commencement of his bankruptcy had the ship or share in his possession, order, or disposition, or was reputed owner thereof, and the mortgage shall be preferred to any right, claim, or interest therein of the other creditors of the bankrupt or any trustee or assignee on their behalf.

(7) The application of this exception must necessarily vary with the facts of each particular case, but it seems that a pledge of stock in trade, bought but not paid for, cannot be considered a transfer in the ordinary course of business;[d] nor do these words point to borrowing

Transfers in the ordinary course of business.

(a) *Exp.* Winter *re* Softley, 44 L. J. Bank. 107; 20 Eq. 746; 33 L. T. 62; 24 W. R. 68.

(b) Union Bank of London *v.* Lenanton, 3 C. P. D. 243; 47 L. J. C. P. 409; 38 L. T. 698.

(c) Coltman *v.* Chamberlain, 39 W. R. 12.

(d) *Exp.* Close *re* Hall, 14 Q. B. D. 386; R. *v.* Thomas, 11 Cox, C. C., 535; 22 L.T. 138.

money on mortgage or special agreement, though such a thing may be frequent among certain classes of persons.[a] As has been seen, the Acts do not apply to letters of hypothecation accompanying a deposit of goods, nor to pawn-tickets[b]; thus a letter of hypothecation given by a factor and warehouseman to his bankers, agreeing to hold certain wools for them as security for advances with interest, and to sell them and pay over the proceeds when received, or if required to deliver the wools to enable the bankers to realize them for payment of the advance, was held to confer a good equitable charge, and not to require registration;[c] and so was an agreement entered into on supplying goods for shipment, giving the vendor a lien for the price on bills of lading and each shipment;[d] and a deed whereby goods then in the hands of bleachers were by them and the owners transferred to a bank to secure current account, containing a covenant to hold those and any other goods from time to time substituted, for the creditor, who was authorized to enter on the premises and seize and sell the goods, was held to confer a valid charge, and to bind substituted goods without registration.[e]

Transfers in the ordinary course of business.

In another case the Secretary of a Company applied to a pawnbroker for a loan on the security of a warrant indorsed by the Company for goods, lying at a wharf, and the pawnbroker made the loan on the condition that he was to be at liberty to lodge the warrant with the wharfinger and obtain in exchange a new warrant, making the goods deliverable to his manager. The secretary of the Company then signed a memorandum stating that he had deposited the warrant for the goods with the pawnbroker as security for the loan and further advances, empowering the pawnbroker to sell the securities if the loan was not paid, whereupon the pawnbroker lodged the warrant with the wharfinger, obtaining a new warrant, making the goods deliverable to his manager. The transaction was held not to be within the Acts.[f] So the exception in the section applies to a delivery order authorizing

(a) Tennant r. Howatson, 13 App. Cases, 489 ; 58 L.T. 616 ; 57 L. J. P. C. 110.

(b) Exp. Close, re Hall, 14 Q. B. D. 386.

(c) Exp. North-Western Bank, re Slee, L. R. 15 Eq. 69 ; 42 L. J. Bank 6; 21 W. R. 69; 27 L. T. 461.

(d) Exp. Watson, re Love, 5 Ch. D. 35 ; 46 L. J. Bank 97 ; 36 L. T. 75 ; 25 W. R. 489.

(e) Merchant Banking Co. r. Spotten, Ir. L. R. 11 Eq. 586.

(f) Re Cunningham, 28 Ch. D. 682; 54 L. J. Ch. 448; 33 W. R. 387; 52 L. T. 214.

a warehouseman to hand goods to persons who have lent money on a verbal charge upon them.[a]

But where traders in consideration of goods being supplied on credit signed a written document undertaking and agreeing to hold their stock at the vendor's disposal, and from time to time, when required to do so, to execute to them a valid and effectual transfer and assurance to provide for payment of all moneys then due, but no bill of sale was ever called for, nor was possession obtained, the document was held void, not having been registered.[b] So an agreement was held not to be a transfer in the ordinary course of business, whereby the owner of a sugar plantation, in consideration of a loan, borrowed from a merchant for the expenses of getting the crop and making the sugar, agreed to deliver the crop of sugar, when made, to the merchant to sell on commission and retain his debt out of the proceeds.[c] And an hypothecation note, given on obtaining an advance, whereby the grantors undertook to hold goods in trust for the lenders, and to hand over the proceeds when received, to the extent of the advance, was held a bill of sale.[d]

The expression " personal chattels " shall mean goods, furniture, and other articles capable of complete transfer by delivery,[1] and (when separately [1] Page 68. assigned or charged) fixtures and growing crops, but shall not include chattel interests in real estate, nor fixtures (except trade machinery as hereinafter defined), when assigned together with a freehold or leasehold interest in any land or building to which they are affixed, nor growing crops when assigned together with any interest in the land on which they grow,[2] nor shares or interests in the stock, funds, or [2] Page 68. securities of any government, or in the capital, or property of incorporated or joint stock companies, nor choses in action,[3] nor any stock or produce upon [3] Page 70. any farm or lands which by virtue of any covenant or agreement or of the custom of the country ought

(a) Grigg v. National Guardian Assurance Co. [1891], 3 Ch. 206.
(b) Exp. Conning, re Steele, 16 Eq. 414.
(c) Tennant v. Howatson, 13 App. Cases, 489.
(d) R. v. Townshend, 15 Cox C.C 466.

(4) Page 71.

not to be removed from any farm where the same are at the time of making or giving of such bill of sale: [4]

(1) Under the repealed Acts these words qualified the whole section, which included only goods which could have been delivered and removed at the time of sale, and were, nevertheless, left in the apparent possession of the original owner.[a] Pictures,[b] and implements of trade,[c] have been held to be personal chattels, within the reputed ownership clause of the Bankruptcy Acts, but heirlooms would seem not to be included in the definition of personal chattels within that clause.[d]

Growing crops.

(2) A considerable alteration in the law was effected by this clause. Growing crops were not within the Bills of Sale Act, 1854,[e] and where a mortgagor presented a petition for liquidation, and his trustee went into possession of the mortgaged lands, and commenced cutting the growing crops, the mortgagee putting a man in possession, and requiring the trustee to give up possession, which he refused to do, an injunction was granted restraining the trustee from cutting crops, and from removing those cut after the mortgagee's demand of possession.[f] So second mortgagees, who had taken possession, were held entitled to growing crops as against the mortgagor's trustee in bankruptcy.[g]

Although growing crops are not within the Acts, unless separately assigned, as soon as they are severed they become personal chattels, and are not protected by an unregistered assignment.[h]

A bill of sale of future growing crops has been held to pass the property in them on their coming into existence;[i] and by sec. 6 of the amendment Act, a bill of sale will be effectual in respect of growing crops separately assigned

(a) Brantom v. Griffiths, 2 C. P. D. 212; 25 W. R. 313; 46 L. J. C. P. 408; 36 L. T. 4; Exp. Payne, re Cross, 11 Ch. D. 539; 27 W. R. 808; 40 L. T. 563.

(b) Exp. Castle, 3 M. D. & D. 117.

(c) Clark v. Crownshaw, 3 B. & Ad. 804.

(d) Shaftesbury v. Russell, 1 B. & C. 666; 3 D. & R. 84.

(e) Brantom v. Griffiths, 2 C. P. D. 212.

(f) Bagnall v. Villar, 12 Ch. D. 812; 28 W. R. 242; 48 L. J. Ch. 695.

(g) Re Gordon, 61 L. T. 299; 6 Mor. 150.

(h) Exp. National Mercantile Bank, re Phillips, 20 W. R. 227; 16 Ch. D. 104; 44 L. T. 265; 50 L. J. Ch. 231.

(i) Clements v. Matthews, 11 Q. B. D. 808; 52 L. J. Q. B. 772.

or charged, where such crops were actually growing at the time when the bill of sale was executed, or of fixtures separately assigned or charged, and any plant or trade machinery on premises in substitution for any of the like fixtures, plant, or trade machinery specifically described in the schedule to the bill of sale, notwithstanding the crops, fixtures, plant, or machinery assigned are not so specifically described, or that the grantor was not the true owner at the time of the execution of the bill of sale.

Although the section declares fixtures to be personal chattels, they are made so only for the purposes of the Act, and not for all other purposes.[a]　It becomes material to consider what are fixtures within the section, for an assignment of personal chattels, although coupled with an interest in realty, will still require registration. Trade machinery is declared personal chattels by sec. 5 of the principal Act, except as to the machinery and articles thereby excluded from the definition of trade machinery, which are not to be deemed personal chattels within the meaning of the Acts; and, where the security can be severed, a bill of sale, void under the Acts, has been held effectual as a security over such excluded articles.[b]

In its primary sense the word fixtures denotes anything　Fixtures. fastened to or connected with the freehold. Articles no further attached to the land than by their own weight are generally to be considered as mere chattels, unless the circumstances are such as to show that they were intended to be part of the land, the onus of proving which rests on those who assert that they have lost their character of chattels; thus a granary resting upon straddles built into the ground, but not attached to it, except by its own weight, is not a fixture.[c]　On the other hand, articles affixed to the freehold even slightly, whether by nails, screws, solder, or other permanent means, or by being fixed in the soil, are fixtures; thus doors, windows, rings, keys, are fixtures,[d] and so are chimneypieces, stoves, or coppers,[e] unless it clearly appears that the articles have all along been treated as chattels, which

(a) Meux v. Jacobs, L. R. 7 H. L. 481; 44 L. J. Ch. 481; 29 W. R. 526; 32 L. T. 171.
(b) Exp. Byrne re Burdett, 20 Q. B. D. 310; 58 L. T. 708; 36 W. R. 345; 57 L. J. Q. B. 263; 5 Mor. 32.
(c) Wiltshear v. Cottrell, 1 E. & B. 674; 17 Jur. 758; 22 L. J. Q. B. 177.
(d) Liford's Case, 11 Co. 50.
(e) Darby v. Harris, 1 Q. B. 895; 1 G. & D. 234; 5 Jur. 988.

must be proved by the person contending that they have never become fixtures.[a]

A bill of sale of fixtures required registration by the express words of the repealed statute, and much uncertainty arose as to whether a mortgage of land, by which fixtures passed, was within the provisions of the Act. By sec. 7 of the principal Act, which applies to all deeds or instruments including fixtures or growing crops executed before or after the commencement of that Act, no fixtures or growing crops shall be deemed to be separately assigned or charged, by reason only that they are assigned by separate words, or that power is given to sever them from the land or building to which they are affixed, or from the land on which they grow, without otherwise taking possession of or dealing with such land or building, or land, if by the same instrument any freehold or leasehold interest in the land or building to which such fixtures are affixed, or in the land on which such crops grow, is also conveyed or assigned to the same persons or person.

Choses in action.

(3) Book-debts are not chattels within the Acts, but debts due or growing due to a grantor in the course of his trade or business, and included in a bill of sale, may remain in his reputed ownership. unless notice is given of their assignment. Book-debts are such debts accruing in the ordinary course of a man's trade as are usually entered by a trader in his trade books.[b] If book-debts are assigned, a separate instrument of transfer is recommended; and it would seem that book-debts cannot be included in a bill of sale subject to the amendment Act. as the only things which may be inserted in the schedule to such a bill of sale are chattels personal.[c] Subject to this, an assignment of all book-debts due and owing, or which during the continuance of the security might become due and owing to the mortgagor, operated to pass the beneficial interest in a debt which came into existence after the assignment.[d]

A share in a partnership is a chose in action, and is not within the expression "personal chattels," although including

(a) Mather v. Fraser, 2 K. & J. 536; 25 L. J. Ch. 361 ; 4 W. R.387; 2 Jur. N. S. 900.

(b) Official Receiver v. Tailby, 18 Q. B. D. 25 ; 35 W. R. 91 ; 55 L. T. 626; 56 L. J. Q. B. 30.

(c) Cochrane v. Entwistle, 25 Q. B. D. 116 ; 59 L. J. Q. B. 418 ; 62 L. T. 852 39 W. R. 597.

(d) Tailby v. The Official Receiver, 13 App. Cases 523; 37 W. R.513; 60 L. T. 162 ; 58 L. J. Q. B. 75.

plant and stock-in-trade;" and so is an assignment, to secure a debt, of all rights under a hiring agreement, by which the assignor had let goods on hire to a third person, with authority to the assignee on default to exercise all powers conferred by the agreement, but not purporting to assign the goods themselves;[b] and even though by the same instrument the goods themselves are assigned.[c] It has, however, been decided that an assignment of, or charge on, a debt secured by a mortgage of chattels, must be accompanied by the same formalities as are essential to make the original security effective.[b]

A testator by his will bequeathed to his wife the right of possession of all his pictures during her life, and subject to this bequest gave them to his son for his own absolute use and benefit. The testator's wife retained the pictures, and the son executed a mortgage assigning all his share and interest under his father's will, and of and in the sums of money hereditaments and premises thereby devised and bequeathed expectant on the decease of his mother. The son during his mother's lifetime became bankrupt, and it was held as against the trustee, who claimed the expectancy in the pictures, that the mortgage was of a chose in action, and not within the Acts.[d]

Choses in action.

Assignments of choses in action, with their validity against assignees and others will be found discussed in the notes to "Ryall v. Rowles." 1 Ves. 348; 2 W. & T. L. Cases.

(4) No purchaser or mortgagee of a tenant's crop can carry it off a farm contrary to the terms of the lease; and it is provided by statute that no assignee of any bankrupt, or under any bill of sale, nor any purchaser of the goods, chattels, stock, or crop of any person engaged or employed in husbandry on any lands let to farm, shall take, use, or dispose of any produce of such lands, or any manure or dressings intended for such lands and being thereon, in any other manner or for any other purpose than such bankrupt or other person so employed in husbandry ought to have taken, used, or disposed of the same if there had been no bankruptcy, assignment, or sale.[f]

(a) *Exp.* Fletcher, *re* Bainbridge, 17 L. J. Bank. 70; 4 Ch. D. 218; 26 W. R. 439; 38 L. T. 229.

(b) *Exp.* Rawlings, *re* Davis, 22 Q. B. D. 193.

(c) *Exp.* Mason, *re* Isaacson, 98 L. T. J. 155.

(d) Jarvis v. Jarvis, 63 L. J. Ch. 10.

(e) *Exp.* Singleton, *re* Tritton, 6 Mor. 250; 61 L. T. 301.

(f) 56 Geo. III. c. 50, s. 11, *see* Lybbe v. Hart, 29 Ch. D. 8; 54 L. J. Ch. 860; 52 L. T. 631.

Personal chattels shall be deemed to be in the "apparent possession" of the person making or giving a bill of sale, so long as they remain or are in or upon any house, mill, warehouse, building, works, yard, land, or other premises occupied by him, or are used and enjoyed by him in any place whatsoever, notwithstanding that formal possession thereof may have been taken by or given to any other person.

This definition, although not expressly repealed by the amendment Act, will cease to have any practical value as affecting bills of sale executed on or after the 1st of November, 1882, and given by way of security for the payment of money, for the validity of such a bill of sale does not now depend on the question whether the chattels it comprises were or were not in the grantor's apparent possession.[a] As, however, the doctrine of apparent possession appears still to apply to bills of sale given otherwise than as security, and questions may arise under the repealed sec. 8 of the principal Act, the cases on the subject are here noted. By that section, a bill of sale not registered within the time and in the manner prescribed is to be deemed fraudulent and void against trustees and execution creditors of the person whose chattels are comprised in such bill of sale, so far as regards chattels which at or after the time of such person's bankruptcy or liquidation, or of execution levied, and after seven days from the time of giving the bill of sale, are in such person's possession or apparent possession.

It should be noted that two classes of apparent possession are mentioned in the sub-section :—firstly, where the chattels subject to the bill of sale are upon premises occupied by the grantor, and secondly, where they are used and enjoyed by him in any place whatsoever. In the first class there must be an actual occupation, the words "occupied by him" meaning that the grantor should occupy in the ordinary sense of the term, and not including cases where he has merely an interest in a lease ; and when the grantor of an unregistered bill of sale was tenant of rooms where the goods comprised in it were placed, but resided elsewhere; and having made default in payment, gave up the keys of the rooms to the grantee, who opened the rooms and put his name on some of the goods

(a) Sec. 8 [1882].

which, however, remained on the premises, it was held that
the grantor did not occupy the rooms, and that the goods
were not to be deemed in his apparent possession. [a] Again,
where the grantor, who had by an unregistered deed mortgaged a freehold house and furniture to secure a debt and
interest, remained in possession, attorning to the mortgagee,
and subsequently let the house furnished with the consent of
the mortgagee, to whom a portion of the rent was to be paid
by the incoming tenant, who took possession ; on the grantor's
bankruptcy it was held that the section did not apply, for the
goods were not upon premises in the occupation of the
grantor, nor were they used or enjoyed by him. [b]

The doctrine of apparent possession differs from that of
order and disposition under the Bankruptcy Act, and the
consent of the true owner is here immaterial. He may demand and endeavour to take possession of the goods ; but to
avoid the section, there must be something done which takes
them plainly out of the grantor's control in the eyes of everybody who sees them. [c]

The doctrine of actual and formal taking of possession has
thus been laid down : "The distinction between formal and
real possession seems to have been grounded upon the
authority of some recent decisions at law which were then
fully considered. The distinction is this ; that if a bailiff is
simply put in possession and remains in possession so as to
prevent the removal of the goods, but allows everything to go
on just as it did before, permitting everything to be used by
the debtor and his family, then the goods still remain in the
apparent possession of the debtor. There must be something
done which, in the eyes of everybody who sees the goods, or
who is concerned in the matter, plainly takes them out of the
apparent possession of the debtor." [d] This decision is
illustrated by the following cases :—

In *ex parte* Lewis, *re* Henderson, [e] the holder of an un- Apparent
registered bill of sale of household furniture took possession possession.
by sending in a broker's man, who remained in the house and
slept in an upper room, but did not remove any of the furni-

(a) Robinson *r*. Briggs, L. R. 6 Exch. 1 ; 40 L. J. Ex. 17 ; 24 L. T. 695.

(b) *Exp.* Morrison *re* Westray, 28 W. R. 524 ; 42 L. T. 158.

(c) Ancona *r*. Rogers, 46 L. J. Ex. 121 ; 35 L. T. 115 ; 1 Ex. D. 285, 24 W. R.
1080.

(d) *Exp.* Jay, *re* Blenkhorn, L. R. 9 Ch. 697 ; 22 W. R. 907, 31 L. T. 260 ; 43 L.
J. Bank. 122, per Mellish, L.J.

(e) L. R. 6 Ch. 626 ; 40 W. R. 845 ; 24 L. T. 785.

ture, or interfere with the use of it by the grantor, who went on using it as before. Placards were posted in the neighbourhood announcing a sale of furniture; but with the exception of reference to a firm of solicitors for particulars, there was nothing from which it would be inferred that the sale was not by the grantor himself. It was held that the goods remained in the apparent possession of the grantor, that the possession by the broker's man was a merely formal possession, and that posting the placards, not shewing that the sale was under a bill of sale, could not take the goods out of the grantor's apparent possession; but when the grantee takes possession of the goods and advertises them for sale as the goods of the grantor sold under a bill of sale, they will no longer be in his apparent possession, though remaining in his house.[a]

Apparent
possession.

In Smith c. Wall,[b] when possession was taken and the business was stopped, the door of the house was locked, the key being kept by the plaintiff's man in possession, and placards were posted outside the house and about the neighbourhood announcing a sale under a bill of sale, but the debtor, who was an infirm old man, was allowed to remain in the house, not being able to get lodgings elsewhere, it was held that more than formal possession had been taken. Where the assignee, under a bill of sale, put a man into possession of the premises to carry on for his benefit the grantor's business, and the man in possession seized the whole stock, employed new servants while retaining some who had been on the premises before, buying fresh stock to a large amount, and the grantor ceased to be on the premises, but his name was still over the door, and his daughter continued to reside there, it was held that the goods did not remain in his apparent possession;[c] for formal possession within the section means that possession should have no effect if the grantor remains in the house and in use and enjoyment of the goods, although some person is put in to hold joint possession; thus, where a man was put in possession of the goods which were in a house belonging to the grantor, who had a key and went in and out as he pleased, although he did not sleep there, his apparent possession was held to continue.[d]

(a) Emmanuel c. Bridger, L. R. 9 Q. B. 286; 43 L. J. Q. B. 96; 30 L. T. 195; Gough c. Everard, 2 H. & C. 1; 32 L. J. Ex. 210; 8 L. T. N. S. 363; 11 W. R. 702.
(b) 16 L. T. 182.
(c) Davies c. Jones (Note (a) 75).
(d) Seni c. Claridge, 7 Q. B. D. 516; 50 L. J. Q. B. 316; 29 W. R. 508; 44 L. T. 501.

But if the grantee openly, really and truly takes possession, **Apparent possession.** then, although the grantor remains in possession, the Act does not apply;[a] thus where the mortgagee sold the goods to the grantor's son, who kept them in premises he rented and occupied, they were held not to be in the grantor's apparent possession, although he continued to live there;[b] although in another case furniture comprised in a bill of sale was held to be in the apparent possession of the grantor, who resided in a house taken by his son, to which the furniture had been removed.[c] Where stock and the goodwill of a business were sold by unregistered deed, and after the sale the goods remained on the premises where the business was carried on, which was managed by the vendor, who continued to live on the premises as servant to the purchaser, but the name over the shop was altered, circulars being issued to all creditors, and the sale advertised in the local papers, it was held as against an execution creditor of the vendor that the stock was not in his apparent possession.[d] Also, when the man placed in possession of the grantor's shop and premises locked them up at night, the servants in the shop being dismissed, and the bill of sale holder made an inventory of the goods, it being notorious in the neighbourhood that possession had been taken, it was decided that the bill of sale holder had seized in such a way as to shew he was dealing with his own property, and had done all that was incumbent on him to take the goods out of the grantor's apparent possession, although it was in evidence that the man in possession did not appear in the shop, but remained in a warehouse out of sight of customers, the business going on as usual, and the shop being served by the grantor and his son.[e] This must, however, be considered an extreme case.

For the purposes of the section, goods in the possession of a bailee for the grantor, such as a gentleman's plate delivered to his banker, or his furniture lodged in a warehouse, are in the possession of the grantor himself; and so long as the grantor is having the goods kept for him and is exercising dominion over them the section will apply.[f] Thus, where the grantor managed a business as servant to the grantee at a weekly salary, and was allowed to reside in the house where

(a) Davies r. Jones, 10 W. R. 779; 7 L. T. N. S. 130.
(b) Swire r. Cookson, 19 L. T. 798.
(c) Re Emery, 21 Q. B. D. 405; 37 W. R. 21 ; 57 L. J. Q. B. 620.
(d) Gibbons r. Hickson, 34 W. R. 140; 54 L. T. 910; 55 L. J. Q. B. 119.
(e) Exp. Mortlock, re Basham, W. N. 1881, p. 161.
(f) Ancona r. Rogers, 1 Ex. D. 285.

the business was carried on, and, as part of his salary, to use the furniture assigned by the bill of sale, the grantee residing elsewhere, it was held that the goods remained in the grantor's apparent possession; [a] but a chattel pledged is not in the apparent possession of the pledgor, for he has no power of disposal or to act as owner. [b]

Apparent
possession

Goods may be in the true and actual possession of one person, but in the apparent possession of another; [c] thus, where a person, being in custody, gave a bill of sale over certain jewels in the hands of the police. they were held to remain in his apparent possession; [d] but goods comprised in an unregistered bill of sale in the possession of the sheriff under an execution are not in the apparent possession of the grantor, even although the mortgagee has himself taken no possession, [e] and so it would seem in the case of seizure by a duly-appointed receiver. [f]   Such possession, however, must be an actual visible possession; thus, if the sheriff's officer took possession in the disguise of a livery servant of the grantor it would not be sufficient. [e]

The possession of chattels by a cestui que trust, in accordance with the provisions of the trust, is in law, for some purposes, the possession of the trustees; [g] and it seems doubtful whether goods which are the separate property of a wife can be deemed in the apparent possession of her husband when husband and wife are living together. [h]

When a wife bought from her husband certain furniture in the house where they lived together, there being no formal delivery of the furniture, which remained as before in the house where the parties resided, it was held that the husband's apparent possession was excluded, for as the situation of the goods was consistent with their being in the possession of either the husband or the wife, the law would attribute possession to the wife, who had the legal title. [i]

(a) Pickard v. Marriage, 1 Ex. D. 364; 45 L. J. Ex. 594; 35 L. T. 343; 24 W. R. 846.

(b) Lincoln Wagon Co. v. Mumford, 41 L. T. 655.

(c) Robinson v. Tucker, 1 Cab. & E. 173.

(d) Exp. Newsham, re Wood. 40 L. T. 104.

(e) Exp. Saffery, re Bremner, 16 Ch. D. 668; 44 L. T. 324; 29 W. R. 749.

(f) Taylor v. Eckersley, 5 Ch. D. 740; 25 W. R. 527 36 L. T. 412.

(g) Barker v. Furlong [1891]. 2 Ch. 172.

(h) Shepherd v. Pulbrook, 4 T. L. R. 642.

(i) Ramsay v. Margrett [1894], 2 Q. B. 18.

Indeed it is not necessary that the grantee should have an exclusive possession to take the goods out of the grantor's apparent possession; [a] and actual possession taken by the grantee of an unregistered bill of sale, even though taken wrongfully, may exclude the operation of the Act; but a wrongdoer or trespasser, as for example, a bill of sale holder, who seizes without a proper demand, must take actual physical possession to remove the goods from the grantor's apparent possession, although where possession is taken legally it will be extended by construction of law beyond the actual physical possession, and a taking possession of one of the things comprised in the deed may amount to possession of all. [b]

" Prescribed " means prescribed by rules made under the provisions of this Act.

By section 21 of the principal Act, rules may be made and altered from time to time, under the provisions of the Judicature Acts. Certain rules have been issued which will be found noted in their places.

4. (1882.) Every bill of sale shall have annexed thereto or written thereon a schedule containing an inventory of the personal chattels comprised in the bill of sale; and such bill of sale, save as hereinafter mentioned, shall have effect only in respect of the personal chattels specifically described in the said schedule; and shall be void, except as against the grantor, in respect of any personal chattels not so specifically described.

Bill of sale to have schedule of property.

It is difficult to reconcile the two clauses of the section, by the first of which the bill of sale shall have effect only in respect of chattels specifically described, while the second saves its avoidance against the grantor in respect of chattels not fulfilling that condition; but the proper construction probably is that the latter clause of the section qualifies the first. Another construction might be that assignments of property not specifically described, although not void as against the grantor, operate only as a licence to seize and have no effect by grant.

(a) Burroughs v. Williams, L. J. N. 1878, 127;
(b) Exp. Fletcher, re Henley, 25 W. R. 573; 36 L. T. 758; 46 L. J. Bank, 41; Ch. D. 809.

D

It will be observed that in the scheduled form, which by sec. 9 of the amendment Act is compulsory, the property assigned is only that which is specifically described; and it has been held that an essential condition of the validity of a bill of sale is a present assignment of chattels capable of specific description;[a] and that the only things which may be inserted in the schedule are chattels personal; thus a bill of sale assigning chattels real with personal chattels is void.[b] Sec. 4 must therefore be read with and subject to sec. 9, and deals with a departure, not from the form, but from the proper description in the schedule. Thus, a bill of sale, in accordance with the form, followed by a schedule purporting to specifically describe the chattels assigned, but with regard to some of them containing no sufficient specific description, would, as to such chattels, come within the saving clause of the section.[c]

By sec. 6 of the amendment Act, a bill of sale shall not be void for want of specific description in the schedule of any growing crops separately assigned or charged where such growing crops were actually growing at the time when the bill of sale was executed, or any fixtures separately assigned or charged, and any plant or trade machinery, when such fixtures, plant or trade machinery are used in, attached to, or brought upon any land, farm, factory, workshop, shop, house, warehouse, or other place in substitution for any of the like articles specifically described in the schedule to the bill of sale.

A schedule was not requisite before the amendment Act, but was frequently adopted for greater accuracy, being prepared in such a form as not to limit the general words of the deed.   It is now compulsory in all cases within the amendment Act, and must be written on or annexed to the bill of sale, and a copy filed;[d] and if no schedule is attached to a bill of sale at the time of its execution, the security is void against an execution creditor.[e]

The chattels intended to be assigned must be described, not generally, but should be specified so as to be capable of identifi-

---

(a) Thomas r. Kelly, 13 App. Cases, 506; 60 L. T. 114; 58 L. J. Q. B. 96; 37 W. R. 353.

(b) Cochrane r. Entwistle, 25 Q. B. D. 116.

(c) Kelly r. Kellond, 20 Q. B. D. 569; 36 W. R. 363.

(d) Sec. 10, sub-sec. 2 (1878).

(e) Griffin r. Union Deposit Bank, 3 T. L. R. 608.

cation; although what will be a sufficient specific description must, it seems, depend, to some extent, on the circumstances of the case. A mere clerical error of description which could not deceive, as for example, " premier plating machine " for " premier platen machine," there being evidence that any one acquainted with the trade would know what article was intended, will not affect the sufficiency of description.[a]

The requirements of the section are an inventory and specific description of the chattels, and specifically described means described with such particularity as is usual in an ordinary business inventory of such chattels in such a place as they are.[b]   A full inventory or catalogue is recommended, for the description must, generally speaking, be sufficient to distinguish the chattels assigned from other chattels of the same class. Thus, the description "household furniture and effects, implements of husbandry," has been held insufficient.[c]   So description only by number and quality will not do, as applied to a trader's stock where other articles of the same kind may be on the premises; and the schedule to a bill of sale of stock-in-trade, describing the goods as " 450 oil paintings in gilt frames, 300 oil paintings unframed, 50 watercolours in gilt frames, 20 watercolours unframed, 20 gilt frames," was held not to be a specific description of the chattels assigned.[b]   And so a description of farm stock, " 21 milch cows," has been held not sufficiently specific, there being nothing to shew that they were the only cows on the premises.[d]

Specific description.

But if this had appeared, such a description would it seems have been sufficient; thus an assignment of all the farming stock on a particular farm described as "all my farming stock comprising four horses, five cows " and other animals particularized only by the number of them was upheld.[e]   So the description of chattels as "roan horse, ' Drummer,' brown mare and foal, three rade carts," was held sufficient in the absence of evidence that the grantor at the time of executing the bill of sale had other articles answering this description.[f]

(a) Simmons r. Hughes, 34 S. J. 650.
(b) Witt r. Banner, 20 Q. B. D. 114; 36 W. R. 115; 57 L. J. Q. B. 141 ; 58 L. T. 34.
(c) Roberts r. Roberts, 50 L. T. 351; 32 W. R. 606; 13 Q. B. D. 794; 53 L. J. Q. B. 313.
(d) Carpenter r. Deen, 23 Q. B. D. 566; 61 L. T. 860.
(e) Jones r. Roberts, 34 S. J. 254.
(f) Hickley r. Greenwood, 25 Q. B. D. 277 ; 38 W. R. 680 ; 59 L. J. Q. B. 413 ; 63 L. T. 288.

Where the objection is taken that there is not a specific description of the goods, the objector in order to succeed must either shew that from the nature of the description the goods cannot be identified, or that they are incapable of identification.[a] Nor is the same accuracy and precision of description required of goods in a particular room of a private house as of goods in the possession of a trader, and in the former case "twelve oil paintings in gilt frames" described as being in a particular room was held a sufficient description.[b]

In such cases specifically described does not mean individually described, for a description by number is not necessarily insufficient; for example, "all silver coffee pots now in my house" would seem sufficient without describing each coffee pot by itself; and the following was held a specific description in a schedule of the things assigned :— "The whole of the chattels and things at present at W. Vicarage, and consisting, *inter alia*, of . . . Study : 1,300 vols. of books as per catalogue. Miscellaneous : silver-plated goods, china tea service, coffee service, knives, forks, dinner sets, table linen, bed linen, beds, bedding, ornaments, crockery," the articles not being otherwise enumerated, and the catalogue not being annexed.[c]

The schedule.   The decisions under the old law would appear to some extent still applicable. Although a list of the chattels either in the deed or in the schedule was not necessary, such a description as would enable them to be identified being sufficient, where a deed contained a covenant to make an inventory, but none was ever made, its absence was, with other circumstances, left to the jury as evidence of fraud.[d] Where, however, the original schedule was destroyed, filing a copy was held sufficient.[e]

Under the repealed Acts it was held that the schedule controlled the general words of the deed ; thus, the words "goods and chattels" or "effects" which, alone, would include the grantor's whole personal estate, might be cut down and qualified by the particular description in the schedule;

(a) Hickley r. Greenwood, 25 Q. B. D. 277 ; 38 W. R. 686 ; 59 L. J. Q. B. 413 ; 63 L. T. 288.

(b) Cooper r. Kendrick, 34 S. J. 96.

(c) Davidson r. Carlton Bank [1893], 1 Q. B. 82 ; 41 W. R. 132 ; 62 L. J. Q. B. 111 ; 67 L. T. 641.

(d) Dewey r. Bayntun, 6 East, 257.

(e) Green r. Attenborough, 3 H. & C. 468 ; 34 L. J. Ex. 88 : 13 W. R. 185 ; 11 L. T. 513.

and a bill of sale, which after assigning specific goods,
then or thereafter in or about premises occupied by
the grantor, proceeded to assign all other the personal
estate whatsoever, of or to which the grantor then was or
thereafter should become entitled, was held not to pass the
term which the grantor had in the premises. [a] In like manner,
a mortgage of a business of dining rooms and restaurant,
together with the trade fixtures, fittings, and other things used
for carrying on the same, was held not to pass loose articles,
such as cooking utensils and furniture used for the purposes
of the restaurant. [b] So where a bill of sale purported to
assign all the household goods and furniture of every kind and
description whatsoever in a house, more particularly mentioned
and set forth in an inventory or schedule of even date, and
given to the mortgagee upon the execution thereof, but the
inventory did not specify all the goods and furniture in the
house, it was held to operate only as an assignment of the
goods and furniture specified in the inventory. [c]

Neither could a schedule enlarge the deed where the words   The schedule.
of the latter were precise; thus, when to a mortgage of a
foundry with the engines, fixtures, machinery, tools and
working plant thereon more particularly enumerated and
described in an inventory to be signed by the parties, and to
be read and construed as forming part of the deed, was
annexed an inventory which mentioned stock-in-trade, as to
which the deed was silent, it was held the stock-in-trade did
not pass, James, L.J., remarking, that even if an express
intention to include articles not coming within the terms of
the deed had been shewn by a separate writing, that could not
make the deed operate in a way inconsistent with its plain
terms, however it might lay ground for rectifying it. [d] It
would seem, however, that a schedule, now being compulsory,
forms part of the deed; [e] though it is treated as distinct
from the deed in section 10, sub-s. 2, of the principal Act, and
it has been held that a catalogue referred to in the schedule,
but not in the bill of sale itself, does not require registration. [f]

(a) Harrison v. Blackburn, 34 L. J. C. P. 109; 17 C. B. N. S. 678; 13 W. R. 135.
(b Dowling v. Steward, W. N. 1885, 98.
(c) Wood v. Rowcliffe, 6 Exch. 407; 20 L. J. Ex. 285; Mee v. Parren, 15 L. T.
N. S. 320.
(d) Exp. Jardine, re McManus, L. R. 10 Ch. 322; 23 W. R. 382; 31 L. T. 802.
(e) Melville v. Stringer, 12 Q. B. D. 132; 53 L. J. Q. B. 176; 32 W. R. 388.
(f) Davidson v. Carlton Bank [1893], 1 Q. B. 82.

If there was an adequate and sufficient description of what
was meant to pass, a subsequent erroneous addition would
not vitiate it, and where a bill of sale assigned all the goods,
&c., in certain premises more particularly described in
the schedule, it was held that the large words in the body of
the deed were not limited by the schedule, which only
described a part of the goods, the schedule being merely by
way of further description;[a] and this rule was extended so
as to include goods bought and inserted in the schedule
before, but not upon the premises until after the execution of
a bill of sale which expressed to assign all the furniture in a
house, and comprised in a schedule annexed.[b] Where, however, the defendant bound himself under a penalty to deliver
to the plaintiff the whole of his mechanical pieces as per
schedule annexed, it was held that the schedule formed part
of the deed, without which it would be insensible;[c] but upon
an assignment of all and every the household goods, &c., the
particulars whereof were stated to be more fully set forth in
an inventory signed by the grantor, and annexed thereto,
although no inventory existed, it was nevertheless held that
the assignment was effectual, it appearing that the particulars
of the chattels comprised in the deed could be ascertained. [d]

The schedule.

If chattels were omitted from the schedule by mistake, the
Court might, perhaps, allow it to be rectified, and extend the
time for registration under sec. 14 of the principal Act; or
for greater caution, a new bill of sale might be given of the
chattels omitted.

The Stamp Act, 1870, repealed by the Stamp Act, 1891,
imposed a duty on every schedule or inventory not indorsed
upon or annexed to the bill of sale,[e] but if a bill of sale
referring to a schedule of things sold is complete and in-
telligible without it, it might have been read, though the
schedule, being unstamped, was inadmissible; thus, when
there was tendered in evidence a bill of sale and schedule,
the former assigning all the goods, &c., in and about certain
premises where the grantor resided, the chief articles whereof
were stated to be more particularly described and enumerated
in a certain schedule annexed, but the schedule was not annexed

(a) Baker r. Richardson, 6 W. R. 663.
(b) Sutton r. Bath, 1 F. & F. 152.
(c) Weeks r. Maillardet, 14 East, 568.
(d) England r. Downs, 2 Beav. 522; 9 L. J. Ch. 313; 4 Jur. 526.
(e) See Note to sec. 18 [1878].

to the deed, and was inadmissible for want of a stamp, it was held that the bill of sale was admissible in evidence without the schedule; [a] nor was a deed legally stamped vitiated by referring to an inventory which was not stamped. [b]

5. (1882.) Save as hereinafter mentioned, a bill of sale shall be void, except as against the grantor, in respect of any personal chattels specifically described in the schedule thereto, of which the grantor was not the true owner at the time of the execution of the bill of sale.

Bill of sale not to affect after-acquired property.

The effect of this and the preceding section will be to avoid, except as against the grantor, assignments of property not specifically described in the schedule, or of which, although so specifically described, the grantor was not true owner at the time of executing the bill of sale; subject to the qualification of sec. 6 of the amendment Act, by which a bill of sale is not void in respect of any growing crops separately assigned or charged where such crops were actually growing at the time when the bill of sale was executed, and any fixtures separately assigned or charged, and any plant or trade machinery, where such fixtures, plant, or trade machinery are used in, attached to, or brought upon any land, farm, factory, workshop, shop, house, warehouse, or other place, in substitution for any of the like fixtures, plant, or trade machinery, specifically described in the schedule to the bill of sale, although such crops, fixtures, plant, or trade machinery did not belong to the grantor at the time of the execution of the bill of sale; and although such substituted plant, fixtures, or machinery are not specifically described in the schedule. It will be observed that the section does not protect additions to the property specifically described; and it has been held that sec. 5, like sec. 4, must be read subject to sec. 9. It does not, therefore, protect even as against the grantor, a bill of sale not in accordance with the form, though when the bill of sale is in accordance with the form, goods specifically described in the schedule, of which the grantor was not the true owner at the time of the execution of the deed would seem to be within the saving clause of the section. [c]

(a) Dyer v. Green, 1 Exch. 71; 16 L. J. Ex. 239.
(b) Duck v. Braddyll, 13 Price, 455, M'Clel. 217.
(c) Kelly v. Kellond, 20 Q. B. D. 569.

Though this section, as well as sec. 4, appears to be aimed at bills of sale covering a floating stock-in-trade, the effect of section 5 is not limited to assignments of after-acquired property, and subject to the exceptions in sec. 6, avoids a bill of sale in every case as regards chattels of which the grantor was not the true owner at the time of executing the bill of sale.[a]

When grantor is true owner.

The words true owner are used in their natural and not in an artificial sense, and the section applies to every case in which a bill of sale, but for the section, would have had effect on property, although the grantor was not the true owner at the time of its execution; as, for instance, when the grantor purports to convey property which is not then his own, but which he acquires subsequently, the conveyance operating by estoppel; or where having parted with all his interest at common law. he might, nevertheless, under the principal Act create an interest in a third person. Thus, a bill of sale, given in 1888, to secure money lent in good faith to the grantor, was held void under the section; the grantor having in 1885 parted with the property by unregistered deed of gift of which the bill of sale holder had no notice.[a]

But if the prior bill of sale is not absolute the case is different, and a grantor of chattels who has already given a bill of sale over them to secure the payment of money, is still the true owner within this section, in respect of his equity of redemption, and may give a subsequent valid bill of sale.[b] And it has been decided that a person having a beneficial interest in chattels, is to that extent the true owner, and may bind it by bill of sale; so a grantor was held the true owner, to the extent of his interest, of chattels settled for the joint use of himself and his wife during their lives with a right of survivorship.[c] And it seems a man does not cease to be the true owner of chattels because they may be subject to some lien or equitable right; thus where one partner, with his co-partner's consent, gave a bill of sale over the firm's property to secure a loan for partnership purposes, it was held that the grantor to the extent of his interest in the goods assigned was the true owner, and that the bill of sale

(a) Tuck *v.* Southern Counties Deposit Bank, 42 C. D. 471; 58 L. J. Ch. 699; 61 L. T. 348; 37 W. R. 769.

(b) Thomas *v.* Searles [1891], 2 Q.B. D. 408; 65 L. T. 39; 60 L.1J. Q. B. 722; 39 W. R. 692.

(c) *Exp.* Pratt *re* Field, 7 Mor. 132; 63 L. T. 289.

holder was entitled to half proceeds of the goods.[a]   Again,
where a person had mortgaged a public-house, including
trade fixtures, and afterwards gave a bill of sale of the
trade fixtures, it was held that the grantee having become
possessed of the equity of redemption in the fixtures by
virtue of the bill of sale, was entitled to them as against an
execution creditor. [b]

So the expression " true owner " includes one who is the
legal owner of goods, though another person is equitably or
beneficially entitled ; thus where the goods of an execution
debtor were by his direction and with his money purchased by
his wife, who gave a bill of sale of them to a person taking in
good faith, she was held to be the true owner within the
meaning of the section, and the bill of sale was supported
against the trustee in the husband's bankruptcy. [c]

As a bill of sale to which the amendment Act applies is
wholly void if registration is not duly renewed, an objection
failed, taken to the title of claimants under a bill of sale given
in 1889, that the grantor had given in 1884 a bill of sale over
the same goods, registration of which had not been renewed,
and it was held the earlier bill of sale having become void,
even as between the parties, before the second deed was
given, that the grantor was then the true owner of the
goods.[d]

The law relating to assignments of after-acquired personal After-acquired property.
chattels by way of security is thus practically repealed, and
a bill of sale purporting to assign after-acquired chattels
generally, is absolutely void, under sec. 9 of the amendment
Act. [e]   And a bill of sale assigning chattels by generic
description does not extend to cover articles of the same kind,
bought in place of those comprised in the bill of sale, but
disposed of by the grantor ;[f] though a covenant to replace
has been upheld.[g]   As questions concerning assignments
of after-acquired property may, however, still arise as
between grantor and grantee, and under bills of sale registered
before the commencement of the amendment Act, the rules
affecting such assignments must still be noticed.

(a) *Exp.* Barnett, *re* Tomplin, 7 Mor. 70 ; 38 W. R. 351 ; 62 L. T. 264.
(b) Usher *v.* Martin, 24 Q. B. D. 272 ; 59 L. J. Q. B. 11 ; 61 L. T. 778.
(c) *Exp.* Willmms, *re* Sarl [1892], 2 Q. B. 591 ; 9 Mor. 263 ; 67 L. T. 507.
(d) Fenton *v.* Blythe, 25 Q. B. D. 417 ; 63 L. T. 453 ; 39 W. R. 70 ; 59 L. J. Q. B. 589.
(e) Thomas *v.* Kelly, 13 App. Cases, 506.
(f) Carpenter *v.* Deen, 23 Q. B. D. 566 ; 61 L. T. 860.
(g) Seed *v.* Bradley [1894], 1 Q. B. 319 ; 42 W. R. 257 ; 63 L. J. Q. B. 387 ; 70
L. T. 214 ; 1 Mans. 167.

Of the questions formerly arising upon bills of sale, one of the most frequent was how far the instrument covered chattels acquired subsequently to its execution. At common law an assignment of chattels to be thereafter acquired, in which there was neither actual nor potential property, was inoperative unless ratified after acquisition of the subject of the assignment, or accompanied by a licence to seize, acted upon by the vendee.[a] When the licence to seize was executed by taking possession, the effect was the same as if the grantor had himself delivered possession.[b]

After-acquired property.

But in equity a different rule has prevailed, and the distinction between the legal and equitable right in property to be afterwards acquired appears to be that an assignment or contract for value relating to future property, without possession, creates an equitable title only, but if possession is actually taken of the property when it comes into existence a legal interest is acquired.[c] A contract for valuable consideration to transfer property to be afterwards acquired, provided, perhaps, it is one which might be the subject of a decree for specific performance, transfers to the vendee or mortgagee the beneficial interest in the property as soon as it is acquired, without any seizure or ratification ; thus, where A. by deed assigned to B. all the machinery in and about a certain mill, and it was thereby provided that all the machinery which during the continuance of the security should be fixed or placed in the mill in addition to or substitution for the former machinery, should be subject to the trusts of the assignment, and A. undertook to do all that was necessary to vest the substituted and added machinery in B. ; in delivering judgment, Lord Westbury said: " If a vendor or mortgagor agreed to sell or mortgage property, real or personal, of which he was not possessed at the time, and he received the consideration for the contract, there was no doubt that a Court of Equity would compel him to perform the contract, and that the contract would, in Equity, transfer the beneficial interest to the mortgagee or purchaser immediately on the property being acquired, assuming that the supposed contract was one of that class of which a Court of Equity would decree the specific performance." [d]

(a) Carr v. Allatt, 27 L. J. Ex. 385; Lunn v. Thornton, 1 C. B. 379; 14 L. J. C. P. 161 ; 9 Jur. 350.

(b) Congreve v. Evetts, 10 Ex. 298 ; 23 L. J. Ex. 273; 18 Jur. 655; Cole v. Kernot, 11 L. J. Q. B. 221.

(c) Morris v. Delobbel-Flipo, [1892] 2 Ch. 352.

(d) Holroyd v. Marshall, 10 H. L. Cases 191 ; 33 L. J. Ch. 193; 11 W. R. 171; 7 L. T. N. S. 172; 9 Jur. N. S. 213.

Contrasted with this case is Reeve v. Whitmore,[a] where
the lessee of a brickfield executed a bill of sale of the bricks,
&c., then in and upon the premises, with a proviso that the
lessee should have the use and enjoyment until default, or the
expiration of one day after notice in writing requiring possession; and the deed contained a power of entry and sale; and
the lessee gave and granted to the grantee, his executors, &c.,
or his or their agents, license at all times during the continuance of the security to enter on the premises, and there
remain, and seize and hold possession of the property then on
the premises as if the same formed part of the chattels
thereby assigned. Lord Westbury decided that the bill of
sale operated only as an assignment of the property on the
premises at the time of its execution, and that although a
contract to assign may, in Equity, operate as an assignment
yet, in order to do so, it must purport to confer an interest
in the future chattels, immediately, by its own force, without
the necessity for any further act of the assignee upon the
future chattels coming into existence; and therefore an
assignment of existing chattels, coupled with words amounting
to a mere licence to seize after-acquired property, will not
operate as an assignment of the latter.[b]

Therefore there must be a clear assignment of chattels to be *After-acquired*
thereafter acquired, and no intention to include them can be *property.*
implied from an assignment of chattels in a house, with a
power to enter and seize all the goods upon the premises, for
such words do not clearly apply to future property.[c]
Formerly it was held that for the contract to operate as an
assignment, the chattels must be so specifically described as
to be identified;[d] and the degree of specific description
required was discussed in cases which do not now seem to call
for particular reference.[e]

It was at length decided that if part of the property could
be identified and part could not, the Court would enforce
the contract against the property capable of ascertainment,

(a) 33 L. J. Ch. 63; 12 W. R. 113; 9 L. T. 311; 4 De G. J. & S. 1.

(b) See also Collyer v. Isaacs, 10 Ch. D. 342; 30 W. R. 70; 51 L. J. Ch. 14; 45
L. T. 567.

(c) Tapfield v. Hillman, 6 M. & G. 245; 12 L. J. C. P. 311; 6 Scott, N. R. 967;
7 Jur. 771.

(d) Belding v. Read, 3 H. & C. 955; 13 L. T. 69; 13 W. R. 867; 11 Jur. N. S.
517; 31 L. J. Ex. 12.

(e) Lazarus v. Andrade, 5 C. P. D. 318; 43 L. T. 30; 29 W. R. 15; 49 L. J. C. P.
817; Clements v. Matthews, 11 Q. B. D. 808; Petch v. Tutin, 15 M. & W. 110;
15 L. J. Ex. 290; Leathum v. Amor, 26 W. R. 739; 47 L. J. Q. B. 581; 38 L. T. 785.

and that it was sufficient if the property could be identified as being referred to by the contract at the time when the contract was sought to be enforced.[a]

Eventually, the question came before the House of Lords, and by their decision distinctions formerly drawn seem abolished. An assignment of specific after-acquired property is now held to be effectual whether the property is capable of ascertainment or not at the time the contract was made, if capable of identification when the subject-matter of the contract has come into existence, and it is sought to enforce the security. So there may be an assignment of specific future property falling within general descriptive words, nor is there any rule that a contract is too vague to be enforced in the sense of embracing much within its terms. Belding v. Read, and other cases, deciding that the property must be so described as to be capable of identification at the time the contract was made are thus overruled.[b] But there may be an assignment so indefinite and uncertain, and in that sense so vague in its terms, that the Courts will not give effect to it because of the impossibility of ascertaining to what it is applicable;[b] and it remains yet to be decided whether an instrument whereby a person charges all present and future personalty, which was formerly held ineffectual,[c] would now be enforced in equity.[b]

After-acquired property

There may be other objections to the title of a claimant to after-acquired property; as for instance where the grantor, a trader, to secure a loan, assigned his premises, together with the goodwill and all the goods, wares, merchandise, stock-in-trade, fixtures, furniture, articles, effects and things belonging to him in respect of his business. The bill of sale declared that after-acquired property of the same description should be included in the security, providing that the articles assigned should remain in the grantor's possession until the mortgagee should enter, and secured to the mortgagee a share of the profits of the business in lieu of interest. The grantor sold some of the goods on credit, and the mortgagee took possession, giving notice to the purchasers to pay him the price, but on the grantor going into liquidation it was held that book-debts were not assigned by the deed, and that the

(a) Coombe v. Carter, 36 C. D. 348; 36 W. R. 293; 57 L. T. 823; 56 L. J. Ch. 981.

(b) Tailby v. Official Receiver, 13 App. Cases, 523.

(c) Tadman v. D Epineuil, 20 Ch. D. 758; 47 L. T. 157; 30 W. R. 702.

unpaid purchase-money was the proceeds of goods allowed to be sold by the grantor for his own profit, and passed to his trustee.[a]

A mortgagee of after-acquired property had priority over execution creditors, and was entitled to an injunction restraining them from dealing therewith;[b] but the equitable estate of the mortgagee under a bill of sale of after-acquired property will be postponed to that of a purchaser in good faith, for value and without notice, who has taken actual possession of the thing sold, for as the grant of chattels to be acquired confers only an equitable interest, if before possession is taken the legal estate and interest become vested in another person without notice of the prior equitable interest, he will become the owner both at law and in equity.[c]

5. (1878.) From and after the commencement of this Act trade machinery shall, for the purposes of this Act, be deemed to be personal chattels, and any mode of disposition of trade machinery by the owner thereof, which would be a bill of sale as to any other personal chattels, shall be deemed to be a bill of sale within the meaning of this Act.

Application of Act to trade machinery.

For the purposes of this Act—

"Trade machinery" means the machinery used in or attached to any factory or workshop ;

1st. Exclusive of the fixed motive-powers, such as the water-wheels and steam engines, and the steam-boilers, donkey engines, and other fixed appurtenances of the said motive-powers ; and,

2nd. Exclusive of the fixed-power machinery, such as the shafts, wheels, drums, and their fixed appurtenances, which transmit the action of the motive powers to the other machinery, fixed and loose ; and,

(a) Browne v. Fryer, 40 L. T. 637.
(b) Holroyd v. Marshall, 10 H. L. Cases, 191.
(c) Joseph v. Lyons, 15 Q. B. D. 280; 34 W. R. 145 ; 54 L. J. Q. B. 1 ; 51 L. T. 740 ; Hallas v. Robinson, 15 Q. B. D. 288 ; 33 W. R 246; 54 L. J. Q. B. 364.

3rd. Exclusive of the pipes for steam, gas, and water in the factory or workshop.

The machinery or effects excluded by this section from the definition of trade machinery shall not be deemed to be personal chattels within the meaning of this Act.

" Factory or workshop " means any premises on which any manual labour is exercised by way of trade, or for purposes of gain, in or incidental to the following purposes or any of them ; (that is to say)

(a.) In or incidental to the making any article or part of an article ; or

(b.) In or incidental to the altering, repairing, ornamenting, finishing, of any article ; or

(c.) In or incidental to the adapting for sale any article.

Trade machinery.

By sec. 6 of the amendment Act, a bill of sale of any trade machinery used in, attached to, or brought upon any land, farm, factory, workshop, shop, house, warehouse or other place, in substitution for any of the like trade machinery specifically described in the schedule, shall not be void, although such substituted trade machinery is not so specifically described, and was not the property of the grantor at the time of the execution of the bill of sale.

It would seem that trade machinery, although to be deemed personal chattels for the purposes of the Acts, does not necessarily become so for all purposes.[a]

The articles excluded from this definition of trade machinery are not personal chattels within the Acts for any purpose whatever; even where they are not affixed to the land with which they are assigned, but to other land not belonging to the grantor.[b]   A deed therefore which is void as a bill of

(a) Meux v. Jacobs, L. R. 7 H. L. 481.
(b) Topham v. Greenside, 37 Ch. D. 281 ; 36 W. R. 461 ; 57 L. J. Ch. 583 ; 58 L. T. 274.

sale may still operate as a valid security over articles excepted
from the definition of personal chattels.[a] There is, however,
much difficulty in deciding what the Legislature intended to
include or exclude, and it remains for judicial decisions to
interpret the words of the section. Trade machinery is not
within sec. 7 of the principal Act,[b] nor, it would seem, if
affixed to the freehold, is it within the operation of the reputed
ownership clause of the Bankruptcy Act.[c]

Trade machinery, if affixed to the land, still passes without   Trade
express mention by a mortgage of the land. So where the   machinery.
owner of land and buildings, used for the purposes of his
business, in which there was fixed trade machinery, mortgaged
them in fee without any reference to fixtures or machinery,
agreeing by the mortgage that the powers conferred by
sec. 19 of the Conveyancing Act, 1881, should be exercised
without the notice required by that Act, it was held that the
mortgage was not a bill of sale or assignment of trade machinery,
which passed only by virtue of being affixed to the freehold;
and that as the deed did not give a power to seize or take
possession of the trade machinery as chattels, but only as
part of the freehold, and did not authorize the mortgagee to
sell the trade machinery apart from the freehold, a valid
security over the trade machinery was given.[b] And the same
was held where there was express reference to fixed trade
machinery, specified in a schedule, the Court inferring that it
was only intended to pass as part of the mortgaged buildings.[d] So an equitable deposit of deeds of leasehold
premises will give a right to fixed trade machinery, even
though accompanied by an agreement to execute a legal
mortgage.[e] But as sec. 7 of the principal Act does not
protect trade machinery, if the mortgagee acquires an
interest in the trade machinery distinct from the land, or
has power to sever and sell the trade machinery separately,
the Acts will apply. Therefore if a mortgagee of land
desires to have the power of selling trade machinery separately he must take a bill of sale.[b]

An agreement authorizing possession of certain premises,
and of everything which should have been built, erected, or

(a) Exp. Byrne, re Burdett, 20 Q. B. D. 310.
(b) Batcheldor v. Yates, 38 Ch. D. 112 ; 57 L. J. Ch. 697 ; 36 W. R. 563 ; 59 L. T. 47.
(c) Whitmore v. Empson, 28 L. J. Ch. 361 ; 3 Jur. N. S. 230 ; 24 Beav. 313 ;
exp. Wilson, re Butterworth, 4 D. & C. 143.
(d) Brooke v. Brooke 1894 , 2 Ch. 600, 71 L.T. 398.
(e) Exp. Lusty, 6 Mor. 18 ; 37 W. R. 304 ; 60 L. T. 160.

placed thereon which would not require registration within the meaning of the Bills of Sale Acts, was held not to cover trade machinery as defined by the section.[a]   An unpaid vendor's lien extends to trade machinery fixed to the freehold, and as the lien is given by law there is nothing to register. and the Acts do not apply.[b]

Under the Bills of Sale Act, 1854, trade machinery was subject to the same rule as ordinary fixtures, and passed with the land;[c] thus where a millowner deposited title deeds by way of mortgage, and then annexed trade machinery to the mortgaged premises by bolts and screws, afterwards giving a bill of sale of the machinery to an assignee who had notice of the mortgage, the machinery was held to pass to the mortgagees as against the bill of sale holder.[d]   It has also been held that an assignment of trade machinery would pass without special mention such things as were an essential part of the machine, although moveable and actually removed for a particular purpose—as a millstone removed for repair; and that if the machine was a fixture, the moveable part of it must also be so held,[e] thus belts for driving fixed machines, which could not be taken off without cutting, or unfixing the machines, were held part of them;[f] but chattels which had never been fitted to the machine, though made to be used with it, would not pass.[g]

Another statutory definition of factory or workshop is given in the Factory and Workshop Act. 1878 (41 Vic. c. 16, s. 93).

6. (1882.) Nothing contained in the foregoing sections of this Act shall render a bill of sale void in respect of any of the following things ; (that is to say),

(a) *Re* London & Lancashire Paper Mills Co., 58 L. T. 798; 57 L. J. Ch. 766.
(b) *Re* Vulcan Iron Works, W. N., 1888, 37.
(c) Climie *v.* Wood, L. R. 4 Exch. 328 ; 37 L. J. Ex. 158 ; 18 L. T. 609.
(d) Longbottom *v.* Berry, L. R. 5 Q. B. 123 ; 10 B. & S. 852 ; 39 L. J. Q. B. 37 ; 22 L. T. 385.
(e) Mather *v.* Fraser, 2 K. & J. 559 ; Cort *v.* Sagar, 3 H. & N. 370 ; 27 L. J. Ex. 378.
(f) Sheffield & S. Yorks Society *v.* Harrison, 33 W. R. 144 ; 54 L. J. Q. B. 15 ; 15 Q. B. D. 358.
(g) *Exp.* Astbury, *re* Richards, L. R. 4 Ch. 630 ; 38 L. J. Bank. 9 ; 17 W. R. 997 ; 20 L. T. 997.

(1.) Any growing crops separately assigned or charged where such crops were actually growing at the time when the bill of sale was executed.

(2.) Any fixtures separately assigned or charged, and any plant, or trade machinery where such fixtures, plant, or trade machinery are used in, attached to, or brought upon any land, farm, factory, workshop, shop, house, warehouse, or other place in substitution for any of the like fixtures, plant, or trade machinery specifically described in the schedule to such bill of sale.

It has been decided that this section, like ss. 4, 5, must be read subject to sec. 9 of the amendment Act, and does not protect against the grantor a bill of sale, even of the excepted chattels, unless made in accordance with the form in the schedule to the Act.[a]

A bill of sale of the chattels mentioned seems to be within the saving of the section although they are not specifically described in the schedule, and were not the property of the grantor at the time of the execution of the bill of sale; but sub-sec. 2 does not protect any additions to the property specifically described. It has been said that if the schedule to a bill of sale, in accordance with the form, specifically described the chattels, and added words covering substituted goods, the form of the deed would be in accordance with the statute, though the schedule would contemplate substitution.[a]

Before the section, a mortgage of a mill with trade machinery had been held to include machinery affixed in substitution for that of a like description on the premises at the time of the mortgage, but destroyed by fire.[b]

Growing crops and fixtures are personal chattels within the Bills of Sale Acts when separately assigned or charged but fixtures (except trade machinery) are not, when assigned with an interest in any land or building to which they are

Substituted chattels.

(a) Thomas v. Kelly, 13 App. Cases, 506.
b) Irish C. S. Building Society v. Mahony, 10 Ir. C. L. R. 363.

Sec. 6.
[1878.]

affixed, nor are growing crops when assigned with any interest in the land on which they grow,[a] and no fixtures or growing crops shall be deemed separately assigned or charged merely because they are assigned by separate words, or that a power of severance is given without otherwise taking possession of the land or building to which they are affixed or on which they grow. [b] Growing crops, although assigned with other goods. are deemed separately assigned within the section.[c] Trade machinery, as defined by sec. 5 of the principal Act, is to be deemed personal chattels. Plant in its ordinary sense is said to include the tools, apparatus, &c., permanently used in carrying on any trade or mechanical business. [d]

Certain instruments giving powers of distress to be subject to this Act

6. (1878.) Every attornment, instrument, or agreement, not being a mining lease, whereby a power of distress is given or agreed to be given by any person to any other person by way of security for any present, future, or contingent debt or advance, and whereby any rent is reserved or made payable as a mode of providing for the payment of interest on such debt or advance, or otherwise for the purpose of such security only, shall be deemed to be a bill of sale. within the meaning of this Act, of any personal chattels which may be seized or taken under such power of distress.[1]

Provided, that nothing in this section shall extend to any mortgage of any estate or interest in any land, tenement, or hereditament which the mortgagee. being in possession, shall have demised to the mortgagor as his tenant at a fair and reasonable rent.[2]

(2) Page 95.

[1] The effect of sec. 4 of the amendment Act will be to add a further difficulty to the use of the attornment clause in mortgages, for the object of such clause has been to enable the mortgagee to seize property not assigned by his security; and

(a) Sec. 4, clause 2 (1878).
(b) Sec. 7 (1878).
(c) Roberts c. Roberts, 13 Q. B. D. 794.
(d) See per Lindley, L.J., Yarmouth c. France, 19 Q. B. D. 656.

THE BILLS OF SALE ACT, 1878.

sec. 6 extends to a distress on the goods of strangers, and
not only to the property of the grantor.[a]

The documents mentioned in the section are to be
deemed bills of sale, but are not bills of sale within sec. 9 of
the amendment Act, and need not be in the scheduled form,
though they are to be treated as bills of sale for the purposes
of registration.[a] It will be observed, moreover, that a
document within the section is deemed a bill of sale
only so far as regards any personal chattels which
may be seized or taken under a power of distress, and
the section does not avoid the document itself for all
purposes.[b] Where no personal chattels are seized or
taken, the section does not apply, or affect the operation of
an attornment clause so far as it creates the relation of landlord and tenant as between mortgagor and mortgagee, for
the clause consists of two severable things; so far as it creates
the relation of landlord and tenant it is not within the Acts,
but so far as it gives a power of distress as incident to that
relation it is a bill of sale and subject to the section.[c] And
the validity of an agreement entered into between a landlord
and tenant, so far as relates to the tenancy, is not affected
because containing a clause giving a power of distress, void
under the Acts.[d] Indeed, an attornment clause in a
mortgage of realty, even if itself void, does not necessarily
avoid the whole deed;[e] and though probably insufficient to
confer any security, it appears to give a mortgagee the right,
as landlord, to proceed to recover possession under R. S. C.
1883, Order III. R. 6, Order XIV. R. 1.[f]

The section applies to attornments by way of security for
money, whether the attornment clause is followed by an
express power of distress, or the right to distrain is claimed
as incident to the demise;[g] though it was formerly
questioned whether an attornment clause not giving any
express power of distress was within the section at all: and
the section was held not to apply to an attornment clause

(a) Green v. Marsh [1892], 2 Q. B. 330.
(b) Exp. Kennedy, re Willis, 21 Q. B. D. 384; 5 Mor. 189; 36 W. R. 793; 57
L. J. Q. B. 841; 59 L. T. 740.
(c) Mumford v. Collier, 25 Q. B. D. 279 ; 38 W. R. 716; 59 L. J. Q. B. 552.
(d) Stevens v. Marston, 39 W. R. 129.
(e) Re O'Dwyer, 19 L. R. Ir. 19.
(f) Hall v. Comfort, 18 Q. B. D. 11; 35 W. R. 84; 55 L. T. 550; 56 L. J. Q. B.
185; Mumford v. Collier, 25 Q. B. D. 279.
(g) Exp. Kennedy, re Willis, 21 Q. B. D. 384.

whereby a mortgagee was empowered to determine the
term and re-enter, although a right of distress attached to the
relationship of landlord and tenant thereby created.[a]

Prior to the section an attornment clause in a mortgage
deed created all the incidents and remedies of an ordinary
tenancy, and the mortgagee might distrain goods on the
mortgaged premises, whether those of the mortgagor or
a stranger; thus, where after a mortgage with an attornment clause the mortgagor let to a tenant who assigned
certain of his goods on the premises, by a bill of sale, on the
original mortgagee seizing the goods as distress for rent in
arrear under the attornment clause, it was held that the
distress was justified, and that the bill of sale holder could
not recover damages for the seizure.[b]

Attornments.　　But the section would now avoid the distress; thus
where, four years after a mortgage containing an attornment
clause, at a fair rent, the mortgagor, being in arrear with his
interest signed a document undertaking to hold the premises
as tenant to the mortgagees at a rent which was not found
to be other than fair and reasonable, but the document was
colourable only in so far as it purported to alter existing
arrangements, there being no change of possession or intention to make a real demise, the rent being reserved only to
further secure principal and interest ; the mortgagees having
seized goods of third parties as a distress, it was held on
their bringing trover that both documents were to be deemed
bills of sale, and were void for want of registration.[c]

A mortgage contained an attornment clause whereby the
mortgagor attorned tenant to the mortgagee from year to
year at a yearly rent payable quarterly, the first payment to
be made on the first of the month next after any interest
should become in arrear, all money recovered by the
attornment clause to be accepted in the first place in
or towards satisfaction of interest in arrear. Default having
been made, the mortgagee distrained, and the mortgagor subsequently became bankrupt. It was held that the distress
was invalid and that the trustee was entitled to the proceeds.[d]　So it has been held that the Acts apply to an

(a) Hall v. Comfort, 18 Q. B. D. 11.
(b) Kearsley v. Phillips, 31 W. R. 909 ; 52 L. J. Q. B. 581 ; 11 Q. B. D. 621 ; 49 L. T. 435.
(c) Green v. Marsh (1892), 2 Q. B. 330.
(d) Exp. Kennedy, re Willis, 21 Q. B. D. 384.

agreement for letting a public-house, by which the landlords (brewers) were empowered to enter on the premises and distrain for the amount due to them for goods supplied to the tenant.[a]

Formerly a security over chattels by assignment or Attornment. demise of a debtor's interest in premises, with a proviso that the premises and chattels should be held by the debtor as tenant from year to year, at a rent which, together with the tenancy, was to cease on payment of all moneys recoverable under the security, a power of entry, without previous demand, being also reserved on default in payment, was held not fraudulent under the Statute of Elizabeth, or the Bankruptcy or Bills of Sale Acts; nor was a mortgage, by which the mortgagor attorned tenant to the mortgagee at a fixed rent with a power of distress, a licence to seize within the repealed Act;[b] and it was decided that a power of distress in an agreement for the hire of chattels was not a fraud on the bankruptcy laws.[c]

It was also, on more than one occasion, decided that an attornment by the mortgagor brought the mortgagee, as landlord, within the protection of sec. 34 of the Bankruptcy Act, 1869.[d] The test in such cases was afterwards decided to be whether the intention was to create a real tenancy, or whether the transaction was a mere device for giving an additional security to the mortgagee in the event of the mortgagor's bankruptcy. If the attornment clause constituted a real relation of landlord and tenant between the parties, a distress levied for the rent fixed by the clause was good as against the trustee in the bankruptcy of the mortgagor.

An attornment clause in a second mortgage might be valid, notwithstanding there was a like clause in a prior mortgage of the same premises, and if the amount of the rents fixed by the two clauses was a fair rent of the property, so that there was no fraud on the bankruptcy laws, valid distraints might be levied by both mortgagees after the commencement of the bankruptcy.[e] And before the amendment Act a mortgage containing an attornment clause was held to pass tenant's fixtures

(a) Pulbrook v. Ashby, 35 W. R. 779.
(b) Morton v. Woods, 38 L. J. Q. B. 81 ; L. R. 4 Q. B. 293 ; 17 W. R.
(c) Leman v. Yorks Wagon Co., 50 L. J. Ch. 293.
(d) Section 42 is the corresponding section of the Bankruptcy Act, 1883.
(e) *Exp.* Punnett, *re* Kitchin, 16 Ch. D. 226 ; 29 W. R. 129 ; 50 L. J. Ch. 212 ; 44 L. T. 226.

placed on the premises after the date of the mortgage, for the mortgagee does not cease to be mortgagee because he is made a landlord.[a]

Attornments.

A mortgage with an attornment clause and an agreement authorizing the mortgagee at any time within three months from the date of the mortgage, without any previous notice, to enter on the premises and determine the tenancy, creates a tenancy from year to year, and not at will; therefore, apart from the section, the mortgagee might have distrained for the rent reserved, although in the meantime the mortgagor became bankrupt;[b] and it was not an objection that the rent was of a fluctuating amount.[c]

(2) It is important to observe that the benefit of the proviso is limited to cases where the mortgagee, "being in possession," leases to the mortgagor; and this has been held to apply only to cases when the mortgagee has taken possession and subsequently demises to the mortgagor, and not where no actual possession has been taken and the demise is created by the mortgage deed itself.[d] Neither the mortgage itself, nor a subsequent document modifying the arrangement under the mortgage for the purpose of further securing money, makes the mortgagee a mortgagee in possession within the section; for what was intended to be protected is a lease in good faith by a mortgagee in possession to a mortgagor, and not a mere lease to secure money.[e] It has been held that the possession of a mortgagor, who withholds possession from the mortgagee after the latter has demanded it, is a wrongful possession.[f] Where the mortgage contains an attornment clause, a mortgagee in possession is liable for wilful default in receipt of the rent.[g]

The words fair and reasonable rent seem to be introduced to prevent the reservation of a rent to the mortgagee equal to the amount of the loan; and in determining what is a fair and reasonable rent, the test will be, is the rent excessive

(a) *Exp.* Punnett, *re* Kitchin, 16 C. D. 226.

(b) *Exp.* Queen's Benefit Building Society, *re* Threlfall, 16 Ch. D. 274; 44 L. T. 74; 50 L. J. Ch. 318; 29 W. R. 128.

(c) *Exp.* Voisey, *re* Knight, 21 Ch. D. 442; 52 L. J. Ch. 121; 47 L. T. 362; 31 W. R. 19.

(d) *Exp.* Kennedy, *re* Willis, 21 Q. B. D. 384.

(e) Green *v.* Marsh [1892], 2 Q.B. 330.

(f) Bagnall *v.* Villar, 12 Ch. D. 812.

(g) *Re* Stockton Iron Works Co., 40 L. T. 29; 10 Ch. D. 335; 27 W. R. 433; 48 L. J. Ch. 417.

considering the nature of the property, and does it
shew of itself that there was no intention to create a real
tenancy.[a] It would seem that if the rent fixed by the clause be
so excessive that the Court comes to the conclusion that it was
not intended to create a real rent or a real tenancy, the clause
and any distress levied under it, even though before the commencement of the bankruptcy, will be invalid as a fraud on
the bankruptcy laws, for the section of the Bankruptcy Act,
giving a landlord or other person to whom rent is due
from the bankrupt a right of distress, does not protect a dis
tress levied for a sham rent ; thus, where a trader executed a
mortgage to secure a current account, attorning tenant to the
mortgagee at a rent of £8,000, when the yearly value of the
property was £140 only, the Court held that the rent reserved
by the attornment clause was so excessive, that it could not
have been intended to create a real tenancy, and that the
attornment clause was invalid against a trustee under the
mortgagor's liquidation.[b]   The rent reserved, however, will
enure as a security as well for the principal as the interest of
the mortgage debt.[c]

7. (1878.) No fixtures or growing crops shall be Fixtures or growing crops not to be deemed sepa-
deemed under this Act to be separately assigned or rately assigned when the land
charged, by reason only that they are assigned by passes by
separate words, or that power is given to sever them the same instrument.
from the land or building to which they are affixed,
or from the land on which they grow, without
otherwise taking possession of or dealing with such
land or building, or land, if by the same instrument
any freehold or leasehold interest in the land or
building to which such fixtures are affixed, or in
the land on which such crops grow, is also conveyed
or assigned to the same persons or person.

The same rule of construction shall be applied to
all deeds or instruments, including fixtures or growing
crops, executed before the commencement of this

(a) *Re* Stockton Iron Works Co., 40 L. T. 29 ; 10 Ch. D. 335 ; 26 W. R. 433 ;
48 L. J. Ch. 417.

(b) *Exp.* Jackson, *re* Bowes, 14 Ch. D. 725 ; 43 L. T. 272 ; 29 W. R. 253 ;
Exp. Williams *re* Thompson, 7 Ch. D. 130 ; 47 L. J. Bank. 26 ; 26 W. R. 274 ;
37 L. T. 764.

(c) *Exp.* Harrison, *re* Betts, 18 Ch. D. 127 ; 30 W. R. 38 ; 45 L. T. 290 ; 50
L. J. Ch. 832.

Act and then subsisting and in force, in all questions
arising under any bankruptcy, liquidation, assignment for the benefit of creditors, or execution of any
process of any court, which shall take place or be
issued after the commencement of this Act.

This section is retrospective only so far as it enacts that a
certain rule of construction as to the meaning to be attached
to the words "separately assigned or charged," shall apply to
bills of sale executed before the commencement of the principal Act.[a] The section restores a rule recognised in Boyd v.
Shorrock,[b] but overruled by subsequent cases. A legal or
equitable mortgage of realty or leaseholds, although unregistered, carries with it trade or tenants' fixtures as a part
of the land, whether on the land at the time of
the mortgage or subsequently affixed.[c] A deposit of a
lease, also, covered tenant's fixtures;[d] and when the
documents of title to leasehold premises were deposited
by way of equitable charge with a person on whose behalf
they, with fixed machinery, &c., upon them, had been
bought, accompanied by a memorandum reciting the terms
of purchase and agreeing on request to execute either a
mortgage or absolute transfer of the property, it was held
against the mortgagor's trustee in bankruptcy that the
mortgagee was entitled to the fixtures, and that the memorandum was not an assignment of trade machinery within the
Acts.[e]

When fixtures are included in security.

On a mortgage of land by sub-demise a qualified property
in fixtures passes to the mortgagee without the right to
remove and sell, unless given in express terms, but the
mortgagor cannot remove fixtures during the continuance
of the mortgage term, though his right to do so revives
when the mortgage is satisfied.[f] But the mortgagee does
not take a better title to the fixtures than the mortgagor himself, thus the mortgage will not cover fixtures attached to

(a) *Exp.* Moore, *re* Armytage, 14 Ch. D. 379 ; 28 W. R. 924 ; 42 L. T. 443 ; 49 L. J. Bank. 60.

(b) 37 L. J. Ch. 144 ; L. R. 5 Eq. 72 ; 16 W. R. 102 ; 17 L. T. 197.

(c) Menx *v.* Jacobs, L. R. 7 H. L. 481 ; Holland *v.* Hodgson, 41 L. J. C. P. 146 ; L. R. 7 C. P. 328 ; 26 L. T. 709 ; 20 W. R. 990 ; Walmsley *v.* Milne, 7 C. B. (N. S.) 115 ; 29 L. J. C. P. 97 ; 6 Jur. N. S. 125.

(d) Williams *v.* Evans, 23 Beav. 239 ; *Exp.* Broadwood, 1 M. D. & D. 631.

(e) *Exp.* Lusty, 6 Mor. 18 ; 37 W. R. 304 ; 60 L. T. 160.

(f) Southport, &c., Banking Co. *v.* Thompson, 37 C. D. 64 ; 36 W. R. 113 ; 58 L. T. 143 ; 57 L. J. Ch. 114.

the land by a tenant to the mortgagor under a letting subsequent to the mortgage.[a]

A limited company mortgaged to their bankers a colliery,
of which they were lessees, together with all fixed engines,
boilers, shafting, gearing, machinery and other fixtures then
or thereafter standing or being upon the mortgaged premises.
Afterwards they agreed with a firm of engine makers to
erect a machine, in the nature of a trade fixture, at the
colliery, the purchase-money to be paid by instalments, and
when fully paid the machine to become the property of
the Company, but until paid for to remain the property
of the makers. The machine was erected, but after default
in paying the instalments, the mortgagors went into liquidation. The Court held the makers of the machine entitled as
against the mortgagees, for though the mortgage was good
between the parties, the stipulation that the machine should
remain the maker's property until paid for was also valid,
and the mortgage could not give the mortgagees a better title
than the mortgagors had.[b] So where a tenant, who had
agreed with the defendants to supply him a boiler to be paid
for by instalments, and to remain their property until paid
for, mortgaged his premises by underlease to the plaintiff, the
defendants afterwards supplying the boiler, which was affixed
to the mortgaged premises, it was held that the plaintiff,
though without notice of the agreement, by leaving the mortgagor in possession, must be taken to have acquiesced in his
making agreements for fixing and removing fixtures for the
purposes of his business, and could not claim the boiler as
against the defendants.[c]

As a mortgage of premises covers fixtures in the absence
of expression of intention that they shall not pass, a mortgage of a mill, together with specified trade machinery of
the kind excluded by sec. 5 of the principal Act from the
definition of personal chattels, but not enumerating or
purporting to charge other fixtures, was held to pass all
fixtures annexed to the mill.[d] Under the repealed Act,
a mere deposit of an assignment of leaseholds and fixtures
did not confer any right to trade fixtures against a

When fixtures are included in security.

(a) Sanders v. Davis, 15 Q. B. D. 218; 33 W. R. 655; 54 L. J. Q. B. 576.
(b) Cumberland Union Banking Co. v. Maryport Hematite Iron and Steel
Co. [1892], 1 Ch. 415; 40 W. R. 280; 66 L. T. 108.
(c) Gough v. Wood 1894], 1 Q. B. 713; 70 L.T. 297; 63 L.J. Q. B. 564; 42 W.R.
409.
(d) Southport, &c., Banking Co. v. Thompson, 37 C. D. 64; 36 W. R. 113; 58
L. T. 143; 57 L. J. Ch. 114.

trustee or execution creditor, a registered assignment of the fixtures being necessary in order to perfect the mortgagee's title,[a] and a mortgage of land with fixtures required registration, if the mortgagee had power to sever and sell separately from the land,[b] or if the fixtures were separately assigned by the operative part of the deed.[c] It is apprehended that if an intention appears to charge fixtures as distinct from the land or building, the former rule will still apply;[d] though the effect of sec. 7 is to exclude from the ruling in *Exp.* Daglish fixtures not coming under the head of trade machinery.[e]

Fixtures.

Before the commencement of the principal Act, where a stone merchant, by an unregistered deed, made a mortgage in fee of land, and a stone quarry therein, together with all the fixed and moveable machinery and fixtures of every description, with power for the mortgagee to sell any part or parts of the mortgaged property either together or in parcels, it was held on the mortgagor's bankruptcy, that a steam crane and tramway upon the property in connection with the quarry, comprised in the mortgage deed, and so attached to the freehold as not to be capable of removal without damage, although not fixtures in the ordinary sense, passed to the mortgagee under the deed; and that inasmuch as the freehold passed by the deed, registration was not required under the Bills of Sale Acts, 1854.[f] But now if a mortgagee of land wishes to have the power of selling trade machinery apart from the land he must take a bill of sale, although trade machinery, if affixed to the freehold, still passes without express mention, by a mortgage of the land. The power of sale given by the Conveyancing Act, 1881, which entitles a mortgagee to sell the mortgaged premises, or any part thereof, either together or in lots, does not confer a right to sell fixed trade machinery apart from the premises so as to operate as a separate assignment.[g] Nor is any such power necessarily

(a) *Exp.* Tweedy, *re* Trethowan, 5 Ch. D. 559; 46 L. J. Bank. 43; 25 W. R. 399; 36 L. T. 70.

(b) *Exp.* Daglish, L. R. 8 Ch. 1072; 42 L. J. Bank. 102; 29 L. T. 168; 21 W. R. 893; *Exp.* Barclay, *re* Joyce, L. R. 9 Ch. 576; 43 L. J. Bank. 137; 22 W. R. 608; 30 L. T. 479.

(c) Begbie v. Fenwick, L. R. 8 Ch. 1074; 19 W. R. 402; 24 L. T. 58; Hawtrey v. Buttlin, L. R. 8 Q. B. 290; 42 L. J. Q. B. 163; 21 W. R. 663; 28 L. T. 532.

(d) Climpson v. Coles, 23 Q. B. D. 465; Waterfall v. Penistone, 6 E. & B. 876; 3 Jur. N. S. 15; 26 L. J. Q. B. 100.

(e) Batcheldor v. Yates, 38 Ch. D. 112.

(f) *Exp.* Moore, *re* Armytage, 14 Ch. D. 379.

(g) Batcheldor v. Yates, 38 Ch. D. 112.

implied where there is express mention of fixed trade machinery, if the machinery is only assigned as part of the land.[a]
But if a power of selling separately is conferred expressly or
by implication, the instrument will, as regards fixed trade
machinery, require registration; and the intention of the parties
must be collected from the whole deed. Thus, where a mill-
wright granted and assigned his freehold business premises
by way of mortgage, together with all and singular the fixed
and moveable plant, machinery, and fixtures, implements and
utensils, then or thereafter fixed to, or placed on, or used in
or about the said hereditaments, the deed also containing a
separate covenant by the mortgagor to keep the plant, machinery, fixtures, &c., in good repair, and insured against loss or
damage by fire, it was held that the mortgage, being unregistered, was void as regards trade machinery, and the mortgagees were restrained from selling it, either together with or
apart from the mortgaged premises.[b]

A lessee who mortgages tenant's fixtures cannot defeat   Fixtures.
his grant by a voluntary surrender of his lease, and the
mortgagee has a right, notwithstanding the surrender, to
enter and sever the fixtures.[c]   Where, however, the grantor,
having assigned growing crops, agreed with his landlord,
who had distrained for rent, to surrender the tenancy
and give possession of the land and crops in consideration of the distress being withdrawn, on which
the landlord withdrew, and on the surrender being completed took possession and cultivated the crops, it was held
that although the surrender could not prejudicially affect
the rights of the mortgagee, an action of trover was not
maintainable, the legal title of the landlord being complete
by the surrender; but that the mortgagee was entitled to be
put in the same position as the tenant before surrender,
subject to his liabilities.[d]

As an assignment of freeholds or leaseholds will pass trade
and tenant's fixtures, and by the section such an assignment is effectual without registration, it will be prudent for a
mortgagee of fixtures or growing crops to ascertain whether
they are affected by any dealing with the land; and to require
a declaration by the grantor that no such charge exists, in
addition to the usual covenant against incumbrances.

(a) Brooke r. Brooke [1894], 2 Ch. 600.
(b) Small r. National Provincial Bank of England [1894], 1 Ch. 686; 42 W. R.
378; 63 L. J. Ch. 270; 70 L. T. 492.
(c) London Loan & Discount Co. r. Drake, 6 C. B. (N. S.) 798; 28 L. J. C. P.
97; 5 Jur. N. S. 1407.
(d) Clements r. Matthews, 11 Q. B. D. 808.

By sec. 4, cl. 2, of the principal Act, stock or produce upon any farm or lands which by virtue of any covenant or agreement, or of the custom of the country, ought not to be removed from any farm where the same are at the time of making or giving a bill of sale, are excluded from the operation of the Acts.

7. (1882.) Personal chattels assigned under a bill of sale shall not be liable to be seized or taken possession of by the grantee for any other than the following causes :—[1]

(1.) If the grantor shall make default in payment of the sum or sums of money thereby secured at the time therein provided for payment, or in the performance of any covenant or agreement contained in the bill of sale and necessary for maintaining the security ;[2]

(2) Page 107.

[1] A bill of sale in the statutory form gives the grantor an absolute interest in the goods, subject to the provisions of the section and to the grantor's right to redeem ;[a] and it has been decided that this section, coupled with the form in the schedule, gives an implied power of seizure in the events mentioned,[b] but a power of seizure and sale in the specified events may still be inserted in the deed.[c] When the sum secured is payable by instalments, the grantee on default in payment of any instalment may, subject to relief under the proviso to this section, sell the chattels assigned, and retain the whole principal unpaid, together with the interest then due, although the bill of sale does not contain an express term making the debt payable on default in paying an instalment.[d]

Remedies of mortgagee.

A mortgagee of personal chattels is entitled to a decree for an account, and in some cases, foreclosure,[e] or to an order for sale and payment of the principal debt, interest, and expenses.[f]

(a) Johnson v. Diprose [1893], 1 Q. B. 512.

(b) Watkins v. Evans, 18 Q. B. D. 386; 56 L. J. Q. B. 200; 35 W. R. 313; 56 L. T. 177.

(c) Exp. Official Receiver, re Morritt 18 Q. B. D. 222; 35 W. R. 277; 56 L. J. Q. B. 139; 56 L. T. 42.

(d) Exp. Woolfe, re Wood [1894], 1 Q. B. 605; 70 L. T. 262; 1 Mans. 87; 63 L. J. Q. B. 352.

(e) Wayne v. Hanham, 9 Hare, 62.

(f) Carter v. Wake, 4 Ch. D. 605; 46 L. J. Ch. 841.

He is entitled to add to his security, and to deduct from the proceeds of sale, his expenses on a sale, and any costs which he may properly incur in defending and maintaining his rights under the security; [a] but these do not become a personal debt of the mortgagor, though he may be compelled to pay them as a condition of redemption. [b]

It seems that a mortgagee or pledgee of personal chattels has, as incident to the security, a power of sale without foreclosure proceedings, upon non-payment of the debt when a day has been fixed for payment, or after proper demand and notice where no day has been fixed, and that a purchaser in good faith from the mortgagee would acquire an absolute title. [c]

If, however, a mortgagee sells recklessly, he will be responsible in damages, [d] for he has been termed a trustee for the grantor, and those claiming under him, of any surplus that may remain after sale of the mortgaged property; [e] but the holder of an absolute bill of sale who has seized and sold is under no liability to the holder of a second bill of sale for losses on the sale. [f] By the " Conveyancing and Law of Property Act, 1881," section 21 (2), any person damnified by an unauthorized, or improper, or irregular exercise of the power of sale conferred by that Act shall have his remedy in damages against the person exercising the power. Where the security is upon goods, the grantor, on redemption, is entitled to credit for damages occasioned by the grantee's negligence in removing or dealing with them. [g]

Any person interested in the equity of redemption, the Redemption time for redemption having arrived, may redeem a mortgage, and on tender of the principal money and interest is entitled to delivery of the title deeds and a conveyance of the property; [h] thus a subsequent mortgagee may redeem prior charges on the property, and so it would seem may judgment creditors who have issued execution, under which, but for the mortgage, the property comprised in it might be

(a) Lumley v. Simmons, 34 Ch. D. 698; 56 L. J. Ch. 339; 35 W. R. 423; 56 L. T. 194.

(b). Exp. Fewings, re Sneyd, 25 Ch. D. 338; 53 L. J. Ch. 545; 50 L. T. 109, 32 W R. 352.

(c) Story Eq. Jur., 12th Ed. s. 1031; Exp. Hubbard, re Hardwick, 17 Q. B. D. 698.

(d) Maugham v. Sharpe, 17 C. B. N. S. 444; 34 L. J. C. P. 19; 12 W. R. 1057; 10 L. T. 870.

(e) Robinson v. Hedger, 17 Sim. 184; 13 Jur. 846; Warner v. Jacob, 20 Ch. D. 220; 51 L. J. Ch. 642.

(f) Maugham v. Sharpe, 17 C. B. N. S. 444; 34 L. J. C. P. 19.

(g) Johnson v. Diprose [1893], 1 Q. B. 512.

(h) Pearce v. Morris, L. R. 5 Ch. 227; 39 L. J. Ch. 342; 21 L. T. 190.

taken.[a] Under an ordinary mortgage with a proviso for redemption on payment by a certain day, the mortgagor cannot redeem before the day, even on tender of interest during the intervening period,[b] though earlier redemption was allowed when instead of a proviso for redemption there was a trust for sale upon non-payment at a certain day, the estate by the terms of the deed being redeemable before the day.[c] But if the mortgagee himself takes proceedings to recover the debt, it seems that the mortgagor could redeem on payment of principal with interest to date.[d]

Redemption. Where a grantee has seized in the events mentioned in the section, the grantor's legal interest in the goods determines, and he cannot maintain trespass, even after tender of the debt with interest. His remedy, within five days of seizure, is to apply under the proviso to the section, and after that date, unless entitled to enter satisfaction under section 15 of the principal Act, to bring an action to redeem.[e] Thus, where the grantee of a bill of sale, given by way of security, seized on default of payment, and after five days began to remove the goods, whereupon the grantor tendered the debt, interest and expenses, which the grantee refused to accept; on the grantor suing in trespass, claiming damages for the removal of the goods, and for injury to them in the course of such removal, also claiming to redeem, it was held that no action of trespass would lie, as at the time of removal the property in and right to possession of the goods were in the grantee, the grantor being only entitled to redeem on payment of the debt, interest, expenses and costs of redemption.[e]

But if the grantor pays or tenders the debt at the appointed day, an action of trespass will lie for seizure;[e] and before this section, permitting seizure only in certain specified events, every condition prior to taking possession must have been fulfilled to make the seizure lawful; and if a demand in writing was precedent to a power of seizure, it must have been made according to the terms of the deed, or the seizure was a trespass, for which an action would lie.[f]

(a) Mildred v. Austin, 8 Eq. 220 ; 17 W. R. 638; 20 L. T. 939.
(b) Browne v. Cole, 14 Sim. 427 ; 9 Jur. 200 ; 14 L. J. Ch. 107.
(c) Harding v. Tingey, 34 L. J. Ch. 13 ; 10 Jur. N. S. 872.
(d) Prescott v. Phipps, 23 Ch. D. 372 ; 49 L. T. 240.
(e) Johnson v. Diprose [1893], 1 Q. B. 512.
(f) Belding v. Read, 3 H. & C. 955, per Channell, B.

THE BILLS OF SALE ACT(1878) AMENDMENT ACT, 1882. 107

Sec. 7.
[1882.]

But if the grantee seizes before default, though he may be responsible in damages, the bill of sale remains a valid security for money becoming due under it.[a]

The measure of damages recoverable for a wrongful seizure, where the deed is not void, is not the actual value of the goods, but the value of the legal interest of the mortgagor in them at the time of seizure.[b] But damages may be given for the wrongful seizure; [c] and where the deed is void the real value of the goods sold, coupled with any proved special damage, would seem to be recoverable; and when the goods have been sold at a loss, or a trespass has been committed, substantial damages may be given, and the Courts have refused to set aside a verdict for vindictive damages.[d] If damages are claimed for trespass, the action should be tried in the Queen's Bench Division, and not in Chancery.[e]

It has been said that a licence in the terms formerly common in bills of sale, empowering the mortgagee, if necessary, to use force and break into any dwelling-house or premises wherever the goods may be, would be void as a licence to commit an offence against the statute, 5 Ric. II. c. 8.[f]

(2) It will be observed that the covenant or agreement in respect of which default in performance will warrant a seizure must be one necessary for maintaining the security. It should also be remembered that a power of seizure upon failure or neglect to perform a covenant would seem not to apply to breach of a negative covenant.[g]

Causes of seizure.

Under the former Bills of Sale Acts it was held that as a compliance with the stipulations of the deed was required for the grantor's protection, he might, of course, waive them; thus, where a bill of sale contained a proviso for re-entry on non-payment for twenty-four hours after demand, and the mortgagee entered and took actual possession before the expiration of the notice, but the grantor raised no objection to his so doing, the seizure was held good against a trustee under the grantor's liquidation.[h]

(a) Monson v. Milner, 8 T. L. R. 447.
(b) Brierley v. Kendall, 17 Q. B. 937 ; 21 L. J. Q. B. 161.
(c) Moore v. Shelley, 8 App. Cases, 285 ; 52 L. J. P. C. 35 ; 48 L. T. 918.
(d) Thomas v. Harris, 27 L. J. Ex. 353.
(e) Wallis v. Sayers, W. N. 1890, 120.
(f) Edwick v. Hawkes, 18 Ch. D. 199 ; 45 L. T. 168.
(g) Hyde v. Warden, 3 Ex. D. 72 ; 47 L. J. Ex. 121 ; 37 L. T. 567.
(h) Exp. Redfern, re Ball, 19 W. R. 1058.

Payment on demand cannot now be required, but if a bill of sale holder chooses to enlarge the time for payment, a default under the terms of the deed will not, it has been said, warrant a seizure; [a] though this has been doubted, and it would seem that a mere promise to enlarge the time, without consideration, will not render illegal a seizure under the terms of the deed, unless there has been some misrepresentation of existing facts by the grantee or his agent, on the faith of which the grantor has altered his position for the worse; thus, where a bill of sale given for a loan payable by instalments, authorized the grantee at any time to take possession, and the grantor requested time for payment of one of the instalments, to which the grantee replied that he would wait a week, but nevertheless seized and sold on the third day after the instalment became due, it was held that there had been no waiver of the grantee's rights under the deed, a mere promise, without consideration, being insufficient to prevent him putting them in force. [b] Nor did an outstanding bill of exchange suspend the rights of a grantee. [c]

Power of
seizure.

When the power was to seize and take possession "immediately after notice," or "immediately upon demand," the grantor had such reasonable time for payment as in the ordinary course of business would suffice to fetch the money, thus, half-an-hour's notice has been held insufficient : [d] and where the bill of sale contained a proviso for redemption if the grantor should instantly on demand, and without delay, on any pretence whatsoever pay the sum due; and it was also provided that the demand might be made personally on the grantor, or by giving or leaving verbal or written notice to or for him at his place of business, &c., so nevertheless that a demand should in fact be made; and in the grantor's absence a demand was made on his son, who stated his inability to meet it, and the grantee immediately seized, it was held that the notice required was such as might be reasonably supposed to reach the grantor and give him an opportunity of comply-

(a) Albert v. The Grosvenor Investment Co., L. R. 3 Q. B. 129 ; 37 L. J. Q. B. 24 ; 8 B. & S. 664 ; Longden v. Sheffield Deposit Bank, 24 S. J. 913, per Field, J.

(b) Williams v. Stern, 42 L. T. 719 ; 5 Q. B. D. 409 ; 28 W. R. 901 ; 49 L. J. Q. B. 663.

(c) Bramwell v. Eglinton, 5 B. & S. 39 ; 35 L. J. Q. B. 163 ; 14 W. R. 739 ; 14 L. T. 735 ; 12 Jur. N. S. 702 ; L. R. 1 Q. B. 494.

(d) Brighty v. Norton, 3 B. & S. 305 ; 9 Jur. N. S. 495 ; 11 W. R. 167 ; 7 L. J. N. S. 422 ; 32 L. J. Q. B. 38 ; but see Wharlton v. Kirkwood, 22 W. R 93 ; 29 L. T. 645.

ing with it within a reasonable time, and that the seizure was
therefore not justified. [a]   So where demand by a person
representing himself as the mortgagee's agent was made on
the wife of the mortgagor, during his absence, and upon non-
payment the mortgaged property was forthwith seized, the
Privy Council decided that such non-payment before the
mortgagor had an opportunity to inquire into the alleged
agency did not constitute default. [b]

Where, however, a bill of sale contained a declaration that
after default should be made in payment according to the
covenants therein contained, or on breach of any covenant of
the borrower therein, and after written demand for payment
should have been made, or on certain other events, it should
be lawful for the mortgagees to seize and sell, and there was
the usual proviso for possession until default, it was held that
the prior clause was not controlled by the subsequent proviso,
and that a seizure on one of the events mentioned was justified independently of default in payment after demand, and
although no demand had been made; [c] and prior to the
amendment Act, if by the terms of the bill of sale the
grantor held the chattels as the mere servant or agent of
the mortgagee, or at his will, the latter was entitled to possession whenever he thought fit to call for it, and might at
once seize, remove and sell the property. [d]

If the mortgagee takes possession before default he will be
subject to an action, for the proviso, formerly inserted
that the grantor might hold possession, operated as a
regrant or bailment of the goods, and the proviso to the
statutory form probably has the same effect; thus,
where it was provided that the deed should become
void on payment of a certain sum on a certain day, or
on some earlier day to be appointed by the grantee by a notice
in writing to be served on the grantor twenty-four hours
before the day of payment, and the grantee served insufficient
notice to pay on a day earlier than that named in the deed,
and afterwards entered and sold the goods, it was held that
the notice being bad, he was a mere trespasser, and that the

Power of seizure.

(a) Massey v. Sladen, L. R. 4 Ex. 13 ; 38 L. J. Ex. 34 ; *Exp.* Trevor, *re* Burg-
hardt, 1 Ch. D. 297 ; 45 L. J. Bank. 27 ; 24 W. R. 301 ; 35 L. T. 600.
(b) Moore v. Shelley, 8 App. Cases, 285.
(c) *Exp.* National Guardian Assurance Co., *re* Francis, 10 Ch. D. 408; 40 L. T.
237 ; 27 W. R. 408.
(d) Mayhew v. Suttle, 4 E. & B. 347 ; 24 L. J. Q. B. 54 ; 1 Jur. N. S. 303.

F

grantor's right to possession of the goods being defeasible only in default on payment, he was entitled to recover the value of his interest in them at the time of the trespass.[a]

(2.) If the grantor shall become a bankrupt,[1] or suffer the said goods or any of them to be distrained for rent, rates, or taxes ;[2]

[1] By section 125, sub-sec. 7, of the Bankruptcy Act, 1869, the word " bankrupt " included a debtor whose affairs were under liquidation, and the word " bankruptcy " included liquidation by arrangement. If, therefore, the grantor became a liquidating debtor, the section would have applied ; but his presenting a petition for liquidation, or compounding with his creditors, would not have had that effect.

Seizure on bankruptcy.

By section 3 (16) (17) Bankruptcy Act, 1890, for the purposes of administration of property, the words " bankruptcy," "bankrupt," and "order of adjudication," are to be interpreted as if they included respectively a composition or scheme of arrangement, a compounding or arranging debtor, and order approving the composition or scheme. It is not at all clear, however, that a composition or scheme would bring the grantor within the sub-section.

Under the bankruptcy laws, it has been decided that a person becomes bankrupt on committing an act of bankruptcy available for and followed by adjudication ; [b] but the commission of an act of bankruptcy without adjudication would seem not to warrant a seizure under the section.[c]

As chattels comprised in a bill of sale given after the commencement of the amendment Act, by way of security for the payment of money, are subject to the reputed ownership clause of the Bankruptcy Act, the power of seizure on the grantor becoming bankrupt affords a very inadequate protection to the mortgagee, for if the chattels are in the reputed ownership of the bankrupt in his trade or business at the commencement of the bankruptcy, that is, at the time of the commission of an act of bankruptcy to which the trustee's title relates, the mortgagee's rights may be defeated, although

[a] Toms v. Wilson, 4 B. & S. 442 ; 32 L. J. Q. B. 382 ; 11 W. R. 952 ; 8 L. T. N. S. 778 ; 10 Jur. N. S. 201.

[b] Fawcett v. Fearne, 6 Q. B. 20 ; 13 L. J. Q. B. 30 ; 8 Jur. 695 ; *exp.* Attwater, *re* Turner, 5 Ch. D. 27, 30, per James, L. J. ; 25 W. R. 206 ; 35 L. T. 682 ; 46 L. J. Bank.

[c] Gilroy v. Bowey, 59 L. T. 223.

he seizes before adjudication.   It would seem, however, that
actual physical possession taken, though not warranted by the
section, would exclude the reputed ownership clause.[a]

(2) Section 13 of the amendment Act, by which chattels are Landlord and
to remain on the premises for five days after seizure, will grantee.
afford an additional opportunity for distraint; and by
sec. 14, a bill of sale to which the amendment Act applies is no
protection in respect of personal chattels included in such bill
of sale, which, but for such bill of sale, would have been liable to
distress under a warrant for the recovery of taxes and poor
and other parochial rates.   This is a new provision, but
whether a bill of sale be registered or not, the chattels it comprises which remain upon the grantor's premises have always,
with some few exceptions, been subject to his landlord's distraint for rent.   So under a reservation of rent payable
quarterly, and always if required a quarter in advance,
whereby rent is payable a quarter in advance throughout, the
landlord on giving reasonable notice of demand was held
entitled to distrain on goods comprised in a bill of sale, which
the grantees had seized and were about to sell.[b]

Fixtures and things in actual use or delivered to a
person to be dealt with in the way of his trade are absolutely privileged from distress: and also, except where the
tenant's term has expired and demand of possession has been
made, any goods or chattels of the tenant or his family
which would be protected from seizure in execution under
the County Court Acts;[c] so also are things in the custody
of the law, as of the sheriff or his vendee,[d] but these
cannot be removed without satisfying one year's arrears of
rent.   Beasts of the plough, sheep, the tools of a man's trade,
or implements of husbandry, are also privileged from
distress, provided there be other sufficient distress upon the
premises.   The landlord's right of distress may be waived by
consent, and if he expressly or impliedly agrees that chattels
placed by a stranger on the tenant's land shall be exempt
from distress, he will not be permitted to distrain.[e]

(a) *Exp.* Fletcher, *re* Henley, 5 Ch. D. 809.
(b) London and Westminster Loan Co. *v.* London and North Western Railway, 41 W. R. 673; [1893] 2 Q. B. 49; 62 L. J. Q. B. 370; 69 L. T. 320.
(c) Law of Distress Amendment Act, 1888, s. 4.
(d) Wharton *v.* Naylor, 12 Q. B. 673; 6 D. & L. 136; 12 Jur. 894; 17 L. J.
Q. B. 278.
(e) Horsford *v.* Webster, 5 Tyrr. 409; 1 C. M. & R. 696.

The grantee may, however, remove the goods before distress levied; for Stat. 11 Geo. II. c. 19. by which landlords are authorized to follow goods fraudulently or clandestinely removed, and penalties are imposed on persons aiding such removal, does not apply to the goods of strangers or mortgagees.[a] Thus a creditor may, with his debtor's consent, take possession of goods and remove them from the premises for the purpose of satisfying his debt, although he knows the debtor to be in embarrassed circumstances, and apprehends a distress.[b]

So if the bill of sale holder, with the grantor's consent, in order to prevent a distress, removes the goods within the period of five days provided by sec. 13, the landlord has no right of action against the bill of sale holder for the loss of rent occasioned by removal, or for double value under the statute.[c]

Landlord and grantee.

Where a bill of sale holder, who had put a man in possession, on being informed by the landlord that rent was in arrear, and that the goods should not be removed until it was paid, continued in possession but made no attempt to remove the goods, but the landlord did not take possession or assume dominion over them, it was held there was no evidence of a conversion by the landlord; and, per Bramwell, B., that an actual prevention of removal by force would not have amounted to a conversion.[d] It was also held that a landlord was not under an obligation to hand any surplus goods or proceeds to the bill of sale holder, although after distraining he received notice that the goods were subject to a bill of sale, which notice he stated he would take care was properly acted on.[e]

Where a bill of sale holder seized goods on the grantor's premises, and with his knowledge but without any express request, and as the Court found for the bill of sale holder's own convenience, allowed them to remain until they were distrained for rent which he paid, he was held not to be

(a) Tomlinson c. Consolidated Credit Corporation, 24 Q. B. D. 135; 38 W. R. 118; 62 L. T. 162; 54 J. P. 644.

(b) Thornton c. Adams, 5 M. & S. 38; Fletcher r. Marillier, 9 A. & E. 457; Bach r. Meats, 5 M. & S. 200.

(c) Tomlinson v. Consolidated Credit Corporation, 24 Q. B. D. 135; Lane r. Tyler, 56 L. J. Q. B. 461.

(d) England r. Cowley, L. R. 8 Ex. 126; 42 L. J. Ex. 80; 28 L. T. 67.

(e) Evans c. Wright, 2 H. & N. 527; 27 L. J. Ex. 50.

entitled to recover from the grantor the money so paid;[a] but this decision appears questionable, and as a general rule, when one person's goods are lawfully seized for the debt of another, the owner is entitled to redeem them and to be reimbursed the money paid, or if the goods are sold to satisfy the debt, the owner may recover their value from the debtor; and this right exists even although there may be no agreement to indemnify, and in that sense no privity between the owner of the goods and the debtor.[b]

The limit on the landlord's right of distress imposed by section 42, Bankruptcy Act, 1883, as amended by section 28, Bankruptcy Act, 1890, under which a distress levied after bankruptcy is available only for six months' rent, extends to the goods of the bankrupt, and not to those of other persons. Thus under a Colonial statute prohibiting distress for rent after sequestration of the tenant's estate, the holder of a bill of sale was held not be entitled to take his goods out of the hands of a bailiff who had levied a distress, on the ground that they formed no part of the estate on which distress was prohibited. [c]

But when the landlord distrains and sells the chattels on the premises, part of which are, and part are not, comprised in the bill of sale, a mortgagee is entitled to stand in the landlord's place, and, under the doctrine of marshalling, to have the goods not comprised in the security first applied in payment of the rent.[d]

When after the expiration of a tenancy for years the holder of a bill of sale of the furniture of the late tenant put and continued a man in possession of the furniture upon the premises, under a power in the bill of sale authorizing him to enter upon the premises in or about which the goods should be and to take possession thereof, and if he should think fit to keep possession thereof, and for that purpose to put and continue a man in possession thereof upon such premises, or if he should think fit to sell the goods, whether upon the premises or after moving them, it was held that the landlord was entitled to treat the bill of sale holder as a mere trespasser.

Landlord and grantee.

(a) England v. Marsden, L. R. 1. C. P. 529; 35 L. J. C. P. 259; 14 W. R. 650, 14 L. T. N. S. 405; 12 Jur. N. S. 700.

(b) Edmunds v. Wallingford, 14 Q. B. D. 811; 33 W. R. 647; 54 L. J. Q. B. 305; 52 L. T. 720.

(c) Railton v. Wood, 15 App. Ca. 363; 59 L. J. P. C. 84; 63 L. T. 13; Crosse v. Welch, 8 T. L. R. 709.

(d) Exp. Stephenson 17 L. J. Bank. 5; De Gex, 690.

and an order was granted restraining him from selling the goods upon the premises or continuing in possession.[a] In another case, the grantor having assigned growing crops, the landlord distrained for rent, and whilst in possession, without notice of the bill of sale, agreed with the grantor, his tenant, to accept a surrender of the tenancy and possession of the crops. He then withdrew the distress, on which the mortgagee seized, but afterwards the landlord, on surrender of the tenancy, entered and took possession of the crops, and in an action by the mortgagee against the landlord it was held that the title of the latter was complete on the surrender, and that although the mortgagee was entitled to be put in the same position as the tenant before surrender, his claim was subject to the rent and the expenses the landlord had incurred in cultivating the crops.[b]

(3.) If the grantor shall fraudulently either remove or suffer the said goods, or any of them, to be removed from the premises ;

Fraudulent removal.

Mere removal will not be sufficient—it must be shewn to be with intent to deprive the mortgagee of his remedy; [c] thus, if the effect of the removal would be to deprive the mortgagee of his security, and leave him to his barren remedy by action, it would seem the removal may be within the subsection; [d] but in all cases it will be a question of fact whether the goods were fraudulently removed; and in a case under the Statute 11 Geo. II. c. 19, although the tenant admitted he removed goods to avoid a distress, the question of fraud was left to the jury.[e]

Before the amendment Act, even where no power of seizure on removal was given by the bill of sale, if the grantor dealt fraudulently with the mortgaged goods left in his possession, as if he attempted to sell them, the mortgagee might immediately commence an action for the recovery of the goods or their value,[f] and to restrain their removal ; and it would seem that he might have taken possession if he could do so peaceably and without violence.[g]

(a) Smith v. Brown, 48 L. J. Ch. 694.
(b) Clements v. Matthews, 11 Q. B. D. 808.
(c) Parry v. Duncan, 7 Bing. 243; M. & M. 533.
(d) Opperman v. Smith, 4 D. & Ry. 33.
(e) John v. Jenkins, 1 Cr. & M. 227.
(f) Fenn v. Bittleston, 7 Exch. 152; 21 L. J. Ex. 41.
(g) Story on Bailments, 306.

THE BILLS OF SALE ACT (1878) AMENDMENT ACT, 1882. 115   Sec 7.

1882]

> (4.) If the grantor shall not, without reason-
> able excuse, upon demand in writing by the
> grantee, produce to him his last receipts for
> rent, rates, and taxes ;

The effect of secs. 13 and 14 of the amendment Act will be *Production of* further to imperil the mortgagee's security, for the landlord *receipts.* and tax collector have five days to levy after the mortgagee has seized, an opportunity they will probably not neglect.

Where the grantor did not upon demand in writing by the grantee, produce a receipt for rent which had only become due a few days, and of which it appeared the landlord had not yet required payment, it was held that the grantor had not failed to produce the receipt without reasonable excuse,[a] But where the mortgagee had, at the grantor's request, paid rent which had not been repaid him, relief was refused, although no instalments were in arrear.[b]

> (5.) If execution shall have been levied against
> the goods of the grantor under any judg-
> ment at law;

This will include a decree,[c] and may include every *Execution* order of the Court or a judge in any cause or matter which may be enforced in the same manner as a judgment to the same effect ;[d] but it should be observed that the tendency of the decisions is to give to the word judgment its strict technical meaning.[e]

Although a sheriff, unless relieved by interpleader, is liable in damages for levying execution on the goods of a stranger, even if in the judgment debtor's possession, and the execution creditor also if his solicitor or agent has expressly directed seizure of the goods; yet the holder of a bill of sale over the judgment debtor's goods has no cause of action against the execution creditor for the seizure when the only direction is by the indorsement on the writ of execution, correctly stating the judgment debtor's address where

(a) *Exp.* Cotton, 11 Q. B. D. 301 ; *see also* Nunn *v.* Kirkwood, 75 L. T. J. 134.

(b) Cowley *v.* Tyler, W. N. 1884, 77.

(c) Judicature Act, 1873, s. 100.

(d) R. S. C. 1883, xlii. 17, 21.

(e) *Exp.* Schmitz, *re* Cohen, 12 Q. B. D. 509 ; 53 L. J. Ch. 1168 ; 50 L. T. 747 ; 32 W. R. 812 ; 1 Mor. 55 ; Cremetti *v.* Crom, 4 Q. B. D. 225 ; 48 L. J. Q. B. 337 ; 27 W. R. 811.

the goods are.[a] And the execution creditor by appearing
on the interpleader summons and taking an issue, does not
make himself liable for the sheriff's acts, if it turns out that
the goods belong to a bill of sale holder.[b]

If a bill of sale holder pays money into Court under an
interpleader order, an issue being directed with the execution
creditor, and the judgment debtor becomes bankrupt, the
money will not pending the issue be paid out to his trustee,
even with the bill of sale holder's consent; for the money
does not represent the goods, they not having been sold, nor
does it form part of the judgment debtor's estate. [c]

And on the judgment debtor becoming bankrupt after an
interpleader order, and his trustee claiming in priority to
the judgment creditor, under the provisions of the Bankruptcy Act, his title was held to be subject to the claims
of a bill of sale holder. [d]

Where on interpleader by the sheriff a claimant alleges
that he is entitled under a bill of sale to the goods seized in
execution, and an order is made for a sale and satisfaction of
the claim out of the proceeds of sale, the claimant is not
entitled to demand from the sheriff any sum not included in
the particulars of claim on which the order was made.[e]

Restraining
mortgagee.

Provided that the grantor may within five days
from the seizure or taking possession of any chattels
on account of any of the above-mentioned causes,
apply to the High Court, or to a Judge thereof in
chambers, and such Court or Judge, if satisfied that
by payment of money or otherwise the said cause of
seizure no longer exists, may restrain the grantee
from removing or selling the said chattels, or may
make such other order as may seem just.

It has been decided that the Court may restrain the
grantee from removing or selling goods seized after the date of
the commencement of the Act under a bill of sale executed and
registered before such date.[f] The application in the first

(a) Condy v. Blaiberg, 55 J. P. 580.
(b) Woollen v. Wright, 1 H. & C. 524; 31 L. J. Ex. 715; 7 L. T. 73.
(c) Shuckburgh v. Pike, 8 T. L. R. 710.
(d) Exp. Halling, re Haydon, 7 Ch. D. 157; 47 L. J. Bank. 25; 37 L. T. 809;
26 W.R. 182.
(e) Hockey v. Evans, 18 Q. B. D. 390; 56 L. J. Q. B. 259; 56 L. T. 179; 35
W. R. 265.
(f) Exp. Cotton, 11 Q. B. D. 301.

instance should be by summons, supported by an affidavit of the facts. If an injunction is granted, the parties affected should not apply *ex parte* to the Divisional Court to set it aside, the proper course being to apply on fresh evidence to the judge who made the order.[a] Having regard to the proviso, a demand for payment should be made, and a reasonable time allowed, before seizure. The object of the proviso appears to be to prevent the extortion too frequently practised on borrowers after default, for which a very complete remedy is afforded.

Where a bill of sale was payable by instalments, on default in payment of any one of which the whole amount secured was to become due, the mortgagees having seized, Hawkins, J., on the grantor's application, directed them to withdraw on payment of the instalment due and costs;[b] and so where, after seizure, the grantor offered to pay the amount due, which the mortgagee refused to accept, the Court restrained a sale, on condition that the amount due was paid.[c]

After seizure for any of the causes mentioned in the section, if the grantor pays or tenders the debt, interest and expenses, he may within five days from the seizure apply for relief under the proviso; but after the lapse of five days he is still entitled to bring an action for redemption on the usual terms of paying the debt, interest and expenses, together with the costs of redemption, unless the circumstances are such as to disentitle the grantee to such costs.[d]

Subject to the proviso at the end of this section and in the statutory form of bill of sale, the Court will not interfere by injunction to prevent a mortgagee pursuing his legal remedies to get possession of the mortgaged property; nor, unless by some binding rule of law a bill of sale is clearly invalid, will the Court grant relief on an interlocutory motion by the grantor to restrain a mortgagee who has taken possession from continuing such possession, except on the grantor bringing into Court the amount claimed by the mortgagee.[e] This, however, is not an invariable rule, and the Court has a discretion in the matter, and will not order the amount claimed by the mortgagee to be brought into Court if it appears that he is claiming too much.[f] But the Court will not interfere,

Restraining mortgagee.

(a) *Exp.* Mulworth, 30 S. J. 63.
(b) *Re* Graves, 27 Sol. J. 215.
(c) *Exp.* Cotton, 11 Q. B. D. 301.
(d) Johnson *v.* Diprose [1893], 1 Q. B. 512.
(e) Hill *v.* Kirkwood, 54 W. R. 358; 62 L. T. 105.
(f) Hickson *v.* Darlow, 31 W. R. 417.

even by interim injunction, with a mortgagee's legal rights on
a mere suggestion that it is possible that a trustee under the
grantor's bankruptcy may be able to impeach the security; [a]
and an interim injunction should only be granted to a day
certain. [b]

A receiver who has not perfected his title by giving the
security required by the order appointing him, will not be
protected in his possession of the goods, [c] but interference
with a duly appointed receiver, although the mortgagee may
have seized prior to the receiver's appointment, is a contempt
of Court : and so will be a removal of the goods comprised in
a valid bill of sale where a receiver is in possession, and if a
question as to its validity is pending between the mortgagee
and the receiver under the grantor's bankruptcy, the mortgagee
should apply to the Court for leave to exercise his legal
rights. [d]

On an undertaking, given on obtaining an interim injunction,
to pay such damages as the Court shall deem to have been sustained by reason of the order, the Court has a discretion and may
refuse to make any order for payment of damages, if those alleged
to have been sustained are trivial or remote, or if great delay
has occurred in applying for them. [e] Thus, when the receiver
under a bankruptcy petition obtained an *ex parte* injunction
against the holder of a bill of sale, which was afterwards
upheld, but no application for damages was made for three
years and a half, the Court declined to order payment of
damages sustained by a distress on the goods while the injunction was in force, holding that the delay was a sufficient answer
to the application. [f] An order for damages may be made where
an interlocutory injunction has been wrongly granted, owing
to a mistake of law, without any misrepresentation, suppres-
sion, or other default by the party obtaining it ; although
this was formerly doubted. [g]

(a) *Exp.* Bayley, *re* Hart, 43 L. T. 181 ; 29 W. R. 28 ; 15 Ch. D. 223.

(b) *Exp.* Abrams, *re* Johnstone, 50 L. T. 184 ; 1 Mor. 32.

(c) Edwards *v.* Edwards, 2 Ch. D. 291.

(d) *Exp.* Andrews, *re* Fells, 4 Ch. D. 509 ; 36 L. T. 38 ; 46 L. J. Bank. 23 ; 25
W. R. 382 ; *exp.* Cochrane, *re* Mead, 20 Eq. 282 ; 44 L. J. Bank. 87 ; 23 W. R.
726 ; 32 L. T. 508.

(e) Smith *v.* Day. 21 Ch. D. 421 ; 31 W. R. 187 ; 48 L. T. 54.

(f) *Exp.* Hall, *re* Wood, 23 Ch. D. 644 ; 32 W. R. 179 ; 49 L. T. 275 ; 52
L. J. Q. B. 907.

(g) Griffith *v.* Blake, 32 W. R. 833 ; 27 Ch. D. 474 ; 53 L. J. Ch. 965 ; 51 L. T. 274.

.8. (1878.) Every bill of sale to which this Act applies shall be duly attested, and shall be registered under this Act within seven days after the making or giving thereof, and shall set forth the consideration for which such bill of sale was given, otherwise such bill of sale, as against all trustees or assignees of the estate of the person whose chattels or any of them are comprised in such bill of sale under the law relating to bankruptcy or liquidation, or under any assignment for the benefit of the creditors of such person, and also as against all sheriffs' officers and other persons seizing any chattels comprised in such bill of sale, in the execution of any process of any Court authorizing the seizure of the chattels of the person by whom or of whose chattels such bill has been made, and also as against every person on whose behalf such process shall have been issued, shall be deemed fraudulent and void so far as regards the property in or right to the possession of any chattels comprised in such bill of sale which, at or after the time of filing the petition for bankruptcy or liquidation, or of the execution of such assignment, or of executing such process (as the case may be), and after the expiration of such seven days are in the possession or apparent possession of the person making such bill of sale (or of any person against whom the process has issued under or in the execution of which such bill has been made or given, as the case may be).

Avoidance of unregistered bills of sale in certain cases.

This section is repealed by sec. 15 of the amendment Act, but the repeal is, it would seem, qualified by sec. 3, and the section will therefore still govern bills of sale given otherwise than as security for the payment of money,[a] and also all bills of sale registered under the principal Act before the 1st of November, 1882.

Application of the section.

(a) Swift v. Pannell, 24 Ch. D. 210.

By sec. 10, sub-sec. 1, of the principal Act, also repealed by sec. 15 of the amendment Act, so far only as regards bills of sale given by way of security for the payment of money, every bill of sale to which the principal Act applies shall be attested by a solicitor of the Supreme Court in the prescribed form.

Considerable doubt arose whether under the section registration was not requisite to support a bill of sale between the parties themselves, and the Common Pleas Division decided that, unless there had been attestation with the formalities prescribed by sec. 10. sub-sec. 1, the instrument would be invalid, even as between the grantor and grantee; but the decision was overruled by the Court of Appeal holding that a bill of sale, though not attested or registered as required by the Act, was good between the parties;[a] indeed, under the repealed statutes, an unregistered bill of sale was good as between the grantor and grantee, and all other persons except those mentioned in the section; thus, it prevailed against the liquidator of a Company,[b] or the unsecured creditors of a deceased person whose estate was being administered;[c] and this rule was not affected by the provisions of sec. 10 of the Judicature Act, 1875.[d] By sec. 68 (3), Bankruptcy Act, 1883, all expressions (in the Act) referring to the trustee under a bankruptcy shall, unless the context otherwise requires, or the Act otherwise provides, include the official receiver when acting as trustee. By sec. 3 (16) (17). Bankruptcy Act, 1890, certain provisions of the Bankruptcy Acts apply as if the trustee under a composition or scheme were trustee in a bankruptcy; and by sec. 21 (3) also apply in cases of administration in bankruptcy of estates of persons dying insolvent. It would seem that such persons might be deemed trustees or assignees within the meaning of section 8 of the principal Act.

Application of the section.   But the principal Act does not apply unless the goods are in the possession or apparent possession of the grantor; thus, a purchase by unregistered receipt from a trustee in liquidation, was upheld against an execution creditor of the debtor, to whom the goods had been let by the purchaser, for the goods

(a) Davis v. Goodman, 5 C.P.D. 128; 49 L. J. C. P. 344; 28 W. R. 559; 42 L. T. 288.
(b) Re Marine Mansions Co., L. R. 4 Eq. 601; 37 L. J. Ch. 115; re Stockton Iron Co., 10 Ch. D. 342, per Bacon V.-C.
(c) Re Knott, 7 Ch. D. 549 n.
(d) Tadman c. D'Epineuil, 20 Ch. D. 217; 30 W. R. 423; 46 L. T. 409; 51 L. J. Ch. 491.

were not in the possession or apparent possession of the person making the bill of sale.[a] So where the grantees of a bill of sale, by verbal agreement, coupled with a receipt and inventory, sold the goods to a purchaser who allowed the former owner to remain in possession, the case was held not to be within the Act;[b] and an unregistered document, by which goods were purchased from a bill of sale holder, was upheld against an execution creditor of the original grantor.[c]

Again, when a person who had given a charge over goods to secure payment to his late partner, afterwards assigned them to a trustee for creditors, and then died leaving a widow, who, with the trustee, contracted engagements which resulted in an execution being levied on the goods, the charge, though a bill of sale, was held not to be void against the execution creditor, whose execution was not a process authorizing the seizure of the chattels of the person by whom or of whose chattels such bill of sale had been made.[d]

Whenever a sale was followed by open delivery and taking possession, registration, unless to obtain the benefit of the repealed sec. 20, was not essential; for to create a necessity for registration there must have been apparent possession of the goods and a lapse of seven days after the bill of sale was made; nor was the case within the section by reason of apparent possession, the seven days not having expired, for the assignee had the period of seven days within which he might complete his title by registration, and if he took and retained a more than formal possession, he acquired a good title, and no registration was necessary.[e] The bankruptcy of the grantor within the seven days allowed for registration did not affect the bill of sale if registered in due time;[f] but it was held under the Bills of Sale Act, 1854, that possession taken under an unregistered bill of sale, after the time for registration had expired, could not avail against the title of a trustee under a subsequent petition, if the grantor had committed a prior act of bankruptcy, though such act of bankruptcy might have been unknown to the grantee at the

When unregistered bills of sale were valid.

(a) Parnacott e. Dieudonné, 2 T. L. R.
(b) Hay e. Nathan, 3 T. L. R. 11.
(c) Hall e. Smith 3 T. L. R. 505.
(d) Cranfield e. Cranfield, 23 L. R. Ir. 555.
(e) Marples e. Hartley, 1 B. & S. 1 ; 30 L. J. Q. B. 92 ; Hollingsworth e. White, 6 L. T. 604, 40 W. R. 616; Piercy e. Humphreys, 17 L. T. 694.
(f) Exp. Kahen, re Hewer, 21 Ch. D. 871 ; 46 L. T. 850; 30 W. R. 954 ; 51 L. J. Ch. 901.

time of taking possession.[a]   It should, however, be observed
that sec. 1 of the Act of 1854 avoided an unregistered bill of
sale, in the event of bankruptcy, so far as regarded chattels in
the apparent possession of the grantor at or after the time
of such bankruptcy, which was decided to mean the commission of an act of bankruptcy to which the title of the trustee
related; but the operation of sec. 8 of the principal Act is
limited to chattels in the apparent possession of the grantor
at or after the time of filing the petition for bankruptcy or
liquidation.

Extent of
avoidance.

It was decided under the Bills of Sale Act, 1854, that the
effect of an execution was to avoid a prior unregistered bill
of sale altogether, and to give the holder of a second registered security a good title against the prior grantee and a
trustee in the grantor's bankruptcy;[b] but it was doubted if
this rule applied under the principal Act,[c] and the result
of the section is to avoid the bill of sale only so far as is
necessary to give due effect to the execution.[d]   Therefore a
bill of sale to which the principal Act applies, although void
as against an execution creditor for non-compliance with the
requirements of the Act, may, after the execution has been
satisfied, prevail against subsequent execution creditors, or a
trustee in the grantor's bankruptcy, if the goods are no longer
in the grantor's apparent possession.   Indeed, when after an
execution creditor had seized the goods comprised in an unregistered bill of sale, the mortgagee took sufficient possession before the filing of a bankruptcy petition, and the
execution was then avoided by relation of the trustee's title
to an act of bankruptcy committed before the levy, it was held
that the execution creditor was ousted altogether, and the bill
of sale holder's title prevailed. [d]

As bills of sale to which the amendment Act applies are
void altogether if unregistered, and not merely as against
a certain class of persons, the refined distinction established
by the preceding cases may not be now of so great practical
importance.

(a) *Exp.* Attwater, *re* Turner, 5 Ch. D. 27 ; 25 W. R. 206; 35 L. T. 682 ; 46 L.J.
Bank, 41.
(b) Richards *v.* James, L. R. 2 Q. B. 285 ; 15 W. R. 580 ; 36 L. J. Q. B. 116 ;
8 B. & S. 302; 16 L. T. 674; Edwards *v.* English, 7 E. & B. 564; 26 L. J. Q. B. 193.
(c) *Exp.* Fourdrinier, 31 W. R. 149 ; 48 L. T. 46 ; 21 Ch. D. 510.
(d) *Exp.* Blaiberg, *re* Toomer, 23 Ch. D. 254 ; 52 L. J. Ch. 461 ; 31 W. R. 906;
49 L. T. 16.

An unregistered bill of sale was void against an execution creditor, notwithstanding he had notice of the bill of sale at the time he became the grantor's creditor.[a]

8. (1882.) Every bill of sale shall be duly attested, and shall be registered under the principal Act within seven clear days after the execution thereof, or if it is executed in any place out of England then within seven clear days after the time at which it would in the ordinary course of post arrive in England if posted immediately after the execution thereof; [1] and shall truly set forth the consideration for which it was given; [2] otherwise such bill of sale shall be void in respect of the personal chattels comprised therein.[3]

Bill of sale to be void unless attested and registered.

(2) Page 124.

(3) Page 134.

(1) Under the Bills of Sale Acts, 1854 and 1866, attestation was not essential to the validity of a bill of sale;[b] but the formality of attestation by a solicitor was introduced by sec. 10, sub-sec. 1, of the principal Act, now repealed, and every bill of sale to which that Act applied must have been attested in the manner prescribed. By sec. 10 of the amendment Act, the execution of every bill of sale by the grantor shall be attested by one or more credible witnesses, not being a party or parties thereto, and unless so attested will be void. " Duly attested " means attested in the manner required by the Act, and by the form in the schedule to the Act.[c]

By the ordinary rule of computation, when clear days are limited for doing an act, time is to be reckoned exclusively of the first and last days, but as registration is required to be within seven clear days, it must be effected on the seventh day, excluding the day of execution. The words used in the section are the same as those in sec. 10, sub-sec. 2, of the principal Act, under which the rule has been as stated, and it would seem therefore, and by analogy to the practice with regard to warrants of attorney, that registration of a bill of sale executed on the first of the month will be in time if registered on the eighth, unless that day happens to be a Sunday, or other day on which the registrar's office is closed, when regis-

Time for registration.

(a) Edwards v. Edwards, 2 Ch. D. 291.

(b) Deffel v. Miles, 15 L. T. 202.

(c) Parsons v. Brand, 25 Q. B. D. 110; 62 L. T. 479; 38 W. R. 344.

tration will be valid if made on the next following day on which the office is open.[a]

In the absence of proof of malice, an action will not lie for damages occasioned by the defendant causing to be registered a document which in fact is not a bill of sale.[b]

The provision for registering bills of sale executed out of England is new, and obviates a difficulty which often arose from the impossibility of registering within the prescribed time bills of sale executed abroad. The requisites of registration are prescribed by sec. 10, sub-sec. 2, of the principal Act, and the cases on the subject will be found collected in the note to that section.

By sec. 14 of the principal Act, any judge of the High Court of Justice, on being satisfied that the omission to register a bill of sale within the prescribed time was accidental or due to inadvertence, may in his discretion extend the time for registration upon such terms as he thinks fit.

The consideration.

(2) A mis-statement of the consideration has always been held a strong, though not conclusive, badge of fraud,[c] but formerly it did not necessarily invalidate a bill of sale as against creditors, if inserted without fraud and with the intention of making the security available only to the extent of the sum actually due.[d]

Under the repealed section of the principal Act the consideration must have been truly stated, and the decisions under that section will therefore still apply. It is difficult to lay down any general rule for adequately setting forth the consideration, and every case must to some extent depend on its particular circumstances; but in cases of difficulty the safest plan is to set out the facts, and not their supposed legal results. It has, however, been decided that the consideration for giving a bill of sale is, if money, the amount actually passing, not necessarily the amount secured; thus, where a bill of sale was given to secure a present advance, and also the amount for the time being due upon a mortgage including further advances, but the recitals omitted a sum which had been advanced on a bill of exchange then current, the omission was held not to amount to a mis-statement of consideration.[e]

(a) Sec. 22 [1878], Williams v. Burgess, 12 Ad. & E. 635 ; 9 Dowl. 544.

(b) Horsley v. Style, 69 L. T. 222 ; 4 Rep. 574.

(c) Exp. Furber, re Pellew, 6 Ch. D. 181 ; 36 L. T. 668 ; exp. Chaplin, re Sinclair, 26 Ch. D. 319 ; 53 L. J. Ch. 762 ; 51 L. T. 345.

(d) Biddulph v. Goold, 11 W. R. 882 ; Kevan v. Mawson, 24 L. T. N. S. 395.

(e) Exp. Challinor, re Rogers, 16 Ch. D. 260 ; 29 W. R. 204 ; 44 L. T. 122.

If the consideration is stated in the way in which it would be ordinarily stated between a mortgagor and mortgagee it is sufficient, for the Act does not intend to throw any greater burden on a bill of sale holder than on an ordinary mortgagee; but the statement of consideration must contain on the face of it what is substantially the whole transaction, and if it does so it is sufficient.[a] Therefore, substantial accuracy will satisfy the requirements of the Act, and although the bill of sale will be avoided by a material mis-statement, whether intentional or the result of accident, unless, perhaps, a mere clerical error, a small inaccuracy in the statement of the consideration will not have that effect;[b] thus stating the consideration as £32, or thereabouts, was held sufficient.[c] And if the bill of sale states as the consideration an amount really stated on accounts between the parties, an arithmetical error, honestly made, in the figures the basis of such account will not be treated as an untrue statement of consideration : so where £10 of the consideration was mentioned as the value of goods sold and delivered to enable the grantor to carry on his business, the consideration was held truly stated though some part of the goods were not delivered until after the bill of sale was executed.[d]

Neither is it necessary to set forth every bargain or stipulation collateral to the consideration,[e] nor need the proposed application of the consideration be stated; thus, where a bill of sale recited that the grantor, having two executions on his premises, and being unable to carry on his business by reason thereof, had applied to the mortgagee to lend him £182 3s., to enable him to pay out such executions, which the mortgagee had agreed to do on having the assignment, and then the deed stated that in pursuance of such agreement, and in consideration of the sum of £182 3s. then paid, the grantor assigned certain chattels, and it appeared the mortgagee, with the grantor's sanction, gave several cheques amounting in the whole to that sum, one being given to the sheriff's officer another to an execution creditor, another to the grantor, while

The consideration.

(a) Roberts v. Roberts, 13 Q. B. D. 794.

(b) Exp. Winter, re Fothergill, 44 L. T. 323 , 29 W. R. 575 ; exp. Probyn, re Barrett, S.J., 1880, 341.

(c) Hughes v. Little, 18 Q. B. D. 32 ; 56 L. J. Q. B. 96 ; 35 W. R. 36 ; 55 L. T. 470.

(d) Griffith v. Williams, 93 L. T. J. 9.

(e) Exp. National Mercantile Bank, re Haynes, 15 Ch. D. 42 ; 28 W. R. 844 ; 41 L. T. 36 ; 49 L. J. Bank. 62.

£25 was paid to the grantor's solicitor for money lent and costs, it was held that in the absence of any suggestion of fraud, the consideration, which was the amount of money paid, was sufficiently set forth.[a]

Again, the consideration was held truly stated where a debtor who owed £235, partly secured by an existing bill of sale, executed a second bill of sale of the same chattels to secure £290, on the understanding that out of such sum he should pay off the existing debt. The bill of sale was expressed to be given in consideration of £290 then paid, without alluding to the intended application of the money; and £290 was in fact advanced to the grantor, who the next day, in pursuance of the arrangement, applied £235 of it in paying off the old debt.[b]

The consideration.

Where a bill of sale recited a debt due to the mortgagee and that the grantor had agreed to execute the bill of sale in order to induce the mortgagee not to institute proceedings against him, the deed was supported although in fact no proceedings had ever been threatened, nor was there any evidence of pressure;[c] and so a bill of sale was held valid when the consideration was stated to be amongst other things a covenant by the mortgagees, which covenant was not given.[d] Again, it was held unnecessary to set forth a verbal agreement not to register a bill of sale in consideration of which a larger bonus was given.[e]

But the true nature of the transaction between the parties must always be set forth; and the Court can inquire into the consideration for a bill of sale, and when a judgment, alleged to have been obtained by collusion, was stated as the consideration, the Court admitted evidence to prove that collusion existed.[f] And where the consideration was an amount stated to have been advanced, but in fact a considerable portion was a mere liability which the mortgagee had arranged with the mortgagor to discharge, the consideration was inquired into

(a) Hamlyn v. Betteley, 5 C. P. D. 327; 42 L. T. 373; 49 L. J. C. P. 405; 28 W. R. 956.
(b) Thomas v. Searles [1891], 2 Q.B., 408.
(c) Exp. Winter, re Fothergill, 44 L. T. 323.
(d) Roberts v. Roberts, 13 Q. B. D. 794.
(e) Exp. Popplewell, re Storey, 21 Ch. D. 73; 47 L. T. 274; 52 L. J. Ch. 39 31 W. R. 35.
(f) Usher v. Martin, 61 L. T. 778.

THE BILLS OF SALE ACT (1878) AMENDMENT ACT, 1882. 127   **Sec. 8.**
1882.

and held not to be truly stated.[a] So a bill of sale was held void expressed to be given for £312 then owing, of which £126 was the grantee's liability on bills of exchange which the grantee agreed to, and afterwards did pay at maturity, for the accommodation of the grantor, the consideration not being truly set forth as the £126 was not "then owing."[b]

Where the grantee held current bills of the grantor for £8,300, but the consideration was stated as £7,575 then owing; it was held, assuming, as was alleged, an agreement for the sum stated to be taken as representing the debt between the parties, that the consideration was not truly stated, for the agreement should have been set out as part of it.[c]

Also, if money, the consideration for the bill of sale, is advanced at different times, it should, in general, be so stated; and where loans amounting to £240 had from time to time, in the months of March and April, been made to a firm consisting of the grantor and other persons, and subsequently, in June and July, other moneys, amounting to £160, had been advanced to the grantor, who had dissolved partnership and taken over the debts and assets of the late firm, the bill of sale reciting that in the month of June last the grantor applied to the mortgagee to lend him the sum of £340, which he consented to do, and then went on to recite a further application and loan of £60, it was held that the consideration not being truly set forth, the registration was void;[d] Indeed, as a rule, if the time of payment is mentioned, it must be truly stated. Thus, where a bill of sale stated the consideration to be paid at or before its execution, but in fact only a small portion was then paid, part being handed some days afterwards to other persons at the grantor's request, it was held that the consideration was not truly stated.[e]

The consideration.

(a) Norman v. Hodges, C. A. Trinity Sittings, 1881. (MS. note.

(b) Mayer v. Mindlevich, 69 L. T. 440.

(c) Cochrane v. Moore, 25 Q. B. D. 57 ; 38 W. R. 588 ; 63 L. T. 153 ; 59 L. J Q. B. 377.

(d) *Exp.* Carter, *re* Threappleton, 12 Ch. D. 901 ; 41 L. T. 37 ; 27 W. R. 945.

(e) *Exp.* Rolph, *re* Spindler, 19 Ch. D. 98 51 L. J. Ch. 88 ; 30 W. R. 52 45 L. T. 482.

G 2

On the other hand, as "payment" does not necessarily mean payment *in præsenti*, a security was supported expressed to be given in consideration of the payment of two sums of money, the first of which had, in fact, been paid some months previously.[a]

The consideration.

In another case the facts were, that in January, 1879, the debtor was indebted to his brother in £200, and by a bill of sale, dated the 17th of that month, in consideration of a past debt of £200, and of £50 then advanced, assigned to his brother certain effects. It appeared that of the £50, £5 had been advanced the previous day, so that on the execution of the deed only £45 was actually paid over, but it was held by the Chief Judge that the statement of the consideration was substantially correct ;[b] and so where the consideration was stated as money paid on or immediately before the execution of the bill of sale, but in fact half of it was paid four days previously on the grantor's written undertaking to give a bill of sale ;[c] and where the consideration expressed to be now paid, had in fact been paid four days previously on the execution of a prior bill of sale, cancelled by the parties as containing clauses inconsistent with the Act, the statement was held sufficient.[d]

For if the facts are stated with substantial accuracy, according to their legal, mercantile, or business effect, it is sufficient, though they may not be stated with perfect verbal accuracy ; thus where a bill of sale recited that the grantees had agreed to lend the grantor £7,350, and that he was already indebted to them in other sums, that it had been agreed between the parties that the grantor should execute the bill of sale as a security for the repayment of the first-named sum with interest, and witnessed that the bill of sale was executed "in pursuance of the said agreement, and in consideration of £7,350 now paid " by the grantees to the grantor, a receipt being indorsed, but in fact no money actually passed between the parties, the sum of £7,350 being the balance due to the grantees in respect of advances made by them to the grantor from time to time, it was held the consideration was suffi-

(a) Carrard *v.* Meek, 29 W. R. 244 ; 43 L. T. 760 ; 50 L. J. Ch. 187.

(b) *Exp.* Smith, L. J. N., 1880, p. 39.

(c) *Exp.* Johnson, *re* Chapman, 26 Ch. D. 338 ; 50 L. T. 214 ; 32 W. R. 603 53 L. J. Ch. 762.

(d) *Exp.* Allam, *re* Munday, 14 Q. B. D. 43 ; 33 W. R. 231.

ciently set forth, inasmuch as the effect of the recitals was to
wipe out the old debt and constitute a new lending on the
terms of the bill of sale.[a]

On 25th October 1885, a bill of sale was given to secure
£220 and interest, stated as £100 advanced in 1882, and £120
then advanced, the facts being that £100 was lent in 1882,
£20 on October 12th, 1885, £20 on October 20th, £66 on
October 22nd, the balance being £7 due for interest on the
first £100, and £7 for rent.   On 22nd April 1886, after the day
fixed for payment, the bill of sale being found void, a new bill
of sale was given to secure the same £220, expressed to be
" in consideration of £220 now paid," no money passing.
The Queen's Bench Division and the Court of Appeal upheld
the bill of sale, deciding that the consideration was truly
stated in a business sense.[b]   These decisions seem inconsistent
with an earlier case holding insufficient the statement in a bill
of sale given to secure a past debt contracted by instalments
extending over two years that the consideration was a sum
" now paid." [c]

Again, where the grantor who had purchased a brewery
from the mortgagee for £2,500, being able to pay £500 only,
agreed that the balance of £2,000 should be secured by a bill
of sale, and accordingly, immediately after the assignment
to him of the brewery, executed a bill of sale expressed to be
made in consideration of £2,000 paid by the mortgagee to the
grantor "immediately before the execution of these presents,"
but no money, except the £500, was paid, the £2,000 being the
unpaid balance of the purchase-money, it was held that the
consideration was properly stated;[d] and when on a sale of
furniture for £600, the purchaser paid £100, giving, to secure
the balance, a bill of sale expressed to be in consideration of
£500 " now paid," it was held sufficient.[e]

In another case the grantor was indebted to the creditors,
and the bill of sale, after reciting that they had agreed to
advance £2,050, witnessed that in consideration of £2,050 the

(a) Credit Company v. Pott, 6 Q. B. D. 295; 29 W. R. 326; 50 L. J. Ex.
101; 44 L. T. 588.
(b) Exp. Nelson, re Hockaday, 35 W. R. 264; 4 Mor. 12.; 55 L. T. 819.
(c) Exp. Berwick, re Young, 29 W. R. 202; 43 L. T. 576.
(d) Exp. Holland, re Roper, 21 Ch. D. 543; 31 W. R. 102; 52 L. J. Ch. 113;
47 L. T. 488.
(e) Staniforth v. Capon, 80 L. T. J. 376.

grantor granted to the creditors the chattels comprised in the bill of sale. On the execution of the deed, £2,050 was handed by the creditors to the grantor, who at once handed back £550 to pay off his liabilities to the grantees. In giving judgment, James, L.J., said: "The consideration must be truly set forth; probably it need not be stated with minute accuracy, but it must be set forth substantially. It has been contended that any collateral stipulations as to the application of the consideration ought to be set forth as part of the consideration; that there should be recitals of the intended application of the consideration. I cannot see that recitals of the motive and object of the advance are required by the Act. Collateral matters and stipulations and the motives of the lender are no part of the consideration for the deed, though they may be an inducement or reason for the advance. Suppose instead of there having been bills due by the grantor to the creditors there had been outstanding in the hands of some other persons bills upon which the creditors were liable, and they had said to the grantor, ' You must take up these bills ' ? or, suppose a loan were made upon the security of farming stock, and the lender said, ' You must pay the rent which is due to your landlord, or my security will be imperilled ' ? Stipulations of that kind would be proper enough, and would be part of the bargain as between the parties, but they would be no part of the consideration which is intended by the Act to be set forth. In my view the Act, while requiring the real, the actual consideration to be set forth, does not require that any bargain between the parties relating to it should be stated. Of course if there was a bargain that the whole sum, which is stated to be the consideration, should be at once returned to the grantee, that would be a sham transaction, and the Court would know how to deal with it."[a]

The consideration.

Again, where a bill of sale stated the consideration to be £560 " this day paid by the mortgagee to the mortgagor," but in fact £500 only was paid to the mortgagor, £20 at his request being paid to the valuer who valued the property for the purpose of the loan, and £40 represented costs of the bill of sale and other documents, which the mortgagor requested the mortgagee to include in the bill of sale, the consideration was held to be set forth within the section.[b]

(a) *Exp.* National Mercantile Bank, *re* Haynes, 15 Ch. D. 42 ; 28 W. R. 848.
(b) Hamilton *v.* Chaine, 7 Q. B. D. 319 ; 29 W. R. 676; 44 L. T. 764; 50 L. J. Q. B. 456.

But the doctrine of these cases will not be extended ; and
a bill of sale was set aside where the consideration was therein
stated to be £700, but it appeared that of this £271 had been
previously paid by the grantee to discharge a prior bill of
sale, and that on a cheque for the balance being handed to
the grantor it had, at her request been cashed, and part of it
paid to one of her creditors, £21 to a solicitor for preparing
the bill of sale, £7 10s. being retained by the grantee for commission on the loan, and expenses in connection therewith, a
promissory note for £10 being given for a like purpose, the
balance only being received by the grantor.[a]   Indeed, the
cases of re Haynes and ex parte Challinor are now binding
authorities only so far as they decide that if part of the consideration is, by the grantor's direction, given at the time of
executing the deed, applied in satisfaction of a then existing
debt owing by him, the money so paid may be properly stated
in the deed to be then paid to him.[b]   But there must be a
debt due or payable, irrespective of the agreement to make
the payment, and money retained with the grantor's consent
to meet future liabilities which are not debts due or payable
cannot be stated as now paid.   So the consideration was held
not truly stated as " now paid " where part only was paid to
the grantor, the remainder being by agreement retained by
the grantee in satisfaction of the grantor's running accept-
ances, of a sum for future hire of the furniture assigned by
the bill of sale, and of an agreed sum for the expenses of the
transaction.[c]

The object of setting forth the consideration has been said The considera-
to be to prevent the giving of a security for a sum stated to tion.
be advanced, when in fact a part of it is retained by the mortgagee ; thus, where a bill of sale was expressed to be given in
consideration of £120 paid on its execution by the grantees to
the grantor, but in fact only £90 was paid, £30 being retained
for interest and expenses, and after the usual attestation
clause was a receipt for £90, signed by the grantor, stating
that the £90, together with the agreed sum of £30 for interest
and expenses, making the sum of £120, being the consideration money expressed to be paid, it was held by the Court of

(a) Exp. Challinor, re Rogers, 16 Ch. D. 260.

(b) Exp. Firth, re Cowburn, 19 Ch. D. 419 ; 51 L. J. Ch. 473 ; 30 W. R. 529 ; 46
L. T. 120.

(c) Richardson v. Harris, 22 Q. B. D. 268 ; 37 W. R. 426.

Appeal, distinguishing the case from *re* Haynes, that the consideration was not truly set forth, on the ground that there was no debt independently of the transaction of loan, the whole liability for interest and expenses arising out of the transaction on the bill of sale, and that the receipt, coming as it did after the attestation clause, could not form part of the deed.[a]

The consideration.

Again, a bill of sale was expressed to be made in consideration of £50 paid at or before the execution, but only £21 was in fact paid, the grantee, at the grantor's written request, retaining £3 10s. for expenses, and seven days later paying £25 to the landlord for rent, as the request alleged "now due." No rent was then due, though half the amount paid fell due two days later, but the remainder did not become due for three months, and it was held that the consideration was not truly stated either as to the time or manner of payment, the £25 not being paid to the grantor, but there being only an agreement to pay on his behalf, and further, it not being paid at or before the execution of the deed.[b] So also the deed was avoided where, out of the advance stated to be paid on the giving of a bill of sale, was deducted the amount due on a previous bill of sale and a small sum for stamps.[c]

It may therefore now be considered settled law that if the amount of the expenses incident to the preparation of a bill of sale, given by way of mortgage, is deducted from the sum stated in it as the consideration, and only the balance is actually paid by the lender to the borrower, the consideration is not stated so as to satisfy the Act ; for the expenses of the preparation of a bill of sale do not become part of the debt due to the mortgagee until after its execution : thus the retainer of 30s. for expenses from the amount stated to be paid was held to vitiate the deed.[d]

And where the consideration was stated as "£114 now paid," of which £10 was, as previously agreed, paid by the grantor out of the advance, for the charges of the grantee's solicitor in preparing the bill of sale, the grantor in fact getting £104 only, the consideration was held not to be truly stated.[e]

(a) *Exp.* Charing Cross Bank, *re* Parker, 16 Ch. D. 35 ; 50 L. J. Ch. 157 ; 44 L. T. 113 ; 29 W. R. 204.
(b) *Exp.* Rolph, *re* Spindler, 19 Ch. D. 98.
(c) *Exp.* Bernstein, *re* Gordon, 74 L. T. J. 245.
(d) *Exp.* Firth, *re* Cowburn, 19 Ch. D. 419.
(e) Cohen *c.* Higgins, 8 T. L. R. 8.

THE BILLS OF SALE ACT (1878) AMENDMENT ACT, 1882. 133

Sec. 8.
[1882.]

If, however, the bill of sale is prepared by a solicitor, acting for both grantor and mortgagee, who receives the consideration money as agent for the grantor, it has been held that the whole consideration money may be stated as paid to the grantor, although the solicitor, after the bill of sale has been executed, retains part of it for his costs, with the consent of the grantor.[a] So where at the time of the loan the borrower repaid the lender the legal expenses of the transaction, in the absence of evidence of a previous agreement to make any deduction, the whole amount of the loan was held properly stated as paid to the borrower.[b] For that is a true statement even though when the money is paid over the grantor choose voluntarily to pay part of it back again in respect of some debt due or accruing;[c] but if he has no option in the matter the case is different; thus where a cheque was drawn for the consideration and indorsed by the grantor, but the grantees refused to pay it until a distress levied by the landlord had been paid out, with the grantor's consent taking away the cheque and executed bill of sale, the same day paying out the landlord, the balance only being given to the grantor, the consideration was held not truly stated as now paid.[d]

Inaccuracies in stating the consideration will not invalidate a bill of sale, if it is apparent from the terms of the instrument what the consideration really was;[e] and so where the recitals shewed the true transaction, stating expenses as part of the advance was held not to avoid the deed; thus where it was recited that the grantor had applied to the mortgagees to advance the sum of £70 less £16 agreed interest and expenses, witnessing, that in consideration of £54, being the said sum of £70 less the said sum of £16 deducted and retained therefrom, and being the agreed interest and expenses in consideration of which the loan was granted, and which said sums of £54 and £16 conjointly (thereinafter called the loan) were by the mortgagees paid to the grantor at or before the execution thereof the receipt of which said sums

The consideration.

(a) *Exp.* Hunt, *re* Cann, 13 Q. B. D. 36.
(b) Cochrane *c.* Dixon, 3 T. L. R. 717.
(c) Richardson *c.* Harris, 22 Q. B. D. 268.
(d) Bishop *c.* Consolidated Credit Corporation, 86 L. T. J. 126.
(e) Roberts *c.* Roberts 13 Q. B. D., 794.

the grantor acknowledged. the bill of sale was upheld. although only £54 was in fact paid.[a]

Some further guide to a statement of the consideration may be found in the following cases, decided under the repealed Annuity Act. 1777, 17 Geo. III. c. 26, which, by sec. 3, provided that in every annuity deed the consideration should be fully and truly set forth and described. Under this statute it was held unnecessary to set out a mere nominal consideration, as 10s. to a trustee, it being like the reservation of a peppercorn rent, and in fact seldom paid;[b] and when an annuity deed was granted by three persons. one of whom was known to be merely a surety, it was held that if all were present when the money was paid, and signed the receipt, the consideration was properly stated as a payment to all.[c] On the other hand. when the consideration was stated as £600 paid. but the real consideration was the payment of £300. and the giving up of a former annuity, it was held insufficient, the objection being not that the consideration was not a good one. but that it was untruly stated.[d]

How a bill of sale may become invalid.

(3) This provision is entirely new. and while under previous statutes an unregistered bill of sale was void only as against a certain class of persons. registration not being essential as between grantor and grantee.[e] by this section a bill of sale to which the amendment Act applies. if not duly registered is absolutely void in respect of the personal chattels comprised therein, even as against the grantor. Indeed it would appear that the object the Legislature had in view was not merely the protection of creditors. but to ensure that whenever the property in chattels is changed as security for a debt, it should be changed in a particular manner.[f]

It will be observed that by this section bills of sale are declared void only in respect of the chattels comprised therein, and therefore covenants contained in them may still be valid; although. as will be seen, a bill of sale void under section 9 is void altogether ;[g] in so far as the rights purporting to be given are incident to the security by bill of sale.[h]

(a) Collis c. Tuson, 46 L. T. 387.
(b) Ince c. Everard, 6 T. R. 545 ; Few c. Backhouse, 3 A. & E. 789.
(c) Cook c. Jones, 15 East, 237.   (d) Washburn c. Birch, 5 T. R. 472.
(e) Davis c. Goodman, 5 C. P. D. 128.
(f) See Hughes c. Morris, 2 De G. M. & G. 355.
(g) Davies c. Rees, 17 Q. B. D. 408 ; 55 L. J. Q. B. 366 ; 34 W. R. 513 ; 54 L. T. 813.
(h) Exp. Byrne, re Burdett, 20 Q. B. D. 310.

.The section is not retrospective, and bills of sale given under the repealed Acts, or it would seem before the commencement of the amendment Act, are still valid as between grantor and grantee, although the registration turns out to have been defective.[a]

A bill of sale, if otherwise regular, will not be invalid for non-registration during the seven days allowed, for the bill of sale holder has the period of seven days within which to complete his title by registration; thus, if goods are seized under an execution, or if the grantor becomes bankrupt within seven days after the making of such bill of sale, the section would not apply, although the form of registering the bill of sale has been gone through, but in a defective manner.[b] If, however, within the seven days, while the goods by the consent of the mortgagee are in the reputed ownership of the grantor in his trade or business, he commits an act of bankruptcy to which the title of his trustee in bankruptcy relates, and of which the mortgagee has notice before seizure, the goods will pass to the trustee; although the contrary was decided before the repeal of sec. 20 of the principal Act.[c] After the lapse of seven days, unless the time is extended under sec. 11 of the principal Act, registration can confer no security.

It may be convenient here to consider in what way a bill of sale will now be avoided. It may be invalid for non-compliance with the Bills of Sale Acts, under the Statute of Elizabeth,[d] or under the bankruptcy laws. By the amendment Act a bill of sale is declared void in the following cases: If not duly attested and registered, or if it does not truly set forth the consideration;[e] if not in accordance with the form in the schedule to the Act;[f] or if made or given in consideration of any sum under £30.[g]

How a bill of sale may be invalid.

Further, a bill of sale will now have effect only in respect of the personal chattels specifically described in the schedule, and will be void, except as against the grantor, in respect of any chattels not so specifically described;[h] or in respect of

(a) Cookson v. Swire, 9 App. Ca. 653.
(b) Banbury v. White, 32 L. J. Ex. 258; 2 H. & C. 300; 11 W. R. 755; 9 Jur., N. S. 913; 8 L. T. 508; Brignall v. Cohen, 21 W. R. 25.
(c) Exp. Kahen, re Hewer, 21 Ch. D. 871. (d) 13 Eliz. c. 5.
(e) Sec. 8 (1882). (f) Sec. 9 (1882).
(g) Sec. 12 (1882) (h) Sec. 4 (1882).

chattels specifically described in the schedule, of which the grantor was not the true owner at the time of its execution;[a] but nothing contained in ss. 4 and 5 of the amendment Act will render a bill of sale void in respect of any of the things excepted by sec. 6 of that Act.

A bill of sale to which the amendment Act applies will be no protection in respect of personal chattels included therein, which, but for such bill of sale, would have been liable to distress under a warrant for the recovery of taxes, poor and other parochial rates.[b]

By the principal Act, certain instruments giving powers of distress are deemed bills of sale, within the Act, of personal chattels which may be taken under such power of distress;[c] and a bill of sale is declared absolutely void when executed within or on the expiration of seven days after the execution of a prior unregistered bill of sale comprising the same chattels as security for the same debt, so far as respects chattels comprised in the prior bill of sale, unless the subsequent bill of sale was given in good faith for the purpose of correcting some material error in the prior deed, and not for the purpose of avoiding the Act.[d]

Also registration is declared void of a bill of sale given subject to any defeasance, condition, or declaration of trust not contained in the body thereof, unless written on the same paper or parchment therewith before registration and truly set forth in the filed copy.[e] Further, the registration of a bill of sale must be renewed once at least every five years, or the registration will become void;[f] in which event if the bill of sale is subject to the amendment Act it will be wholly void even as between the parties.[g]

Possession under void deed.

Possession taken and retained under a void bill of sale will not protect the goods,[h] where the whole agreement between the parties is contained in the bill of sale, for that is the only evidence of their bargain, and if the agreement in writing is void there is nothing to which possession can be referred.[i] But a debtor who is aware of the invalidity of a bill of

(a) Sec. 5 (1882).
(b) Sec. 14 (1882).
(c) Sec.6 (1878).
(d) Sec. 9 (1878).
(e) Sec. 10, sub-sec. 3 (1878).

(f) Sec. 11 (1878).
(g) Fenton v. Blythe, 25 Q. B. D. 417.
(h) Exp. Parsons, re Townsend, 16 Q. B. D. 532.
(i) Newlove v. Shrewsbury, 21 Q. B. D. 41.

sale may give his creditor a right to seize the goods comprised in it, and to acquire a property or beneficial interest in them, irrespective of the bill of sale; though if he only intends to carry out on his part the provisions of the bill of sale, and to permit the creditor to exercise his rights under it, no right in addition to or other than those created by the bill of sale will be conferred.[a] However, if chattels covered by a void bill of sale are sold, and the grantor assents to the application of the purchase-money, his trustee in bankruptcy, apart from any question of fraudulent preference, cannot recover it;[b] and where a bill of sale holder, whose security was defective as against an execution creditor, seized the goods and afterwards sold them, it was held, and affirmed by the House of Lords, that the purchaser had a good title against an execution creditor of the original mortgagor, for that after seizure and sale the original bill of sale was satisfied and gone, and the Acts did not apply; for the exercise of a power of sale, when there was no person entitled as against the mortgagee, put an end to the bill of sale, and conferred an absolute title on the purchaser.[c]

Even if a bill of sale be invalid, a grantor who has taken a benefit under proceedings based on the validity of the bill of sale, by which the position of the mortgagee has been changed, cannot afterwards be heard to say that the bill of sale is void. So when the grantor of a bill of sale filed a petition, and in his statement of affairs returned the grantees as secured creditors, and they, having sold the property assigned, proved for the balance, on which the grantor paid a composition sanctioned by the Court, he was held estopped from setting up the invalidity of the bill of sale, that being inconsistent with his conduct in paying a composition on the balance of the debt after taking credit for the amount realized by the security.[d] On the same principle, if a trustee applies to the Court of Bankruptcy to set aside a bill of sale of goods, which have been sold by the grantee, and for payment over of the proceeds, he cannot afterwards sue for the difference between the sale price and the true value of the goods, for he elects to waive the tort. In such cases he

When grantor estopped from avoiding bill of sale.

(a) Furber v. Cobb, 18 Q. B. D. 494; 56 L. T. 689; 35 W. R. 398.

(b) Parsons v. Dewsbury, 3 T. L. R. 354.

(c) Cookson v. Swire, 9 App. Cases, 653.

(d) Roe v. Mutual Loan Fund Association, 19 Q. B. D. 347; 56 L. J. Q. B. 541; 35 W. R. 723.

should claim the value of the goods and damages, [a] although the Court of Bankruptcy under the Bankruptcy Act, 1869, would not award damages for acts committed prior to the commencement of the trustee's title. [b]

Although a bill of sale complies with all the provisions of the Bills of Sale Acts, it may be impeached as fraudulent against creditors, either under the Statute of Elizabeth (13 Eliz. c. 5) or the bankruptcy laws.

Fraudulent conveyances.

The Statute of Elizabeth enacts that every gift or grant of chattels, made for any intent to delay, hinder or defraud creditors or others of their just remedies, and every suit, or judgment and execution made with a like intent, shall, as against the person so delayed or defrauded, be utterly void, frustrate and of none effect. By sec. 6, there is exempted from the operation of the statute any alienation lawfully made for good, which here means valuable, consideration, and *bonâ fide* to any person not having at the time of such alienation notice of such fraud. To bring the case within the exception, there must be valuable consideration and good faith, for a conveyance, though made for valuable consideration, may be fraudulent in law if made to defeat creditors. [c] Gross inadequacy of consideration is evidence of fraud, although where the object is to establish or negative the existence of fraud, evidence may be adduced to shew that a deed voluntary in form was made for valuable consideration; or that no consideration was given for a conveyance purporting to be founded on valuable consideration. [d]

The Statute of Elizabeth does not apply as between the grantor and grantee, or privies or consenting parties, [e] or as between strangers other than creditors; [f] and therefore a conveyance, fraudulent under the statute, is good against the person making it; although a sham transfer of chattels, without deed, for the purpose of defrauding creditors, has been held not to pass the property in them even between the parties, and the original owner recovered them in an

---

(a) Smith r. Baker, L. R. 8 C. P. 350; 42 L. J. C. P. 155; 28 L. T. 637.
(b) *Exp.* Eatough, *re* Cliffe, 28 W. R. 433; 42 L. T. 95.
(c) Cadogan r. Kennett, Cowp. 432.
(d) Townend r. Toker, 1 Ch. 446; 35 L. J. Ch. 608; 14 L. T. N. S. 531; 12 Jur N. S. 477; R. r. Scammonden, 3 T. R. 474; Gale r. Williamson, 8 M. & W. 405.
(e) Olliver r. King, 25 L. J. Ch. 427; White r. Morris, 11 C. B. 1015.
(f) Robinson r. M'Donnell, 2 B. & Ald. 134   Bessey r. Windham 6 Q. B. 166; 14 L. J. Q. B. 7.

action of trover.[a]   But the statute does not extend to any estate or interest in goods, conveyed or assured upon good consideration, and in good faith, without notice of the fraud ; and if, before avoidance, the transferee assigns to a purchaser for value, the transaction will be protected ;[b] for a conveyance which by statute is void against certain persons, may be perfectly good between the parties from the time of its operation until it is avoided, so as to pass the property in the chattels assigned.[c]   When once avoided, it is taken as if it had never existed,[d] so far as is necessary to deal with the property for the satisfaction of creditors, but for other purposes the conveyance may stand ;[e] thus a deed by a bankrupt, void against creditors, may subsist for other purposes, so that any surplus remaining after satisfying the creditors would be subject to the trusts declared by it.[f]

A past debt is a sufficient consideration within this statute ; and when coupled with a present substantial advance, may rebut a presumption of an intent to delay creditors ;[g] and a *bonâ fide* assignment by way of mortgage of the whole of the assignor's property, present and future, to one person as security for a past debt and future advances is not void within the Statute of Elizabeth.[h]

To invalidate an assignment made for valuable considera- *Fraudulent conveyances.* tion, it is necessary to shew an actual intent to defeat or delay creditors within the purchaser's knowledge, and this intent may be inferred from the circumstances of the case.   If the deed is in such a form as to defeat creditors, and was executed and taken with that intention, it will be invalid, though full consideration was given for it ;[i] thus, where a trader whose goods had been seized under a *fi. fa.* executed a bill of sale of them to the defendant, who paid out the sheriff, and the jury found that the object of the transaction was to protect the goods from other creditors, the bill of sale was set aside.[j]

(a) Bowes c. Foster, 2 H. & N. 779 ; 4 Jur. N. S. 95 ; 27 L. J. Ex. 262.
(b) Morewood c. S. Yorkshire Railway, 3 H. & N. 798 ; 28 L. J. Ex. 114 ; Halifax, &c., Bank c. Gledhill, 39 W. R. 104 ; 1891] 1 Ch. 31 60 L. J. Ch. 181 63 L. T. 623 ; re Brall 1893 , 2 Q. B. 381.
(c) R. c. Creese, 2 C. C. R. 105.
(d) Hue c. French, 26 L. J. Ch. 317.
(e) French c. French, 6 De G. M. & G. 95 ; 25 L. J. Ch. 612.
(f) Exp. Bell, re Webb, 1 G. & J. 282.
(g) Martindale c. Booth, 3 B. & Ad. 498 ; Riches c. Evans, 9 C. & P. 640.
(h) Exp. Games, re Bamford, 12 Ch. D. 314 ; 27 W. R. 744 ; 40 L. T. 789.
(i) Hale c. Metropolitan Saloon Omnibus Co., 28 L. J. Ch. 777 ; Bott c. Smith, 21 Beav. 511.
(j) Graham c. Furber, 14 C. B. 410 ; 2 C. & P. 152 ; 18 Jur. 226 ; 23 L. J. C. P. 51 ; Reed c. Blades, 5 Taunt. 212 ; Latimer c. Batson 4 B. & C. 652.

As, irrespective of the bankruptcy laws, a debtor may lawfully prefer one of his creditors to the others,[a] and before the seizure of his property under an execution can convey a valid title to any person without notice of delivery of the writ to the sheriff,[b] a bill of sale if otherwise *bonâ fide*, and for valuable consideration, will not be invalid merely because its effect is to delay a particular creditor, or to defeat an expected execution,[c] nor will such an effect invalidate a deed executed for the benefit of one or more creditors, unless the transaction is merely a cloak for retaining a benefit to the grantor, or made for the mere purpose of defeating creditors.[d]

Thus, where a creditor, having taken in execution the goods of a debtor who had confessed judgment, bought them by public auction, taking a bill of sale from the sheriff for valuable consideration, and afterwards let them to the former owner at a rent which was actually paid, he was held to have a title which could not be impugned as fraudulent by other creditors having executions against the same debtor.[e]

So, apart from the bankrupt laws, if possession of goods has been taken under a bill of sale, part of the consideration for which was money advanced in good faith for the purpose of obtaining security for a pre-existing debt, the transaction has been said not to be invalid though the creditor was aware at the time of the advance that the debtor had committed a felony, and intended, with the money advanced, to leave the country.[f]

Voluntary conveyances.

A gift of chattels, coupled with delivery of possession, is sufficient to pass the property to the donee without deed or writing; but if the transaction be not for valuable consideration, it will be voidable unless coupled with delivery of possession or made by deed;[g] and a gift by words of a chattel capable of delivery, the donee assenting and communicating his assent to the donor, does not pass the

---

(a) Benton v. Thornhill, 7 Taunt. 149.

(b) 19 & 20 Vic. c. 97, s. 1; Sale of Goods Act, 1893, s. 26.

(c) Wood v. Dixie, 7 Q. B. 892; 9 Jur. 796; Pickstock v. Lyster, 3 M. & S. 371; Westbury v. Clapp, 12 W. R. 511; 3 N. R. 453; Gladstone v. Padwick, L. R. 6 Ex. 203; 40 L. J. Ex. 154; 19 W. R. 1064; 25 L. T. 96.

(d) Alton v. Harrison, L. R. 4 Ch. 623.

(e) Watkins v. Birch, 4 Taunt. 241; Cookson v. Fryer, 1 F. & F. 328.

(f) Bagot v. Arnott, 2 Ir. C. L. 1.

(g) Irons v. Smallpiece, 2 B. & Ald. 551; Shower v. Pilck, 4 Exch. 478; 19 L. J. Ex. 113.

property in the chattel without delivery.[a] But there may
be a sufficient delivery where words of present gift are used,
and the donee is left in possession. Furniture in the house
where the claimant and her husband resided was the property
of the claimant's father, who, at the house, and in the room
where the furniture was, verbally gave it to the claimant.
He then left the house, the claimant being in the room there,
but no other delivery was made of the furniture, which continued to remain in the house. An execution creditor of the
claimant's husband having seized the furniture, she claimed,
and it was held there had been such a change of possession,
consequent on the gift being made, as to complete the gift
without the formality of handing over the furniture by
manual delivery.[b]

A voluntary alienation made with the intention of defeating
creditors is void by the very words of the statute; and although
the mere fact of a settlement being voluntary has never been
held sufficient to avoid it, if the natural result of the
assignment would be to defeat or delay creditors, an intent to
do so may be presumed; for instance, if after deducting the
property which is the subject of the voluntary settlement,
sufficient available assets are not left for payment of the
assignor's debts, then there is a presumption of an intent to
defeat creditors; or if the person making the settlement was
not in a position actually to pay his creditors, or was about to
embark in undertakings which might result in liabilities, it
may be inferred that he intended, by making the voluntary
settlement, to defeat and delay them;[c] although the necessary effect of the deed in delaying creditors is only an element
in determining the settlor's intent.[d]

What bills of sale are deemed fraudulent.

Another test suggested is that there must be unpaid debts
which were existing at the time of the assignment, or the
assignor must have been so largely involved at the time, or have
contracted debts which would so shortly fall due, as to induce
the court to believe that his intention was to defeat or delay his
creditors.[e] But a voluntary settlement whereby the settlor

(a) Cochrane v. Moore, 25 Q. B. D. 57; 39 W. R. 555; 63 L. T. 153.
(b) Kilpin v. Ratley [1892], 1 Q. B. 582, 61 L. T. 707.
(c) Freeman v. Pope, L. R. 5 Ch. 538; 39 L. J. Ch. 689; 23 L. T. 208; Spirett v. Willows, 3 De G. J. & S. 293.
(d) Exp. Mercer, re Wise, 17 Q. B. D. 290; 54 L. T. 720; 55 L. J. Q. B. 558.
(e) Holmes v. Penney, 26 L. J. Ch. 170; 3 K. & J. 90; 5 W. R. 132; 28 L. T. 166; 3 Jur. N. S. 80.

takes the bulk of his property out of the reach of his creditors
shortly before engaging in trade of a hazardous character,
may be set aside on behalf of creditors who became such after
the date of the settlement, even if there are no creditors
whose debts arose before the date of the settlement; [a] although
in one case a deed executed with intent to defraud future,
but not present creditors, has been supported; [b] but this does
not seem to be in accordance with the authorities.

An assignment of chattels, together with leaseholds, may
be deemed voluntary within the Statute 13 Elizabeth, c. 5,
although the assignee takes the burden of the covenants. [c]

Fraudulent conveyances.

In Twyne's Case, [d] which remains a leading authority at
the present day, six resolutions were delivered by the Court,
declaring, as signs and marks of fraud, the generality of a
gift, the donor's continuance in possession, the secrecy of the
transaction, that it was made pending writ, a trust between
the parties, and that unusual clauses were contained in the
deed; and Lord Coke, sagely advising those about to take a
bill of sale, says: " Let it be made in a public manner, and before the neighbours, and not in private, for secrecy is a mark
of fraud. Let the goods and chattels be appraised by good
people to the very value, and take a gift in particular in satisfaction of your debt. Immediately after the gift take possession of them, for continuance of possession in the donor
is the sign of trust." The tendency of modern decisions,
however, is to decide every case on a consideration of all the
circumstances. If the deed being absolute, the grantor continues in possession until an execution or bankruptcy, a strong
though not conclusive presumption arises of fraud, and a
secret trust for the grantor's benefit; [e] but on a conditional
bill of sale, continuance in possession, when consistent with
the deed, is not even *primâ facie* evidence of fraud, [f] unless
such possession is a contrivance to defeat creditors. [g] As

(a) Mackay c. Douglas, L. R. 14 Eq. 106; 41 L. J. Ch. 539; *exp.* Russell, *re* Butterworth, 19 Ch. D. 588; 46 L. T. 113; 30 W. R. 584; 51 L. J. Ch. 621.

(b) Smith v. Tatton, 6 L. R. Ir. C. L. 32.

(c) Ridler c. Ridler, 22 Ch. D. 74; 31 W. R. 93; 48 L. T. 396; 52 L. J. Ch. 343.

(d) 3 Rep.; 1 S. M. L. Cases, 9th Ed. 1.

(e) Edwards c. Harben, 2 T. R. 587; Reed c. Blados, 5 Thunt. 212; Paget c.
Purchard, 1 Esp. 205.

(f) Pennell c. Dawson, 18 C. B. 355; Martindale v. Booth, 3 B. & Ad 498;
Hale c. Metropolitan Saloon Omnibus Co., 28 L. J. Ch. 777; Reed v. Wilmot, 7
Bing. 577.

(g) Nunn c. Wilsmore, 8 T. R. 521.

secrecy is a badge of fraud, so notoriety raises a presumption
of good faith. [a]

To prove a bill of sale fraudulent, declarations made by the
grantor at the time of executing it are admissible, but not
those made at another time, [b] but the will of a deceased
person, though not proved, has been admitted as a declaration
to shew the good faith of a bill of sale. [c] So also a solicitor
employed to obtain the execution of a deed, and who is one of
the attesting witnesses, is not precluded on the ground of a
breach of professional confidence from giving evidence as to
what passed at the time of execution by which the deed may
be proved invalid; [d] and as communications between a solicitor
and client are privileged only if passing between them in professional confidence in the legitimate course of professional
employment, and not if made before the commission of a
crime for the purpose of being guided or helped in the commission of it, the evidence of a solicitor of communications by
his client, made for the purpose of obtaining advice to assist
him in defeating a creditor's claim by a bill of sale, was help
rightly received on a charge against the client and another
person of conspiring to defeat the creditor's claim. [e] But as the
grantor himself is liable to a prosecution, upon the statute 13
Eliz. c.5, if party or privy to a fraudulent conveyance, he is not
bound to answer questions as to the true object of the transaction. [f]

A creditor may bring an action to set aside a deed under
the Statute of Elizabeth at any time within the period
allowed by the statutes of limitation for recovering his debt. [g]

A bill of sale, though valid under the Statute of Elizabeth,
may be avoided as an act of bankruptcy, but an assignment
which is fraudulent within the Statute of Elizabeth is also void
as against the policy of the bankruptcy laws.

Evidence of fraud.

(a) Latimer e. Batson, 4 B. & C. 652.

(b) Phillips r. Eamer, 1 Esp. 357 ; Coole r. Braham, 3 Exch. 183 ; 18 L. J.
Ex. 105.

(c) O'Sullivan e. Burke, 9 Ir. C. L. Rep. 106.

(d) Crawcour e. Salter, 18 Ch. D. 30; 45 L. T. 62 ; 30 W. R. 21 ; 51 L. J. Ch. 4.

(e) R. e. Cox, 14 Q. B. D. 153 ; 33 W. R. 396.

(f) 3 Co., 80 b. ; Michael e. Gray, 1 F. & F. 409.

(g) Re Maddever, 52 L. J. Ch. 733 ; 33 W. R. 286 ; 52 L. T. 35.

Under the bankruptcy laws,[a] an assignment by a debtor of the whole of his property, or of the whole with a merely nominal exception, or an exception of property which would not pass to a trustee in bankruptcy,[b] or it seems of property not readily available[c] in consideration of a pre-existing debt, is fraudulent and an act of bankruptcy.[d]

What bills of sale are void under the bankruptcy laws.

An assignment of this nature is fraudulent as against creditors, for the debtor's estate gains nothing by the transaction, but where there is some substantial equivalent the case is different. A sale for value,[e] therefore, or a mortgage made in good faith to secure an advance, or an existing debt, with a binding agreement for a substantial further advance which is subsequently made, to enable the debtor to meet his engagements or carry on his business, will be good against his trustee;[f] but in order that the execution of a bill of sale of substantially all the grantor's property as security for a pre-existing debt and future advances may not be an act of bankruptcy, it is necessary that there should be an agreement to make further advances, and it is not sufficient that further advances should have been in the contemplation of the parties, the deed being stamped so as to cover them, and they having been actually made after the execution of the deed.[g] It is not, however, necessary that the agreement to make further advances should be legally binding, and a promise may be sufficient, if it appears that the arrangement was made in good faith, and was not a scheme to secure payment of the existing debt.[h]

(a) Bankruptcy Act, 1883, s. 4 (1) A debtor commits an act of bankruptcy in each of the following cases:—(a) If in England or elsewhere he makes a conveyance or assignment of his property to a trustee or trustees for the benefit of his creditors generally; (b) if in England or elsewhere he makes a fraudulent conveyance, gift, delivery, or transfer of his property, or of any part thereof; (c) if in England or elsewhere he makes any conveyance or transfer of his property, or any part thereof, or creates any charge thereon which would under this or any other Act be void as a fraudulent preference if he were adjudged bankrupt. The provisions of the Bankruptcy Act, 1869, were in substance the same, omitting clause (c).

(b) Exp. Hawker, re Keeley, L. R. 7 Ch. 214; 41 L. J. Bank. 34; 20 W. R. 322; 26 L. T. 54.

(c) Exp. Russell, re Butterworth, 19 Ch. D. 588.

(d) Worsley v. De Mattos, 1 Burr. 467; Lindon v. Sharp, 6 M. & G. 895; 2 Scott, N. R. 730; 13 L. J. C. P. 67; Smith v. Cannan, 2 E. & B. 35; 17 Jur. 911; 22 L. J. Q. B. 291.

(e) Exp. Bolland, re Price, 41 L. J. Bank. 60; 20 W. R. 862; Rose v. Haycock, 1 A. & E. 460; 3 N. & M. 645.

(f) Pennell v. Reynolds, 11 C. B. N. S. 709; 5 L. T. 286; Lomax v. Buxton L. R. 6 C. P. 107 40 L. J. C. P. 150; 24 L. T. 137; 19 W. R. 78; Hutton v. Cruttwell, 1 E. & B. 15; 17 Jur. 392; 22 L. J. Q. B. 78.

(g) Exp. Dann, re Parker, 17 Ch. D. 26; 29 W. R. 771; 44 L. T. 760; 51 L. J. Ch. 290.

(h) Exp. Wilkinson, re Berry, 22 Ch. D. 788; 48 L. T. 405; 31 W. R. 640; 52 L. J. Ch. 657.

The test in all such cases is, not whether the further advance was large or small, but, was the fresh advance made with the intention of enabling the borrower, if a trader, to carry on business, and had the lender reasonable grounds for believing that the advance would enable the borrower to do so? If these questions can be answered in the affirmative the execution of the deed is not an act of bankruptcy; and the Court ought not to look at the uncommunicated intention of the borrower, nor at the actual result of the loan.[a] The same test has been stated, in other words, to be whether the further advance was really made for the purpose of obtaining security for a pre-existing debt; [b] and thus was avoided a bill of sale given to an execution creditor, who, to prevent his execution being impeached, agreed to withdraw and to make an advance to enable the debtor to pay off creditors who threatened bankruptcy, on having a bill of sale of all the debtor's property to secure his old debt and the advance. [c]

Neither will the assignment be invalid, although for a past debt arising from a previous loan, if made in pursuance of an absolute agreement entered into at the time of the loan.[d] But, if the giving of the bill of sale is purposely postponed until the debtor is in a state of insolvency, in order to prevent the destruction of his credit which would result from registering the deed, such a transaction will not be protected, for the postponement is evidence of an intention to commit an actual fraud on the general body of the creditors ; [e] and in all cases the person setting up such a prior agreement must prove its existence and good faith, and the reason for any delay in carrying it out. Thus, where a debtor shortly before his bankruptcy executed a bill of sale of substantially all his property, in pursuance of a previous agreement, for valuable consideration, to execute a further security, " if required," and the request to execute the bill of sale was not made until several writs were out against the debtor, the bill of sale was held void against the trustee in the debtor's subsequent bankruptcy.[f]

What bills of sale are void under the bankruptcy laws.

(a) *Exp.* Johnson, *re* Chapman, 26 Ch. D. 396.

(b) *Exp.* Greener, *re* Vane, 91 L. J. Bank. 76 ; 36 L. T. 781 ; *Exp.* Ellis, 2 Ch. D. 707 ; 45 L. J. Bank. 159 ; 34 L. T. 705.

(c) *Exp.* Clater, *re* Wilkinson, 96 L. T. 648.

(d) Harris *v.* Rickett, 28 L. J. Ex. 197 ; Mercer *v.* Peterson, L. R. 3 Ex. 104 ; *exp.* Izard, *re* Cook, L. R. 9 Ch. 271 ; 43 L. J. Bank. 31 ; 22 W. R. 342 ; 30 L. T. 7.

(e) *Exp.* Fisher, *re* Ash, L. R. 7 Ch. 636 ; 41 L. J. Bank. 62 ; 26 L. T. 931 ; 20 W. R. 840 ; *Exp.* Burton, *re* Tunstall, 13 Ch. D. 102 ; 28 W. R. 266 ; 41 L. T. 571.

(f) *Exp.* Kilner, *re* Barker, 41 L. T. 520 ; 13 Ch. D. 245 ; 28 W. R. 269.

As has been observed, if at the time of giving the bill of sale, or if founded on a previous agreement, at the time such agreement was made, the debtor receives an equivalent which may have the effect of enabling him to meet his engagements or continue business, the assignment will be protected.[a] That equivalent need not be in money. If the debtor has something done for him to enable him to carry on his business, e.g., where a drawer of bills took them up at the acceptor's request,[b] or where a creditor consented to take the debtor's acceptance at seven days for a balance of account,[c] or released goods stopped in transitu,[d] or supplied goods on credit,[e] it was held sufficient to prevent the assignment operating as an act of bankruptcy. Forbearance, however, will not constitute such an equivalent as to protect a transfer for a past debt, where the creditor's proceedings would result in an act of bankruptcy; and where a trader executed a bill of sale of all his property to secure an existing debt, for which judgment had been obtained, and the creditor, in consideration of an undertaking to give the bill of sale upon demand, had forborne to levy execution, it was held that as the execution if levied would have constituted an act of bankruptcy, and rendered the debtor's property divisible amongst his creditors, the forbearance was no equivalent, and that the bill of sale was void against the debtor's trustee, the Lords Justices observing, that if such a transaction could be supported it would render nugatory the provisions of the Bankruptcy Act.[f]

What bills of sale are void under the bankruptcy laws.

Neither will forbearance to seize under a bill of sale of the whole of the grantor's property, given for value, be a sufficient equivalent as against the trustee in bankruptcy of the grantor, for the giving of a new bill of sale in lieu of the first, and the new bill of sale given under such circumstances, without any fresh advance to the grantor, is an act of bankruptcy.[g] Nor can a bill of sale, if legally fraudulent as an act of bankruptcy, be supported on the ground that it was given in substitution

(a) Heath v. Cochrane, 37 L. T. 280 ; 46 L. J. Q. B. 727 ; Bittlestone v. Cooke, 6 E. & B. 296 ; 25 L. J. Q. B. 281 ; 2 Jur. N. S. 758.

(b) Exp. Reed, re Tweddell, L. R. 14 Eq. 586 ; 20 W. R. 622 ; 26 L. T. 558.

(c) Philps v. Hornstedt, L. R. 1 Ex. D. 62.

(d) Exp. Threlfall, re Williamson, 46 L. J. Bank. 8 ; 35 L. T. 675 ; 25 W. R. 127.

(e) Exp. Sheen, re Winstanley, 1 Ch. D. 560 ; 45 L. J. Bank. 89 ; 24 W. R. 68 ; 34 L. T. 48.

(f) Exp. Cooper, re Baum, 10 Ch. D. 313 ; Woodhouse v. Murray, L. R. 4 Q. B. 27 ; 9 B. & S. 720 ; 38 L. J. Q. B. 28 ; 17 W. R. 206 ; 19 L. T. 570.

(g) Exp. Payne, re Cross, 11 Ch. D. 539 ; exp. Stevens, 20 Eq. 786 ; 44 L. J. Bank. 136 ; 23 W. R. 908 ; 33 L. T. 135.

for a former bill of sale for which there had been an equivalent,[a] nor is the previous bill of sale admissible, even to prove good faith unless duly stamped.[b]

Where the transfer is of part only of the debtor's property, the question would appear to be whether insolvency, or in case of a trader, stoppage of business, is a necessary consequence of putting the instrument into force,[c] but the validity of such a transaction will in a great measure depend upon all the circumstances of the case and the proportion of the property assigned to the debtor's whole estate.[d] The mere existence of a past consideration in this instance is not evidence of fraud, for every one must have power to make over some part of his property, but if the transaction has for its object a fraud on creditors, it is an act of bankruptcy.[e]

Further, by section 48 (1), Bankruptcy Act, 1883, every conveyance or transfer of property, or charge thereon made, every payment made, every obligation incurred, and every judicial proceeding taken or suffered by any person unable to pay his debts as they become due from his own money, in favour of any creditor, or any person in trust for any creditor, with a view of giving such creditor a preference over the other creditors, shall, if the person making, taking, paying, or suffering the same, is adjudged bankrupt on a bankruptcy petition presented within three months after the date of making, taking, paying, or suffering the same, be deemed fraudulent and void as against the trustee in the bankruptcy.

Fraudulent preference.

This section shall not affect the rights of any person making title in good faith and for valuable consideration through or under a creditor of the bankrupt.

The Bankruptcy Act, 1869, section 92, was substantially the same as section 48 (1) Bankruptcy Act, 1883, substituting " shall become " for " is adjudged " bankrupt, and omitting sub-section 2 ; providing that the section should not affect the rights of a purchaser, payee, or incumbrancer in good faith, and for valuable consideration. It was decided that a

(a) *Exp.* Foxley, *re* Nurse, L. R. 3 Ch. 515 ; 16 W. R. 891 ; 18 L. T. 862.

(b) Williams *v.* Gerry, 10 M. & W. 290.

(c) Hale *v.* Allnutt, 18 C. B. 505 ; 25 L. J. C. P. 267 ; *exp.* Wensley, 1 De G. J & S. 273 ; 32 L. J. Bank. 23 ; 11 W. R. 241 ; 7 L. T. 588 ; 9 Jur. N. S. 315; Young *v.* Fletcher, 3 H. & C. 732 ; 34 L. J. Ex. 154 ; 13 W. R. 722 ; 12 L. T. 392 ; 11 Jur. N. S. 449.

(d) *Exp.* Evans, *re* Edwards, 30 L. T. 364; *exp.* Field, *re* Marlow, 24 W. R. 267.

(e) Siebert *v.* Spooner, 1 M. & W. 714 ; 2 Gale, 135 ; *exp.* Pearson, L. R. 8 Ch. 667 ; 21 W. R. 688 ; 28 L. T. 796 ; 42 L. J. Bank. 41 ; Edwards *v.* Glyn, 28 L. J. Q. B. 350 ; 2 E. & E. 29.

fraudulent preference under the repealed section, was not necessarily an act of bankruptcy;[a] but this was not free from doubt;[b] and as before observed, a fraudulent preference is declared an act of bankruptcy by section 4, sub-sec. 1(c) Bankruptcy Act, 1883.

In determining whether giving a bill of sale within the time limited constitutes a fraudulent preference, the words of the section raise two questions : First, was the grantor unable, from his own money, to pay his debts as they became due; secondly, did he give the bill of sale with a view to prefer the creditor ? It will be observed that transactions in favour of creditors are alone affected by the section.[c]

Fraudulent preference.

In order that a payment or transfer should be void as a fraudulent preference, it is sufficient that preferring the creditor should have been the substantial, effectual, or dominant view with which the payment or transfer was made, and it is not necessary that it should have been the sole view.[d] This view to prefer may be rebutted by circumstances, and although regard should be had rather to the words of the section than to decisions before the Act,[e] it would seem still to be law that if made in pursuance of a previous binding contract[f] or in consequence of apprehended civil or criminal proceedings,[g] or to avoid a distress,[h] or if in consequence of a demand or pressure by the creditor,[i] without collusion,[j] the transfer will not necessarily constitute a fraudulent preference. A threat of civil proceedings against a man who, to the knowledge of the creditor, is about to become bankrupt, as it can have no real influence upon him, will not

(a) *Exp.* Stubbins, *re* Wilkinson, 17 Ch. D. 58 ; 50 L. J. Ch. 547; 29 W. R. 653 ; 44 L. T. 877 ; *exp.* Luck, *re* Kemp, 49 L. T. 809 ; 32 W. R. 296.

(b) Pulling *v.* Tucker, 4 B. & Ald. 382 ; *Exp.* Halliday, L. R. 8 Ch. 283 ; 21 W. R. 348 ; 28 L. T. 324.

(c) *Exp.* Kelly, 11 Ch. D. 306 ; 48 L. J. Bank. 65 ; 40 L. T. 404 ; *exp.* Stubbins, 17 Ch. D. 58 ; *re* Mills, 5 Mor. 55 ; 58 L. T. 871.

(d) *Exp.* Hill, *re* Bird, 23 Ch. D. 695 ; 32 W.R. 177 ; 49 L.T. 278 ; 52 L.J. Ch. 930.

(e) *Exp.* Griffith, *re* Wilcoxon, 23 Ch. D. 69 ; 48 L. T. 450 ; 52 L. J. Ch. 717 ; 31 W. R. 878.

(f) Bills *v.* Smith, 34 L. J. Q. B. 68 ; 13 W. R. 407 ; 12 L. T. 22 ; 11 Jur. N. S. 154 ; *Exp.* Blackburn, L. R. 12 Eq. 358 ; 40 L. J. Bank. 79 ; 19 W. R. 973 ; 25 L. T. 76.

(g) *Exp.* Taylor, *re* Goldsmid, 18 Q. B. D. 295 ; 56 L. J. Q. B. 195 ; 35 W. R. 148.

(h) Mavor *v.* Croome, 1 Bing. 261 ; Stevenson *v.* Wood, 5 Esp. 200.

(i) *Exp.* Tempest, *re* Craven, 40 L. J. Bank. 22 ; 23 L. T. 650 ; L. R. 6 Ch. 70; *Exp.* Topham, L. R. 8 Ch. 614 ; 42 L. J. Bank. 57 ; 21 W. R. 655 ; 28 L. T. 716 ; Jones *r.* Harher, L. R. 6 Q. B. 77 ; 40 L. J. Q. B. 59 ; 19 W. R. 248 ; Smith *r.* Pilgrim, 2 Ch. D. 127 ; 34 L. T. 408.

(j) *Exp.* Arnold, *re* Wright, 3 Ch. D. 70 ; 35 L. T. 21 ; 24 W. R. 977 ; 45 L. J. Bank. 130, per James L. J. ; *exp.* Reader, 20 Eq. 763 ; 32 L. T. 36 ; 44 L. J Bank. 139.

protect the transaction;[a] but in order that the transaction
should be found a fraudulent preference it is essential that
there should be evidence of a view to prefer, and it is not
sufficient that the creditor was in fact preferred; thus, a
transfer or payment made with a view to avoid exposure or a
criminal prosecution, is not a fraudulent preference.[b]   A
debtor having borrowed money from his wife gave her a bill
of sale as security, which a month afterwards was found to
be void as containing clauses not in accordance with the
form.   Two days after calling his creditors together he gave
his wife a valid bill of sale, and, subsequently becoming
bankrupt, his trustee applied to set the bill of sale aside as a
fraudulent preference.   On the hearing it was found that the
second bill of sale was given with the intention of making
good the mistake in the first, and, by inference, with an intention to prefer.   But the decision was reversed on appeal, as it
did not necessarily follow that the substitution of a good for
a bad bill of sale was with a view to prefer, the intention in
fact being to correct a mistake, which rebutted the presumption of a view to prefer.[c]

Where, by virtue of a bill of sale, chattels become the pro-   Fraudulent
perty of the mortgagees, and are not in the reputed ownership   preference.
of the grantor at the commencement of his bankruptcy, it is
immaterial whether the transaction by which the mortgagees
obtain actual possession of such chattels would, if there had
been no bill of sale, amount to a fraudulent preference.[d]

Under the Bankruptcy Act, 1869, a further question arose,
for although a bill of sale was given in favour of a creditor by
a person unable to pay his debts, who became bankrupt within
the prescribed time, the transaction might be protected by the
last clause of sec. 92, and secs. 94 and 95 of the Bankruptcy
Act, 1869, if the creditor could prove that he took the bill of
sale for value and in good faith, that is without any knowledge that he was being preferred;[e] but the burden of
proving this rested upon him.[f]   As has been noticed, the
Bankruptcy Act, 1883, abolishes this protection.

(a) Exp. Hall, re Cooper, 19 Ch. D. 580 ; 51 L. J. Ch. 556 ; 46 L. T. 519.
(b) Exp. Taylor, re Goldsmid, 18 Q. B. D. 295 ; 56 L. J. Q. B. 195 ; 35 W. R. 148.
(c) Exp. Tweedale, [1892], 2 Q. B. 216 ; 66 L. T. 233 ; 9 Mor. 110 ; 61 L. J. Q. B.
505.
(d) Exp. Symmons, re Jordan, 28 W. R. 803 ; 14 Ch. D. 693 ; 42 L. T. 106.
(e) Butcher v. Steard, L. R. 7 H. L. 839 ; 44 L. J. Bank. 129 ; 33 L. T. 541 ; 24
W. R. 462 ; exp. Kevan, re Crawford, L. R. 9 Ch. 752 ; Tomkins v. Saffery, 3
App. Cases, 213, 220 ; 26 W. R. 62 ; 37 L. T. 758.
(f) Exp. Tate, 25 W. R. 52 ; 35 L. T. 531.

Section 49 of the Bankruptcy Act, 1883, provides that subject to the foregoing provisions of the Act, with respect to the effect of bankruptcy on an execution or attachment, and with respect to the avoidance of certain settlements and preferences, nothing in the Act shall invalidate, in the case of a bankruptcy (a) any payment by the bankrupt to any of his creditors, (b) any payment or delivery to the bankrupt, (c) any conveyance or assignment by the bankrupt for valuable consideration, (d) any contract, dealing, or transaction by or with the bankrupt for valuable consideration, provided that both the following conditions are complied with, namely (1), the payment, delivery, conveyance, assignment, contract, dealing or transaction, as the case may be, takes place before the date of the receiving order; and (2), the person (other than the debtor) to, by, or with whom the payment, delivery, conveyance, assignment, contract, dealing, or transaction was made, executed, or entered into, has not at the time of the payment, delivery, conveyance, assignment, contract, dealing, or transaction, notice of any available act of bankruptcy committed by the bankrupt before that time.(a)

Protected transactions. Where a person relies on the protection of the section the burden of proof is on him to prove absence of notice of an act of bankruptcy.(b)

Under the Bankruptcy Act, 1883, available act of bankruptcy means any act of bankruptcy available for a bankruptcy petition at the date of the presentation of the petition on which the receiving order is made;(c) and by sec. 43 the bankruptcy of a debtor whether the same takes place on the debtor's own petition or upon that of a creditor or creditors, shall be deemed to have relation back to, and to commence at the time of the act of bankruptcy being committed, on which a receiving order is made against him, or, if the bankrupt is proved to have committed more acts of bankruptcy than one, to have relation back to, and to commence at the time of the first of the acts of bankruptcy proved to have been committed by the bankrupt within three months next preceding the date of the presentation of the bankruptcy petition. By sec. 6, sub-sec. 1 (c), the act of bankruptcy on which the petition is grounded must have occurred within three months before its

(a) This section is in substance the same as sections 94, 95, Bankruptcy Act, 1869.
(b) *Exp.* Cartwright, *re* Joy, 44 L. T. 883 ; *exp.* Schulte, *re* Mataulé, L. R. 9, Ch. 409 ; 30 L. T. 478 ; 22 W. R. 462.
(c) B. A. 1883, s. 168 (1).

presentation. A deed executed more than three months next preceding the presentation of the petition on which the receiving order is made is therefore not impeachable as an act of bankruptcy.[a]

Under the Bankruptcy Act, 1869, an act of bankruptcy available for adjudication must have occurred within six months next before the presentation of the petition on which the adjudication was made,[b] and by sec. 11 of that Act the trustee's title related in certain events, to any prior act of bankruptcy committed within twelve months next preceding adjudication.

An existing adjudication is conclusive against the holder of a bill of sale executed by the bankrupt, that the act of bankruptcy on which the adjudication was professedly founded was in fact committed, but a third party whose title to property is affected by the adjudication may appeal from it.[c] The same effect would seem now to follow the making of a receiving order.[d]

Effect of bankruptcy on bills of sale.

A trustee cannot avoid a bill of sale valid against the bankrupt, except where by the statutes he takes a higher title than the bankrupt ; thus, where a debtor wrote his creditor informing him he had forged his name to a bill of exchange, and entreating him to take up the bill to save the debtor from prosecution and ruin, offering, if he would do so, to give him a bill of sale to secure the amount of an existing debt and the further advance, upon which the creditor paid the bill, taking a bill of sale, and seizing and selling the goods ; on the debtor being adjudicated bankrupt, it was held that, though the transaction might have been illegal, yet, as the creditor had obtained possession, both parties being *in pari delicto*, the debtor, if he had remained solvent, could not have rescinded the contract, and there being no offence against the bankrupt laws his trustee stood in no better position.[e]

Under the Bankruptcy Act, 1869, a trustee in bankruptcy could not resort to the Court of Bankruptcy in all cases where he sought to set aside a bill of sale ; as he takes only

(a) Allen v. Bonnett, L. R. 5 Ch. 577 ; 23 L. T. 447 ; 18 W. R. 874.

(b) *Exp.* Gilbey, *re* Bedell 8 Ch. D. 248 ; 47 L. J. Bank. 49 ; 26 W. R. 768.

(c) *Exp.* Learoyd, *re* Foulds, 10 Ch. D. 4 ; 39 L. T. 525 ; 48 L. J. Bank 17 ; 27 W. R. 277.

(d) B. A. 1883, s. 142 (2).

(e) *Exp.* Caldecott, *re* Mapleback, 4 Ch. D. 150 46 L. J. Bank 14 ; 35 L. T. 503 ; 25 W. R. 103 ; 13 Cox C. C. 374.

the bankrupt's title, except when the statute places him in a better position.

It has been said that the jurisdiction conferred by the Bankruptcy Act. 1883, sec. 102, is identical with that given by sec. 72, Bankruptcy Act, 1869;[a] and the former decisions would, therefore, to some extent, seem still applicable.

Jurisdiction of Court of Bankruptcy. When a trustee takes only that which the bankrupt himself would have taken, the Court should not exercise jurisdiction and the matter should be left to the ordinary tribunals ; but when by the operation of the bankrupt laws the trustee claims by a higher and better title than the bankrupt, the case should be dealt with by the Court of Bankruptcy ; as when it is sought to set aside the transaction on the ground of the relation of the trustee's title, or of fraudulent preference[b] or, it would seem of fraud under the Statute of Elizabeth ; [c] but if as against a stranger to the bankruptcy he seeks to set aside the deed on a ground which would have been available to the bankrupt, e.g., actual fraud. or the like, he should take proceedings by action.[d] In such cases the Court has a judicial discretion to be exercised with regard to all the circumstances ; thus where questions of character are involved, and a large amount is at stake, the matter should be directed to be tried in the High Court.[e] Nor by the Bankruptcy Act, 1883, sec. 102, can a County Court adjudicate upon any claim not arising out of the bankruptcy,[f] which might. heretofore, have been enforced by action in the High Court. unless all parties to the proceeding consent, or the money. money's worth, or right in dispute does not, in the opinion of the judge, exceed in value £200.

Neither has the Court of Bankruptcy jurisdiction to entertain personal claims between third persons, or claims to property as between them, although the determination of such

(a) *Exp.* Beesty, *re* Lowenthal, 13 Q. B. D. 238 ; 53 L. J. Q. B. 524 ; 51 L. T. 431 ; 33 W. R. 138 ; 1 Mor. 117.

(b) *Exp.* Brown, *re* Yates, 11 Ch. D. 148 ; 40 L. T. 402 ; 27 W. R. 651 ; 48 L. J. Bank. 78.

(c) *Exp.* Butters, *re* Harrison, 14 Ch. D. 265 ; 43 L. T. 2 ; 28 W. R. 876, per James L. J. ; *Exp.* Price, *re* Roberts, 21 Ch. D. 557 ; 51 L. J. Ch. 131 ; per Brett, L. J.

(d) *Exp.* Dickin, *re* Pollard, 8 Ch. D. 377 ; 26 W. R. 731 ; 38 L. T. 860 ; 48 L. J. Bank. 36 ; *Exp.* Musgrave, *re* Wood, 10 Ch. D. 9 ; 48 L. J. Bank. 39 ; 27 W. R. 372 ; 39 L. T. 647.

(e) *Exp.* Armitage, *re* Learoyd, 17 Ch. D. 13 ; 44 L. T. 262 ; 29 W. R. 772 ; *Exp.* Price, *re* Roberts, 21 Ch. D. 553 ; *exp.* Hazelhurst, *re* Beswick, 58 L. T. 691 ; 5 Mor. 105.

(f) *Exp.* Scott, *re* Hawke, 16 Q B. D. 503 ; 55 L. J. Q. B. 302 ; 34 W. R. 168 ; 54 L. T. 54 ; 3 Mor.

claims might also decide which of such third parties should prove against the bankrupt's estate.[a] If, however, a stranger to the bankruptcy is willing to submit to the jurisdiction of the Court of Bankruptcy, the trustee should not object,[b] and any objection to jurisdiction must be taken at the earliest moment.[c]

The holder of a valid registered bill of sale may, in the event of the grantor's bankruptcy, elect to rest on his security, or he may realize it by sale, or apply to the Court to have it realized under the direction of the Court, proving and receiving dividend for any deficiency.[d] He also has a right to prove for his whole debt, on giving up his security;[e] but if he seeks to prove before realizing his security, he must state in his proof the particulars, and value at which he assesses the same, and will be entitled to dividend only in respect of the balance due to him, after deducting such assessed value.[f] The schedules to the Bankruptcy Act, 1883, entitle a secured creditor in certain cases to amend the valuation of the security in a proof; and also empower the trustee to require its realization if dissatisfied with the assessed value. But a secured creditor may by notice in writing require the trustee to elect whether he will or will not exercise his power of redemption or realization, and if the trustee does not within six months after receipt of the notice signify his election to exercise the power he shall not be entitled to exercise it, and the equity of redemption, or other interest in the property comprised in the security which is vested in the trustee, shall vest in the creditor, and the amount of his debt shall be reduced by the amount at which the security has been valued.[g]

If a security is given up, and the mortgagee proves for his whole debt, a subsequent mortgage is not advanced, but the security enures for the benefit of the general body of creditors;[h] and so where the trustee in the mortgagor's bankruptcy purchased the first mortgage it was held not to be

Remedies of grantee on grantor's bankruptcy.

(a) *Exp.* Lyons, L. R. 7 Ch. 494 ; 41 L. J. Ch. 41 ; 20 W. R. 560 ; 26 L. T. 401.

(b) *Exp.* Fletcher, *re* Hart, 9 Ch. D. 381 ; 39 L. T. 187 ; 26 W. R. 851.

(c) *Exp.* Swinbanks, *re* Shanks, 11 Ch. D. 525 ; 48 L. J. Bank. 120 ; 27 W. R. 485 ; 40 L. T. 825.

(d) B. A., 1883, sec. 9 (2), Sched. ii. 9 ; B. R. 1886, 73

(e) B. A., 1883, Sched. ii. 10.

(f) B. A. 1883, Sched. ii. 11.

(g) B. A. 1883, Sched. ii. 12, 15 , Sched. i. 10, 12.

(h) Cracknall c. Janson, 6 Ch. D. 735 , 26 W. R. 904 , 46 L. J. Ch. 652 , 37 L. T. 118.

extinguished, so as to advance a second incumbrancer, who, however, was still entitled to redeem.[a]

A bill of sale holder who under the provisions of a scheme sanctioned by the Court withdrew all claim against the estate of the grantor who had become bankrupt, was held to be remitted to his original rights equally with the other creditors on the scheme being set aside.[b]

When the result of moving to set aside a bill of sale would not be for the benefit of creditors at large, but of an individual creditor who claims a security, the trustee ought not himself to take proceedings for the recovery of the property, nor will the individual creditor generally be allowed to take them in his name.[c]

Where the chattels comprised in an unregistered bill of sale had been transferred by joint tenants, one of whom assigned his interest to the other, who became bankrupt, the latter's moiety only was held to pass to the trustee.[d]

If by the neglect of the bill of sale holder his security becomes worthless, sureties for the debt will be discharged to the extent of the security thus lost.[e]

Payments under void deed.

When the holder of an unregistered bill of sale which was declared void had paid out executions which were good against the grantor's trustee, he was held entitled to be repaid out of the proceeds of the goods the amounts so paid;[f] and an unregistered bill of sale holder who has paid off prior incumbrances, which would have ranked against the estate, has been held entitled to be recouped on his security being set aside against the trustee under the grantor's liquidation;[g] but such a payment must be made in good faith, and if for the purpose of securing the property for the debtor's benefit, will not be protected.[h]

Although a bill of sale is not void under the Statute of Elizabeth, or as an act of bankruptcy, the chattels it comprises which at the commencement of the bankruptcy are in

(a) Bell v. Sunderland Building Society, 24 Ch. D. 618; 53 L. J. Ch. 500; 49 L. T. 555.

(b) Exp. Jarvis, re Spanton, 10 Ch. D. 179; 48 L. J. Bank. 45; 39 L. T. 651; 27 W. R. 297.

(c) Exp. Cooper, re Zucco, L. R. 10 Ch. 510; 44 L. J. Bank. 121; 23 W. R. 782; 33 L. T. 3; see re Arnold, 9 Mor. 1; 40 W. R. 288; 66 L. T. 121.

(d) Exp. Brown, re Reed, 39 L. T. 336; 9 Ch. D. 389; 27 W. R. 219; 48 L. J. Bank. 10.

(e) Wulff v. Jay, L. R. 7 Q. B. 756; 41 L. J. Q. B. 322; 27 L. T. 118; 19 W. R. 1112.

(f) Exp. Mutton, re Cole, 41 L. J. Bank. 57; 14 Eq. 178; 20 W. R. 882; 26 L. T. 918.

(g) Exp. Harris, re James, 44 L. J. Bank. 31; 19 Eq. 253; 31 L. T. 21.

(h) Exp. Hall, re Townsend, 14 Ch. D. 132; 28 W. R. 556; 42 L. T. 162.

the possession, order, or disposition of the grantor in his
trade or business, may pass to the trustee, if something has not
been done by the bill of sale holder to avoid the operation of
s. 44 (2) [a][a] of the Bankruptcy Act, 1883.[a]

9. (1878.) Where a subsequent bill of sale is *Avoidance of certain successive bills of sale.* executed within or on the expiration of seven days after the execution of a prior unregistered bill of sale, and comprises all or any part of the personal chattels comprised in such prior bill of sale, then, if such subsequent bill of sale is given as a security for the same debt as is secured by the prior bill of sale, or for any part of such debt, it shall, to the extent to which it is a security for the same debt or part thereof, and so far as respects the personal chattels or part thereof comprised in the prior bill, be absolutely void, unless it is proved to the satisfaction of the Court having cognizance of the case, that the subsequent bill of sale was bonâ fide given for the purpose of correcting some material error in the prior bill of sale, and not for the purpose of evading this Act.

The section does not invalidate a subsequent bill of sale
executed more than seven days after the execution of a prior
unregistered bill of sale of the same chattels.[b]

Apart from the section a successive bill of sale will be
avoided if obtained by fraud, thus where the plaintiffs who
had given the defendants a bill of sale, void under section 9
of the amendment Act, attended at their offices on request,
and being informed they must give a new bill of sale did so;
the Court held that the second bill of sale was obtained by a
trick and set it aside, finding the defendants meant the
plaintiffs to understand that unless they gave a new bill of
sale their furniture could be seized under the old one, which
as the defendants knew was bad under a decision with which
the plaintiffs were unacquainted.[c]

Under the repealed Acts, it was attempted to avoid the
necessity for registration by an agreement between the grantor

(a) See note to sec. 20 (1878), page 233.
(b) Currard r. Meek, 29 W. R. 244; Wilson c. Watherspoon, 71 L. J. 230.
(c) Bouchette c. Consolidated Credit Corporation, 5 T. L. R. 653.

and grantee, made at the time of giving the bill of sale, to give and accept successive bills of sale, the last only to be registered ; and such an arrangement was good against execution creditors,[a] although void against a trustee in bankruptcy,[b] unless founded on a new consideration.[c]

The giving of each successive bill of sale in substitution, was held to annul and cancel the deed that stood earlier in the series;[d] but it would seem that the mere cancellation of a bill of sale does not revest any property in the goods in the mortgagor, if the cancellation is with the view of obtaining a better security, unless there is an intention to release;[e] thus a bill of sale given after the grantor was adjudged bankrupt, in substitution for an earlier bill of sale, the grantee not knowing of the bankruptcy, was held not to affect the grantee's title under the first deed, the second having been taken under a mistake of fact;[f] and where the grantor having executed a bill of sale, subsequently gave the mortgagee another bill of sale over the same goods for the same debt, reciting that it was given on account of doubts as to the validity of the first deed, it was held that the second bill of sale must be deemed to have been intended only to be effectual in the event of the first being invalid, and did not therefore cancel it.[g]   But if it is found that the intention of the parties by the new deed was to put an end to the old, there cannot be implied a condition that the second deed shall be valid, and although void the first deed cannot be relied on.[h]

Form of bill of sale.

9. (1882.) A bill of sale made or given by way of security for the payment of money by the grantor thereof shall be void unless made in accordance with the form in the schedule to this Act annexed.

(a) Ramsden v. Lupton, L. R. 9 Q. B. 17 ; Smale v. Burr, L. R. 8 C. P. 64 ; 42 L. J. C. P. 70 ; 21 W. R. 193 ; 27 L. T. 555.

(b) Exp. Cohen, re Sparke, L. R. 7 Ch. 20 ; 41 L. J. Bank. 17 ; 25 L. T. 475 ; 20 W. R. 69 ; Exp. Stevens, 44 L. J. Bank. 136 ; Stansfield v. Cubitt, 27 L. J. Ch. 266 ; 4 Jur. N. S. 80 : 2 D. & J. 222 ; Exq. Furber, re Pellew, 6 Ch. D. 181.

(c) Exp. Hall, re Jackson, 46 L. J. Bank. 39 ; 25 W. R. 382 ; 35 L. T. 947 ; 4 Ch. D. 682 ; Exp. Harris, re Pulling, 42 L. J. Bank. 9 ; 21 W. R. 44 ; 27 L. T. 501 ; L. R. 8 Ch. 48.

(d) Ramsden v. Lupton, L. R. 9 Q. B. 17.

(e) Gummer v. Adams, 13 L. J. Ex. 40.

(f) Exp. Hasluck, re Bargen [1894], 1 Q. B. 444 ; 69 L. T. 763 ; 10 Mor. 301 ; 63 L. J. Q. B. 209.

(g) Cooper v. Zeffert, 32 W. R. 402.

(h) Bresnovich v. Levison, 87 L. T. J. 37.

This provision has been a fruitful source of litigation; and has proved fatal to the validity of many bills of sale.[a]

The section is intended to make void absolutely, and not merely against all but the grantor, every bill of sale given by way of security for the payment of money by the grantor unless made in accordance with the form in the schedule; and must be taken to have prohibited bills of sale to which the form is not applicable;[b] so that if the arrangement between the parties cannot be made in accordance with the form in the schedule, it cannot be made at all;[c] the amendment Act applying to every bill of sale given by way of security for the payment of money by the grantor, whether that money is lent or otherwise due or payable to the grantee, for whatever reason the grantor binds himself to pay and gives the bill of sale as security.[d] Thus a bill of sale, absolute in form, but given by way of security for a loan, is wholly void.[e]

It would seem therefore that inventories of goods with receipt attached, receipts, powers of attorney, licences to seize and agreements conferring a right in equity to personal chattels, which are declared bills of sale by sec. 4 of the principal Act will no longer be available as securities, for they cannot fulfil the conditions prescribed by this section. But the documents which by section 6 of the principal Act shall be deemed bills of sale, are not within this section, and need not be in the scheduled form, though they are to be treated as bills of sale for the purposes of registration under section 8 of the amendment Act.[f] By sec. 1, Bills of Sale Act, 1890, instruments hypothecating or declaring trusts of certain imported goods during the interval between the discharge of the goods from the ship in which they are imported and their deposit in a warehouse or delivery to a purchaser were not to be deemed bills of sale within the meaning of sec. 9; but such instruments, when of the kind mentioned in sec. 1 Bills of Sale Act, 1891, are now excluded from the operation of the Acts.

Form of bill of sale.

(a) Form, page 260.
(b) Thomas v. Kelly, 13 App. Cases, 506.
(c) Exp. Parsons, re Townsend, 16 Q. B. D. 532.
(d) Hughes v. Little, 18 Q. B. D. 32; 56 L. J. Q. B. 96; 35 W. R. 36; 55 L. T. 176.
(e) Exp. Foulay, re Linton, 10 Mor. 259.
(f) Green v. Marsh 1892, 2 Q. B. 330.

I

The section avoids the bill of sale altogether, and not merely as to the personal chattels comprised therein, thus a covenant contained in the bill of sale for payment of principal and interest is also void;[a] and a void bill of sale cannot operate even as a licence to seize.[b]

But under the apparent form of a single agreement or covenant written on one piece of paper and sealed with one seal, there may be several contracts or obligations, and though one of these fall the others may be upheld;[a] thus where a deed is a bill of sale of chattels personal, but includes a mortgage of chattels real, it may, though void as a bill of sale, be valid in so far as it is a mortgage of chattels real;[c] and an agreement between landlord and tenant may be valid so far as relating to the tenancy, though conferring a power of distress which is void under the Acts.[d] So where personal chattels and other property are mortgaged by a deed not in accordance with the form in the schedule to the Act, such deed, though void as to the personal chattels, may be valid as to the other property, if it is possible to sever the security; and a deed void as a bill of sale, assigning the several chattels and things specifically described in the schedule, was held good as to scheduled articles which were excepted by sec. 5 of the principal Act from the definition of personal chattels.[e] Again, an assignment of a hire agreement for pianos was held severable from a transfer, by the same instrument, of the pianos themselves.[f] But this rule will not give validity to a bill of sale whereby things other than personal chattels are attempted to be assigned; and the Court refused to sever an assignment of chattels real and personal so as to uphold the assignment of personal chattels as a bill of sale in accordance with the form.[g]

The object of the section has been said to be twofold — first, that the borrower should understand the nature of the security; secondly, that a creditor on merely searching the

(a) Davies v. Rees, 17 Q. B. D. 408; per Bowen L. J.
(b) Griffin v. Union Deposit Bank, 3 T. L. R. 608.
(c) Re O'Dwyer, 19 L. R. Ir. 19.
(d) Stevens v. Marston, 39 W. R. 129.
(e) Exp. Byrne, re Burdett, 20 Q. B. D. 310; re Bansha, &c., Co., 21 L. R. Ir. 181.
(f) Exp. Mason, re Isaacson, 98 L. T. J. 155.
(g) Cochrane v. Entwistle, 25 Q. B. D. 116.

register should be able to understand the borrower's position, without having to get legal assistance as to the meaning of the security; for the Legislature intended that the loan of money on the security of a bill of sale should be a simple transaction. Every bill of sale must be substantially like the form in the schedule; nothing substantial must be subtracted from it, and nothing actually inconsistent may be added;[a] for though the section does not make every word of the form imperative, it enacts not only what a bill of sale must contain, but what it must not contain.[b] No defect in form can be supported by the affidavit filed on registration or by extraneous evidence.[c]

A divergence becomes substantial or material which *Exp.* Stanford. is calculated to give the bill of sale a legal consequence or effect, either greater or smaller than that which would attach to it if drawn in the form which has been sanctioned, or if it departs from the form in a manner calculated to mislead those whom it is the object of the statute to protect. If the instrument as drawn would in virtue of either addition or omission have any legal effect which either goes beyond or falls short of that which would result from the statutory form, or, in respect of such variance, would be reasonably calculated to deceive those for whose benefit a statutory form is provided, it will be void under the section, for whatever form the bill of sale takes, the form adopted by it, in order to be valid, must produce not merely the like effect, but the same effect—that is to say, the legal effect, the whole legal effect, and nothing but the legal effect which it would produce if cast in the exact mould of the schedule.[d] And this being a test laid down by the full Court of Appeal, is taken as qualifying previous decisions, and must in all cases be applied to determine the validity of a bill of sale under the section.[e]

But the judgment in *ex parte* Stanford must be read with reference to cases where the error in form is one relating to the contract, and must not be taken as intended to lay down a rule that nothing is a material departure from the form.

(a) Davis v. Burton, 11 Q. B. D. 537; 32 W. R. 423; 52 L. J. Q. B. 636.
(b) Thomas v. Kelly, 13 App. Cases, 506.
(c) Bird v. Davey 1891 1 Q. B. 29; 39 W. R. 10; 60 L. J. Q. B. s; 63 L. T. 711.
(d) *Exp.* Stanford, *re* Barber, 17 Q. B. D. 259; 34 W. R. 507; 55 L. J. Q. B. 341; 54 L. T. 894.
(e) Kelly v. Kellond, 20 Q. B. D. 569; 36 W. R. 363; 57 L. J. Q. B. 330; 58 L. T. 2-3.

unless it alters the effect of the instrument : thus it is matter of substance that the attesting witness should be described on the face of the instrument, which is void if such description is omitted.[a]

Therefore, although agreements for payment, insurance, and such terms as are agreed upon for the maintenance or defeasance of the security may be inserted, the statutory form should be adhered to as closely as possible, every departure being attended with risk; for no agreement can be included which does not reasonably come within the description given in italics within the brackets of the form.[b]

Maintenance of security.

It will be observed that the scheduled form permits the insertion of terms agreed on by the parties for the maintenance or defeasance of the security, while one of the causes of seizure mentioned in sec. 7 of the amendment Act is for default in performance of any covenant or agreement contained in the bill of sale, and necessary for maintaining the security. It would thus seem that stipulations, if coupled with a power of seizure on default in performance, must be not only for the maintenance of, but necessary for maintaining the security, but that the bill of sale may also contain other terms agreed on for the maintenance or defeasance of the security, if no right of seizure follows a breach, and the stipulations do not contravene the provisions of the Act. It has, indeed, been held that the insertion of terms agreed to by the parties for maintaining the security, but which are not necessary for its maintenance, will not avoid the deed if power is not given to seize for a default in the performance of such terms.[c]

But the parties cannot insert agreed terms unless they are for the maintenance or defeasance of the security,[d] and if a stipulation is not necessary for the maintenance of the security it cannot be made so by agreement of the parties.[e]

Maintenance of the security appears to mean, not the maintenance of a sufficient security less than that agreed to be given, but the maintenance of the security created by the

---

(a) Parsons v. Brand, 25 Q. B. D. 110.

(b) Melville v. Stringer, 13 Q. B. D. 392; 53 L. J. Q. B. 482; 32 W. R. 890; 50 L. T. 774.

(c) Topley v. Corsbie, 20 Q. B. D. 350; 57 L. J. Q. B. 271; 58 L. T. 342; 36 W. R. 352.

(d) Blaiberg v. Beckett, 18 Q. B. D. 96; 35 W. R. 34; 56 L. J. Q. B. 35; 55 L. T. 876.

(e) Furber v. Cobb, 18 Q. B. D. 494; 56 L. T. 689; 35 W. R. 398; 56 L. J. Q. B. 273.

bill of sale, and this is maintained only when the subject
matter of the charge and the grantee's title to it are preserved
in as good a condition as at the date of the bill of sale. [a]

What is meant by the term "defeasance of the security"
is in strictness a condition in the nature of a defeasance, that
is, something which defeats the operation of the deed.[b]

But though some provisions for the maintenance of the
security may, in consequence of the general law applicable to
contracts, not be capable of enforcement, their mere introduction will not necessarily invalidate the deed, unless
contrary to some express provision of the Act, though they
may be invalid and superfluous.[c] Nor will the deed be avoided
by mere verbal deviations from the statutory form which do
not alter its legal effect ; thus a bill of sale has been supported
containing recitals, referring to the parties as mortgagor and
mortgagee, and omitting the words "by way of security," the
recitals shewing that to have been the object of the deed.[d]

A grantor cannot, however, convey or assign as beneficial
owner, the introduction of those words being an attempt to
incorporate the covenants in sec. 7 Conveyancing Act, 1881,
including the covenant for quiet enjoyment contained in that
section, which is inconsistent with sec. 13 of the amendment
Act.[e]

If a bill of sale contains two sets of clauses which, even if
producing the same legal result, are expressed in different
words, so as to make their interpretation a puzzle to any one
who reads them, they make the bill of sale invalid, as being
calculated to mislead ; as for instance where powers of seizure
are given wider than permitted by sec. 7, and are then
attempted to be limited by the statutory proviso.[f] And the
result will be the same if the agreements are so ambiguous
as to be misleading ; thus a bill of sale was avoided which
contained terms for payment of principal, including the
interest then due, by equal weekly payments, and from and

Ambiguity in bill of sale.

(a) Furber v. Cobb, 18 Q. B. D. 494; 56 L. T. 689; 35 W. R. 398; 56 L. J. Q. B.
273.

(b) Blaiberg v. Beckett, 18 Q. B. D. 96; 35 W. R. 34; 56 L. J. Q. B. 35; 55
L. T. 870.

(c) Exp. Official Receiver, re Morritt, 18 Q. B. D. 222; 35 W. R. 277; 56 L. J.
Q. B. 139; 56 L. T. 42.

(d) Roberts v. Roberts, 13 Q. B. D. 794.

(e) Exp. Stanford, re Barber, 17 Q. B. D. 259.

(f) Furber v. Cobb, 18 Q. B. D. 494.

after default, to pay specified interest on the principal by
monthly payments as the principal money became due.[a] But
a bill of sale must be construed in the same manner as any
other document,[b] and is not necessarily misleading because
different tribunals fail to agree in the construction to be given
to it;[c] and if the scheduled form is filled up according to the
instructions given in the brackets, then the bill of sale is in
accordance with the form, whatever may be the construction
to be put upon it.[d]

Nor can covenants be inserted to perform stipulations not
apparent on the face of the deed—for example, to perform the
covenants in a deed recited by the bill of sale;[e] or to pay
interest on mortgages affecting the premises where the goods
assigned then were, or to which they might be removed, even
though no right of seizure is given on breach.[f] And the
deed must shew the true agreement between the parties, and
should not be dependent for its real effect on some other
document; thus, a bill of sale given under and subject to a
contract for payment of compound interest was held void
through embodying only such part of the bargain as could
properly be included in a bill of sale.[g]

Defeasance of the security.

It has also been decided that if a bill of sale, proper in form,
is accompanied by another document containing clauses not
allowed by the Acts, and the whole conditions of the transaction are to be gathered from the effect of the two documents,
the bill of sale is void; as where with a bill of sale to secure
£200, payable by instalments, was given a promissory note for
£280, also payable by instalments, providing that on failure to
pay any instalment, the whole balance should at once become
due;[h] although it would seem that this decision is best
supported under sec. 10, sub-sec. 3 of the principal Act.[i] A

(a) Curtis v. National Bank of Wales, 5 T. L. R. 339.
(b) Weardale Coal and Iron Co. v. Hodson [1894]; 1 Q. B. 598; 42 W. R. 424; 63 L. J. Q. B. 391; 70 L. T. 632.
(c) Hazlewood v. Consolidated Credit Co. 63 L. T. 71; 25 Q. B. D. 555; 39 W. R. 54; 60 L. J. Q. B. 12.
(d) Edwards v. Marston [1891] 1 Q. B. 228, per Lord Esher, M. R.
(e) Lee v. Barnes, 17 Q. B. D. 77; 34 W. R. 640.
(f) Watson v. Strickland, 19 Q. B. D. 391; 35 W. R. 769; 56 L. J. Q. B. 594.
(g) Sharp v. McHenry, 38 Ch. D. 427; 57 L. J. Ch. 961; 57 L. T. 606.
(h) Simpson v. Charing Cross Bank, 34 W. R. 568.
(i) Counsell v. London & Westminster Loan &c., Co., 19 Q. B. D. 512; 36 W. R. 53; 56 L. J. Q. B. 622.

promissory note so given is not avoided, and the amount secured by it may be recovered, even though the bill of sale is held void.[a]

One characteristic of the form is that the name of the grantee must be given, but no particular description is enforced by the Act ; and if the name or description inserted is such as, without the aid of extrinsic evidence, would in the case of any mercantile instrument be sufficient, the bill of sale is not avoided by reason of some ambiguity in the description of the grantee.[b]

But the section deals only with the form of the bill of sale; thus though the form provides for statement of consideration, and for the insertion of agreements for defeasance of the security, an untrue statement of consideration or, it seems, the omission of a condition, would not make a bill of sale, otherwise regular, not in accordance with the form.[c]

As the form provides for payment to the person in whose favour the bill of sale is made, although it seems the security may be given for a joint loan, and perhaps to a trustee, a bill of sale was held not to be in accordance with the form when made between the grantor and four sets of mortgagees, to secure different sums owing to each, and a further advance by them all, the grantor covenanting separately with each mortgagee to pay on demand the sum owing to each, power being given to the mortgagees to sell and repay all money owing if default should be made in payment of any sum secured, or if any other default or event mentioned as a cause of seizure in sec. 7 of the amendment Act should be made or happen.[d] But it seems that a bill of sale may be given by the legal owner of goods without the concurrence of the person equitably or beneficially entitled, and the legal owner has been held the true owner within the meaning of section 5 of the amendment Act.[e] *Parties.*

An essential condition of the deed is a present assignment of goods capable of specific description and present assign- *Description of chattels assigned.*

(a) Monetary Advance Co. *v.* Cater, 20 Q. B. D. 785; 57 L. J. Q. B. 463; 59 L. T. 311.
(b) Simmons *v.* Woodward [1892] A. C. 100; 66 L. T. 534; 40 W. R. 641; 61 L. J. Ch. 252.
(c) Heseltine *v.* Simmons, [1892] 2 Q. B. 547; 67 L. T. 611; 41 W. R. 67; 62 L. J. Q. B. 5; 57 J. P. 53.
(d) Melville *v.* Stringer, 13 Q. B. D. 392.
(e) *Exp.* Williams, *re* Sarl [1892], 2 Q. B. 591.

ment, and therefore a bill of sale is altogether void under the section if purporting to assign chattels and things specifically described in the schedule, together with all other chattels and things of the mortgagor then or thereafter on his premises during the continuance of the security.[a] Before this decision of the House of Lords the rule had been otherwise stated.[b] So a bill of sale assigning chattels specifically described and all other chattels and things substituted for them, pursuant to the covenant thereinafter contained, was held void, though containing no covenant for substitution.[c] It has, however, been held permissible to agree to replace any articles damaged or worn out with others of equal value, to be included in the security.[d]

The assignment must be of personal chattels only, and these alone can be inserted in the schedule, thus a bill of sale was held void under the section by which a farmer assigned the personal chattels specifically described in the schedule together with his tenant right, valuation, goodwill, tillages, and interest in the farm and premises, the schedule specifically describing the personal chattels and adding general words covering the other property assigned.[e]

Certainty of
sum secured.

To accord with the form a fixed sum must be stated as the amount secured, which, with rateable interest, calculated up to the time when the principal shall be called in, can be recovered by the grantee. There must be no attempt to alter the sum secured, and nothing must be added to it except by way of rateable interest; [f] thus a bill of sale cannot be made to cover further advances of an uncertain amount, which may or may not be made.[g] For the same reason a bill of sale cannot now be given by way of indemnity, where the amount which will ultimately become payable, or its time of payment, is for any reason left uncertain.[h]

But this rule against uncertainty of the amount secured does not prevent power being given to the mortgagee to pay, and charge with interest upon the chattels assigned, rent,

(a) Thomas v. Kelly, 13 App. Cases, 506.
(b) Roberts v. Roberts, 13 Q. B. D. 794; Bouchette v. Attenborough, 3 T. L. R. 813; Crosser v. Maxwell, W. N. 1885, 95; cf. Levy v. Polack, 52 L. T. 551.
(c) Hadden v. Oppenheim, 60 L. T. 462.
(d) Seed v. Bradley [1894], 1 Q. B. 319.
(e) Cochrane v. Entwistle, 25 Q. B. D. 116.
(f) Davis v. Burton, 11 Q. B. D. 537.
(g) Cook v. Taylor, 2 T. L. R. 800.
(h) Hughes v. Little, 18 Q. B. D. 32.

insurance and the like which the mortgagor may neglect to
pay;[a] although if the bill of sale makes such payments and
interest recoverable by seizure, it will be void ; thus an agreement whereby sums which might be paid by the mortgagee
were to be added to and recoverable in the same manner as
the principal money was held not in accordance with the
form.[b]

The interest is an essential part of the form, and a bill of *Interest.*
sale must comprehend not only the principal, but the interest;[c]
though the interest may be such as is agreed upon, calculated at a rate per month, or otherwise, and may be payable
by instalments, which need not be equal, but must be rateable, otherwise there will be a variance from the form.
Thus where a bill of sale for £115 advanced, with £15 agreed
interest and bonus, payable by twelve equal instalments, contained the statutory proviso, and set out the causes of seizure,
with the addition that the mortgagee might remove or sell in
the specified events, it was held that as on failure to pay one
instalment, the mortgagee might realize his security for the
whole amount, the interest was not rateable and therefore the
bill of sale was void.[d] Again, calculation of interest in a
lump sum to become payable on failure to pay any instalment
was held not to be in accordance with the form.[e]

It is very doubtful whether a bonus, as such, or a fixed *Bonus.*
sum for interest can now lawfully be reserved by a bill of
sale, although there are early decisions holding that the
insertion of a lump agreed sum was no objection to the bill
of sale, even though the interest varied from month to month, [f]
and that it was unnecessary to state the rate of interest in so
many words when the instrument shewed what the utmost
rate of interest could be ;[g] but these cases, probably, would

(a) *Exp.* Stanford, *re* Barber, 17 Q. B. D. 259 ; Goldstrom *v.* Tallerman, 18 Q.
B. D. 1 ; 56 L. J. Q. B. 22 ; 35 W. R. 68 ; 55 L. T. 866 ; Topley *v.* Corsbie, 20
Q. B. D. 350.

(b) Real, &c., Advance Co. *v.* Clears, 20 Q. B. D. 304 ; 36 W. R. 250 ; 57
L. J. Q. B. 164 ; 58 L. T. 610 ; Bianchi *v.* Offord, 17 Q. B. D. 484 ; 55 L. J. Q. B
480.

(c) Simmons *v.* Woodward (1892), A. C. 100.

(d) Myers *v.* Elliott, 34 W. R. 338 ; 16 Q. B. D. 526 ; 55 L. J. Q. B. 233 ; 54
L. T. 552.

(e) *Exp.* Abrams, *re* Johnstone, 50 L. T. 184 ; Roe *v.* Mutual Loan Association, 56 L. T. 431.

(f) Thorp *v.* Cregeon, 33 W. R. 844 ; 55 L. J. Q. B. 80.

(g) Wilson *v.* Kirkwood, 48 L. T. 821.

not now be followed, and a bill of sale for payment of £50 and interest thereon at the rate of £17 10s. for three years, with a covenant to pay the principal sum, together with the interest then due by 36 equal specified monthly payments, was held void, as not stating any rate of interest for the loan, thus leaving the borrower to calculate the rate.[a] It seems that interest cannot be given upon interest;[b] and capitalized interest certainly cannot be reserved; thus the following bill of sale was held void :—The deed assigned chattels specified in the schedule by way of security for £300, money advanced, and the capitalized interest thereon, being at the rate of 60 per cent. per annum ; the grantor agreeing to pay £480, being the principal and capitalized interest, by certain instalments at dates named also to deliver to the mortgagee the receipts for rent, rates and taxes when demanded in writing or otherwise, and not to make any assignment for the benefit of creditors, or file a petition for liquidation or composition. There were other covenants of a stringent character, and a proviso that if the grantor should break any of the covenants, all moneys secured should immediately become payable, concluding with the proviso against seizure, as in the statutory form.

Bonus.

In the course of the judgment, Lord Esher, M.R., said—" If upon failure to pay the first instalment the whole of the interest which the grantee, on performance of the contract, is ultimately to receive becomes immediately payable, the bill of sale would, I think, be contrary to the form in the schedule for interest is payable upon money only so long as it is due, and it is contrary to the nature of interest to make it payable before it is due because a condition has not been performed or a certain event has happened." The Court also decided the bill of sale to be void as enabling the grantee to seize the goods, upon failure to comply with a verbal demand for receipts for rent, rates and taxes, which stipulation was impliedly forbidden by sec. 7, sub-sec. 4, Fry, L.J., observing : " It is said that this is a covenant necessary for maintaining the security, but a covenant cannot be valid if it is prohibited by the Legislature; and this covenant alters that relation between the parties which the law intended to allow."[c]

(a) Blankenstein v. Robertson, 24 Q. B. D. 543 ; 50 L. J. Q. B. 315.

(b) Dresser v. Townsend, 81 L. T. J. 230.

(c) Davis v. Burton, 11 Q. B. D. 537.

It appears therefore that if powers of seizure are given for causes not specified in sec. 7 of the amendment Act, whether given directly, or by acceleration of payment of the sum secured on breach of covenant, the bill of sale will be void.[a] So the following bill of sale was decided to be contrary to the form in the schedule:—In consideration of a sum paid, and £10 bonus, the grantor assigned chattels by way of mortgage, agreeing forthwith to pay the sum secured, being the money paid, and bonus, with interest at 5 per cent., costs, and other payments—the receipts for which were to be delivered to the grantee. There was a power of seizure on default, or if the grantor should do or suffer anything whereby he should render himself liable to become a bankrupt, or remove or suffer the chattels to be removed from the premises, or if execution should be, or should have been levied against his goods, the expenses of entry and seizure, with a fee of 5 per cent. on the amount then due, to be added to the sum secured; the deed also containing clauses for further advances, concluding with a proviso in the statutory form—the Chief Judge held, having regard to the bonus and powers to seize in events other than those specified in sec. 7, that the bill of sale was void, and that its defects were not cured by the final proviso.[b]

Powers of seizure.

Certainty in the sum secured and in the rateable interest reserved is thus essential. So also is certainty in the time of payment, for as the form in the schedule provides for stipulated times or time of payment, payment on demand is inadmissible;[c] or within a stipulated time after demand in writing, not to be made before a specified time;[d] and so is payment 24 or 48 hours after demand;[e] although the time for payment may be fixed by reference to any known event, or may perhaps include a time to be ascertained by the happening of a contingency, but not to depend on the mere choice and volition of the holder of the bill of sale.[f] A bill of sale dated 5th January, 1887, containing a covenant for payment by equal

Time of payment.

(a) Barr v. Kingsford, 56 L. T. 861.
(b) Exp. Pearce, re Williams, 25 Ch. D. 656; 49 L. T. 475; 53 L. J. Ch. 500; 32 W. R. 157.
(c) Hetherington v. Groome, 13 Q. B. D. 789; 51 L. T. 412; 33 W. R. 103; 53 L. J. Q. B. 570.
(d) Sibley v. Higgs, 15 Q. B. D. 619; 54 L. J. Q. B. 525; 33 W. R. 749.
(e) Bishop v. Beale, 1 T. L. R. 140; Clemson v. Townsend, 1 C. & E. 418.
(f) Hetherington v. Groome [;   B. .789.

instalments on the 5th July and 5th January, without stating the year, was held sufficiently certain as the dates stated could be read "next ensuing."[a]

Time of payment.

A single payment is admissible, and there is no obligation to divide repayment into any number of equal portions.[b] Indeed, there would seem no objection to stipulating for payment on the day succeeding the date of the bill of sale; and it is unobjectionable to provide for payment of principal by instalments with rateable interest, stipulating that on default the whole of the instalments shall at once become due;[c] for without any express provision a grantee on default of payment of an instalment, is entitled, subject to sections 7, 13, to sell and retain the whole principal unpaid, together with the interest then due.[d] Nor need payment be by equal sums, and the form does not require computation of the whole interest at once; nor need principal and interest be repayable together, thus the principal may be first payable;[e] and there is no objection to postponing payment of the principal until the interest has been paid; the question whether repayments are applicable to principal or interest being one of construction in each case,[f] the fact that a calculation is involved to determine the number of instalments not being objectionable, the statutory form itself seeming to necessitate such calculation.[g]

So long as the time of payment is specified, it seems a variation in the manner of payment is admissible; thus a bill of sale was upheld where payment was agreed on for a specified time, provided that if the grantor should not break any of the covenants, and should not become bankrupt, and should pay principal and interest by equal monthly instalments on specified dates, the grantee should accept payment by such instalments.[h]

The true principle to be gathered from this class of cases is that wherever the time of payment is by any circumstances rendered uncertain, whether by reason of payment being on demand or otherwise, payment cannot be deemed to be at a

(a) Grannell v. Monck, 24 L. R. Ir. 241.

(b) Watkins v. Evans, 18 Q. B. D. 386.

(c) Lumley v. Simmons, 34 Ch. D. 698.

(d) Exp. Woolfe, re Wood [1894], 1 Q. B. 605.

(e) Goldstrom v. Tallerman, 18 Q. B. D. 1; Exp. Rawlings re Cleaver, 18 Q.B.D. 489; 35 W. R. 281; 56 L. T. 593; 56 L. J. Q. B. 197.

(f) Edwards v. Marston [1891], 1 Q. B. 225; 39 W.R. 165; 60 L. J. Q. B. 202; 64 L. T. 97.

(g) Exp. Hasluck, re Burgen [1894], 1 Q. B. 444.

(h) Exp. Payne, re Coton, 35 W. R. 476; 56 L. T. 571; 4 Mor. 90.

specified time or times. Thus a bill of sale was held not to comply with the form when given in consideration of the grantee having at the grantor's request become guarantee and signed a promissory note, the grantor assigning chattels as security for any moneys which the grantee might be called upon to pay with interest, agreeing that he would pay the grantee any sums as aforesaid, with interest then due by monthly payments of £2 on the first of every month ; for it might be that the grantee would never have to pay, and if he had both amount and time of payment were uncertain.[a]

As many cases involve the question whether clauses objected to are for the maintenance or defeasance of the security it becomes necessary to summarise the decisions, bearing in mind the principles already dealt with.

Maintenance or defeasance of security.

An agreement has been held reasonable and necessary for maintaining the security whereby the grantor agreed to pay all premiums for insuring and keeping insured the chattels against loss or damage by fire, and forthwith after every payment in respect of such insurance to produce,[b] and if required, deliver to the mortgagee the receipt or voucher for the same, the Court remarking that for payment of premiums a more stringent covenant than for payment of rent might reasonably be required.[c] So also a bill of sale was supported which permitted entry if the grantor should not, without reasonable excuse, upon demand in writing by the mortgagee, produce to him, amongst other things, the policy of insurance or the receipt for the current premium.[d] Nor, is a bill of sale void because it contains a covenant by the grantor to insure, and in default, that premiums paid under its powers by the mortgagee shall on demand be repaid by the grantor with interest, and until repayment shall be a charge on the mortgaged property;[e] and a bill of sale was upheld empowering the mortgagee on the mortgagor's default to pay all premiums, and to pay rent, rates, taxes, charges, assessments and outgoings which might become due and payable in respect of the premises in which the chattels might be, providing that all payments so made, together with interest at a named rate, should be a charge on the assigned chattels which should not

(a) Hughes v. Little, 18 Q. B. D. 32.
(b) Watkins v. Evans, 18 Q. B. D. 386; 56 L. J. Q. B. 200; 35 W. R. 313; 56 L. T. 177.
(c) Hammond v. Hocking, 12 Q. B. D. 291 ; 53 L. J. Q. B. 205 ; 50 L. T. 267.
(d) Duff v. Valentine, W. N. 1883, 225.
(e) Exp. Stanford, re Barber, 17 Q. B. D. 259 ; 55 L. J. Q. B. 341; 54 L. T. 894.

be redeemed until full payment, the mortgagor covenanting
to repay such payments with interest.[a]

Again, a bill of sale was supported containing an agreement
that the grantor should replace any chattels or things which
should be worn out with others of equal value;[b] and an
agreement by the grantor not to permit or suffer the chattels
to be destroyed or injured, or to deteriorate in a greater
degree than by reasonable wear and tear, and forthwith to
replace, repair, and make good the same was said to be in
accordance with the form.[c] So an agreement to keep the
chattels in good repair and in perfect working order and
insured, with power on default for the grantee to insure, repair
and keep the same in repair, and to enter on the premises, all
moneys expended by him for such purposes, with interest, to
be repaid by the grantor on demand, and in the meantime to
be a charge on the chattels, was held for the maintenance of the
security, and in accordance with the form, not being coupled
with any power to seize for breach or non-observance.[d]

At nisi prius a bill of sale was upheld whereby the
grantor agreed not to permit or suffer himself to be sued for
any debt or debts justly due or owing, nor permit or suffer
any writ of execution or distress to be levied against the
chattels assigned, nor any proceedings in bankruptcy to be
taken against him, nor to remove or suffer the chattels
assigned to deteriorate, except by reasonable use and wear,
and to replace them when deteriorated, to insure in a specified
office, with power to the mortgagee to add premiums paid to
his security, reserving a power of seizure on breach of any
of the covenants, which were thereby agreed as necessary for
maintaining the security.[e] This case appears inconsistent
with other authorities, and does not seem to have been
followed ; but it has again been decided that a bill of sale is
not invalidated by a power of seizure, in case the grantor
should do or suffer any matter or thing whereby he shall
become bankrupt, as such a power is in effect equivalent to the
provision of sec. 7, sub-sec. 2 ;[f] although a power of seizure

(a) Goldstrom v. Tallerman, 18 Q. B. D. 1.
(b) Seed v. Bradley [1894], 1 Q. B. 319 ; Consolidated Credit Corporation, re
Gosney, 16 Q. B. D. 24; 34 W. R. 106; 55 L. J. Q. B. 61; 54 L. T. 21.
(c) Furber v. Cobb, 18 Q. B. D. 494.
(d) Topley v. Corsbie, 20 Q. B. D. 350.
(e) Furber v. Abrey, 1 Cab. & E. 186.
(f) Exp. Allam, re Munday, 14 Q. B. D. 43 ; Exp. Pope, re Paxton, 60 L. T.
428.

if the grantor should take the benefit of any Bankruptcy Act was held not in accordance with the form, as conferring larger rights than those given by sec. 7, which limits the cause of seizure to the grantor becoming bankrupt, while the words used would include a composition. [a]

A covenant not to remove the goods from the premises without the consent of the mortgagee has been supported where not followed by any power to seize on breach,[b] and Sir James Hannen expressed an opinion that such a covenant, as well as an unqualified covenant to produce receipts for rent, rates and taxes on demand, might be necessary for the maintenance of the security.[c]   And it has again been decided that an agreement to produce receipts for rent, rates and taxes, without any exception for reasonable excuse, no express power of seizure being given for the breach of it, was for the maintenance of the security and in accordance with the scheduled form.[d]

There does not seem to be any objection to inserting such covenants for title as may be agreed upon by the parties, *Covenants for title.* thus a covenant for further assurance by the grantor for himself and all persons claiming through or under him has been supported ;[e] and although a wider form of covenant purporting to bind the grantor and every other person claiming any interest in the chattels was held to avoid the deed,[f] bills of sale containing such a form of covenant have been upheld.[g]

Subject to the provisions of sec. 13, the grantee of a bill of sale is entitled, when the bill of sale is in the exact statutory form, to seize and sell the goods in the event specified in sec. 7.[h]   Where there is no express power of sale the grantee may for the causes named in the section sell and give a good title to a purchaser, the mortgagor having at any time before sale a right to stop the sale and redeem the chattels on payment of the money due and expenses.[i]

There appears some difference of opinion as to the source

(a) Gilroy v. Bowey, 59 L. T. 223.
(b) Exp. Payne, re Coton, 4 Mor. 90.
(c) Furber v. Cobb, 18 Q. B. D. 494 ; Exp. Pope, re Paxton, 60 L. T. 425.
(d) Turner v. Culpan, 36 W. R. 278; 58 L. T. 340.
(e) Exp. Rawlings, re Cleaver, 18 Q. B. D. 489.
(f) Liverpool, &c., Society v. Richardson, 2 T. L. R. 602 ; 55 L. J. Q. B. 155 n.
(g) Sedwick v. Hillier, 21 S. J. 661.
(h) Watkins v. Evans, 18 Q. B. D. 386.
(i) Exp. Official Receiver, re Morritt, 18 Q. B. D. 222.

of this power of sale, some members of the Court of Appeal holding that the power of sale conferred by sec. 19 of the Conveyancing Act, 1881, applies, subject to the restrictions of sec. 20 of that Act and the provisions of the Bills of Sale Acts, except in cases where the nature of the security or the terms of the instrument shew that such implied power of sale is unnecessary.[a] On the other hand, opinions were expressed that the Conveyancing Act did not apply at all, and that the amendment Act, coupled with the statutory form, gave an implied power of sale.[b] The distinction is not without importance, as if the Conveyancing Act applied the power of sale would arise only after default as defined by sec. 20 of that Act, unless the operation of that section was excluded by the bill of sale, as might be done.[a] However, by the last decision on the subject, it would seem settled that the Conveyancing Act does not apply to bills of sale.[c]

Powers of sale. Although an implied power of sale exists, the form permits provisions to be added giving or regulating a power to enter, seize and sell the chattels,[a] provided they are not so framed as to mislead and do not alter the rights which the parties would otherwise have had. In the Appendix Part III., will be found forms of powers of sale upheld on appeal. The scheduled form is printed at page 260.

But a power to seize and sell on default in payment has been held bad as contrary to the provisions of sec. 13, the Court observing that there could have been no motive in inserting such an express power, except the desire to mislead the grantor.[d]

Nor can the parties agree that the mortgagee may have the chattels valued and purchase them at such valuation,[e] or that the mortgagee may affix to premises in the occupation of the grantor bills or placards having reference to the chattels assigned,[f] or that the mortgagees may retain their commission as auctioneers as if they were selling on behalf of the grantor.[g] But it has been held free from objection to give

(a) *Exp.* Official Receiver, *re* Morritt, 18 Q. B. D. 222.
(b) Watkins *v.* Evans, 18 Q. B. D. 386.
(c) Calvert *v.* Thomas, 19 Q. B. D. 204 ; 56 L. J. Q. B. 470 ; 35 W. R. 616.
(d) Hetherington *v.* Groome, 13 Q. B. D. 789
(e) Lyon *v.* Morris, 19 Q. B. D. 139 ; 56 L. T. 915.
(f) Bardell *v.* Daykin, 3 T L. R. 526.
(g) Furber *v.* Cobb, 18 Q. B. D. 494.

power to sell the goods by private treaty or public auction on or off the premises.[a]

A power of sale carries with it an implied trust of the purchase moneys;[b] and it has been decided that the clauses common in mortgages relieving the purchaser from being bound to see whether there has been a default cannot be inserted in bills of sale.[c] Indeed, a term that the receipt of the mortgagee should be a sufficient discharge to the purchaser, who should not be required to see to the application of the purchase money, has been said not to be in accordance with the form.[d]

The grantee of a bill of sale is entitled on selling to retain his proper costs and expenses, and it has been held admissible to stipulate that the grantee, after seizure, might retain out of the sale moneys, the costs of discharging any distraints execution, or incumbrance on the chattels, and of their removal, warehousing, valuing, or sale:[e] although an agreement that the grantee shall be at liberty to retain all expenses attending the sale or incurred in relation to the security,[f] or to which he may be put,[g] will avoid the deed, such clauses being too vague, and capable of including costs incurred before as well as after the execution of the bill of sale. Nor can the parties stipulate that after redemption the bill of sale shall remain in the custody and be the property of the mortgagee.[h]

It seems that a bill of sale omitting the proviso from the statutory form is void under this section.[i]

As before pointed out it is necessary that the name, *Attestation.* address, and description of the attesting witness should appear in the attestation clause on the face of the bill of sale, which otherwise will not be in accordance with the statutory form, thus the deed was held void where the attesting witness merely signed his name without adding address or description, although the affidavit filed on registration correctly described both :[j] and the same result followed where the

(a) Bourne r. Wall, 39 W. R. 510; 64 L. T. 530.

(b) Exp. Rawlings, re Cleaver, 18 Q. B. D. 489.

(c) Blaiberg r. Beckett, 18 Q. B. D. 96.

(d) Gibbs r. Parsons, L. J. N. 1887, 96.

(e) Exp. Official Receiver, re Morritt, 18 Q. B. D. 222.

(f) Calvert r. Thomas, 19 Q. B. D. 204; 56 L J. Q. B. 470; 35 W. R. 616.

(g) Macey v. Gilbert, 57 L. J. Q. B. 161.

(h) Watson r. Strickland, 19 Q. B. D. 391.

(i) Re Prideaux, per Hawkins, J. (MS. note) ; Thomas v. Kelly, 13 App. Cases, 519, per Lord Macnaghten.

(j) Parsons r. Brand, 25 Q. B. D. 110; Blankenstein r. Robertson, 24 Q. B. D. 543.

K

Sec. 1.
[1891.]

name and address of the witness were stated, but his occupation was omitted.[a] The address required to be stated may be the place of business of the witness, where he is ordinarily to be found, and need not be his private residence; *e.g.*, A.B., clerk to the D. Bank of London, 6, D. Street, Charing Cross.[b] Where there were three grantors, and two attestation clauses by the same witness, in the first of which he stated his name, address, and description, but in the second only signed his name, the deed was upheld, it appearing from the bill of sale itself that the two names were of the same person.[c] No defect in form can be supplied from the affidavit or by extraneous evidence, and if any evidence is necessary to shew that the name of the attesting witness in two attestation clauses is of the same person, he being described in one only, the deed will be void; but if on looking at the bill of sale there is an irresistible inference that the attesting witness is the same in each case, as for example, by comparison of handwriting, the form is complied with.[c]

In the Appendix Part III., will be found various clauses in bills of sale contested under the section.

Exemption of
securities on
imported goods
from 41 & 42
Vic. cap. 31,
and 45 & 46
Vic. c. 43.

1. (1891.) Section 1 of the Bills of Sale Act, 1890, shall be amended so as to read as follows: An instrument charging or creating any security on or declaring trusts of imported goods given or executed at any time prior to their deposit in a warehouse, factory, or store, or to their being reshipped for export, or delivered to a purchaser not being the person giving or executing such instrument, shall not be deemed a bill of sale within the meaning of the Bills of Sale Acts, 1878 and 1882.

A modification of the law respecting the instruments mentioned in the section was effected in consequence of an interpretation of the existing law which was said to create considerable difficulty in commercial transactions, holding certain documents bills of sale which were not intended to be within the operation of the Acts.

A Bill was accordingly introduced to exclude from the Bills of Sale Acts documents relating to goods between the

(a) Coulson *v.* Dickson, 25 Q. B. D. 110; 62 L. T. 479; 38 W. R. 388.
(b) Simmons *v.* Woodward [1892]. A.C. 100.
(c) Bird *v.* Davey [1891], 1 Q. B. 29.

time of their importation and warehousing or delivery to a
purchaser, in the same way that other documents used in
the ordinary course of business are excepted by sec. 4
of the principal Act from the definition of bill of sale.

But, as passed, the Bills of Sale Act, 1890, did not purport
to exclude instruments of the class mentioned from the operation of the Acts, and only provided that they should not be
deemed bills of sale within section 9 of the amendment Act.
To remedy this defect the Bills of Sale Act, 1891, was passed
on the 21st July, 1891, amending section 1 of the Act of
1890, and the excepted instruments are no longer to be
deemed bills of sale.[a]   By sec. 2, Bills of Sale Act, 1890,
nothing in the Act is to affect the operation of the reputed
ownership clause of the Bankruptcy Act.

10. (1882.) The execution of every bill of sale by Attestation.
the grantor shall be attested by one or more credible
witness or witnesses, not being a party or parties
thereto.   So much of section ten of the principal
Act as requires that the execution of every bill of
sale shall be attested by a solicitor of the Supreme
Court, and that the attestation shall state that before
the execution of the bill of sale the effect thereof
has been explained to the grantor by the attesting
witness, is hereby repealed.

Before the Bills of Sale Act, 1878, attestation was not
necessary,[b] but by sec. 8 of the amendment Act a bill of sale
is void unless duly attested; which means in the manner
required by the Act and form; thus the name, address and
description of the witness or witnesses must appear on the
face of the instrument.[c]   The repealed first sub-section of
sec. 10 of the Bills of Sale Act, 1878, introduced the formality
of attestation by a solicitor, and required him to state in the
attestation clause that he had explained the bill of sale to the
grantor.   In practice the presence of a solicitor was some
guarantee to the genuine character of the transaction, and the
object of the Legislature in abolishing such a sanction is not

(a) Section 1 Bills of Sale Act, 1890, will be found in the Appendix, page
261.
(b) Deffell v. Miles, 15 L. T. N. S. 293.
(c) Parsons v. Braud, 25 Q. B. D. 110.

k 2

176   THE BILLS OF SALE ACTS, 1878 AND 1882.

very clear, nor can the substitution of a credible witness be deemed altogether satisfactory. The words " credible witness " in the 5th section of the Statute of Frauds were held to mean such persons as were not disqualified by mental imbecility, interest, or crime, from giving testimony in a court of justice ; and as incompetency from crime or interest is abolished by 6 & 7 Vic. c. 85, it would appear that all persons of sane mind are credible witnesses. If, on the other hand, the literal meaning of the words is adopted considerable confusion must arise, for it is undoubtedly the province of the tribunal having cognizance of the cause, to determine whether the witnesses are credible, from their demeanour and other circumstances.

Before the provision in the section, it had been decided that a party to a bill of sale could not be an attesting witness.[a]

The repeal of sub-sec. 1 of sec. 10 of the principal Act would seem limited to bills of sale to which the amendment Act applies.[b]   Bills of sale given otherwise than by way of security for the payment of money, should still therefore be attested with the formalities prescribed by the principal Act.[c]

Mode of registering and attesting bills of sale.

10. (1878.) A bill of sale shall be attested and registered under this Act in the following manner :

> (1.) The execution of every bill of sale shall be attested by a solicitor of the Supreme Court, and the attestation shall state that before the execution of the bill of sale the effect thereof has been explained to the grantor by the attesting solicitor.[d]

This sub-section is repealed by sec. 10 of the amendment Act, but the repeal would seem to be qualified by sec. 3 ;[e] and bills of sale given otherwise than to secure the payment of money still require attestation in the prescribed manner.[f]

(a) Seal v. Claridge, 7 Q. B. D. 516.

(b) Swift v. Pannell, 24 Ch. D. 210.

(c) Casson v. Churchley, 53 L. J. Q. B. 335 ; 50 L. T. 568.

(d) The following is suggested as a form of attestion :—

Signed, sealed and delivered by the said grantor, A. B., in my presence ; the effect of the above-written bill of sale having been explained to the said grantor before his execution thereof, by me, the attesting solicitor.

C. D., (Address),
A Solicitor of the Supreme Court of Judicature.

(e) Swift v. Pannell, 24 Ch. D. 210.

(f) Casson v. Churchley 53 L. J. Q. B. 335.

As to this class of bills of sale, the sub-section is to be read as
included in and incorporated with sec. 8 of the principal Act;
therefore, unless the prescribed form of attestation is followed,
such bills of sale will be invalid against the persons named in
the latter section, but valid as between the grantor and
grantee.[a] It is, however, only required that the attestation
clause should state that the effect of the deed has been
explained by the solicitor; thus, that the grantor has been
fully informed of the nature and effect of the bill of sale, was
held sufficient,[b] and it is not necessary by the section
that the explanation should in fact have been given;
indeed, if such explanation was necessary, sec. 8 of the
principal Act does not make the bill of sale void against any
one by reason of the omission; but it would seem that a
solicitor attesting that he had given an explanation, where
in fact he had not done so, would be liable to be struck off
the rolls.[c]

The provisions as to attestation and explanation of bills   *Attestation by
of sale by a solicitor were inserted not merely for the grantor's   Solicitor.*
benefit but for the protection of creditors, as a guarantee of
the genuine character of the transaction and as a security
against fraud.[d]

Before the amendment introduced by this sub-section the
law interfered to protect a person who had by misplaced confidence been induced to sign a document by which he was
injuriously affected; thus, where a mortgagor, a man in
humble circumstances and without legal advice, conveyed the
mortgaged property to his solicitor, it was held that the deed
was invalid, unless all the circumstances had been explained to
the mortgagor, and that the onus of proving this rested on the
solicitor.[e] And where a money lender advertised loans on
easy terms, at five per cent., but charged more than cent. per
cent. in the bill of sale, the borrower's denial of any knowledge
of an increase in the rate of interest was said to throw on the
bill of sale holder the onus of showing that he had clearly
explained to the borrower the terms on which the loan was
made.[f]

(a) Davis v. Goodman, 19 L. J. C. P. 344.
(b) Corkhill v. Lambert, 70 L. T. J. 46.
(c) *Exp.* National Mercantile Bank, *re* Haynes, 28 W. R. 848; Hill v. Kirkwood, 28 W. R. 358.
(d) Davis v. Goodman, 19 L. J. C. P. 344.
(e) Prees v. Coke, L. R. 6 Ch. 645.
(f) Moorhouse v. Woolfe, 46 L. T. 374; cf. Helsham v. Barnett, 21 W. R. 309.

It would seem immaterial that the attestation is by an uncertificated solicitor,[a] and a bill of sale was held sufficiently attested within the meaning of the sub-section, although the attesting solicitor did not practise on his own account and was managing clerk of the solicitors who acted generally for the grantee.[b] Indeed, the Act does not seem to require the presence of an independent solicitor, thus the solicitor for the grantee, who had prepared the bill of sale, may attest it,[c] and the attestation of a solicitor acting for both parties was held sufficient.[d] It was, however, held by the Court of Appeal, affirming the decision of Huddleston, B., that a party to the deed could not attest it. and therefore attestation of a bill of sale by the grantee, although a solicitor, was invalid.[e] The principle of this decision has been adopted in sec. 10 of the amendment Act. which provides that a party to the bill of sale shall not be an attesting witness.

Registration of bill of sale.

(2.) Such bill, with every schedule or inventory thereto annexed or therein referred to, and also a true copy of such bill and of every such schedule or inventory, and of every attestation of the execution of such bill of sale, together with an affidavit of the time of such bill of sale being made or given, and of its due execution and attestation,[1] and a description of the residence and occupation of the person making or giving the same (or in case the same is made or given by any person under or in execution of any process, then a description of the residence and occupation of the person against whom such process issued), and of every attesting witness to such bill of sale,[2] shall be presented to and the said copy and affidavit shall be filed with the registrar

(1) Page 179.

(2) Page 181.

(a) Holgate v. Slight, 21 L. J. Q. B. 74; 2 L. M. & P. 662.
(b) Hill v. Kirkwood, 28 W. R. 358.
(c) Penwarden v. Roberts, 30 W. R. 427; 46 L. T. 161; 51 L. J. Q. B. 312; 9 Q. B. D. 137.
(d) Vernon v. Cooke, 49 L. J. C. P. 767.
(e) Seal v. Claridge, 7 Q. B. D. 516.

within seven clear days after the making or
giving of such bill of sale, in like manner as
a warrant of attorney in any personal action
given by a trader is now by law required to
be filed : (3)

(1) The true copy required by the section is a copy which is
essentially true, thus the copy may be sufficient though containing errors, if no one can be misled as to its effect, and where
in passages in the copy, including the power of sale, the principal sum was referred to as "the said sum of £   ,"
which blanks were not in the original, the copy was held a
true copy.[a] Nor will a mere clerical error in the copy
invalidate registration ; as for instance the mis-spelling of a
name,[b] or the omission of a few words from the filed copy,
where it is clear from the context that no one could be misled,[c]
or an obvious mistake in the date, as where in the affidavit
1806 was inserted as the date of execution for 1876,[d] or consideration, as where £1,000 was inserted instead of £100,[e]
and where a bill of sale was executed on the 31st of December,
1860, and the jurat of the affidavit purported to have been
sworn on the 10th of January, 1860, it was held that the
defect, being a mere clerical error, might be amended.[f]

Requisites of
copy bill of sale
and affidavit.

It was formerly sufficient to state that the bill of sale was
given on the date of execution, although the consideration
money was not then paid.[g] The true date of execution must
be given, but an error in date will not be material if it
is one which is obviously a mistake, and can be corrected from
the affidavit itself ; and the requirements of the section will
be complied with if the affidavit states that the bill of sale was
executed on the day it bears date.[h] The execution of a bill
of sale at the foot of a schedule annexed to it has been held
sufficient.[i]

Where the schedule to a bill of sale described certain
articles by number "as per catalogue," it was held that the

(a) Sharp e. Brown, Sharp e. McHenry, 57 L. T. 698 ; 38 Ch. D. 427.
(b) Gardner e. Shaw, 19 W. R. 753 ; 24 L. T. 319 ; Corbett e. Rowe, 25 W. R. 59.
(c) Exp. Kahen, re Hewer, 21 C. D. 871 ; Exp. McHattie, re Wood, 10 Ch. D. 398.
(d) Lamb v. Bruce, 45 L. J. Q. B. 538 ; 24 W. R. 645 ; 35 L. T. 425.
(e) Elliott e. Freeman, 7 L. T. N. S. 715.
(f) Hollingsworth e. White, 10 W. R. 619.
(g) Darvill e. Terry, 6 H. & N. 807 ; 30 L. J. Ex. 335.
(h) Lamb e. Bruce, 35 L. T. 425.
(i) Melville e. Stringer, 12 Q. B. D. 132.

section treated the schedule as something distinct from the
bill of sale, and the catalogue being only referred to in the
schedule, and not in the bill of sale itself, did not require
registration.[a]

The affidavit, which should comply with the provisions of
the rules[b] must be filed at the same time as the bill of sale,[c]
and state the due execution and attestation of the bill of sale
in the prescribed manner, but it is not an objection that the
deponent speaks only to his belief.[d]

But if the affidavit is by reason of a material omission
incomplete on the face of it, registration has been held
defective, as, for example, where the Commissioner's name
was not signed to the jurat, the Court, holding that the
powers given by O. XXXVIII., R. 14, to receive irregular
affidavits did not cure the defect.[e]

Affidavit of attestation.   Questions have arisen under sub-sec. 1 of this section as to
the sufficiency of the affidavit of due attestation under the
principal Act, and it has been held that it must state from the
knowledge of the person who made the oath, that the bill of
sale was executed by the grantor in the presence of the
person attesting its execution, nor is it sufficient to verify
his signature to the attestation clause ; thus, an affidavit
was held insufficient in which the deponent stated that he was
present and saw the grantor execute the bill of sale, the
effect thereof having been first explained to him by the
person, whose handwriting he verified, as it did not swear
that the solicitor was present when the bill of sale was
executed.[f] And so was a similar affidavit, which stated in
addition that the deponent was one of the attesting witnesses,
and that the name of the solicitor set and subscribed as the
other witness attesting the execution was in his handwriting.[g]

It was not, however, necessary in so many words to state
that the solicitor attested, and it was sufficient if this could be
inferred from the whole affidavit ;[h] and it was held that the

(a) Davidson v. Carlton Bank [1893], 1 Q. B. 82.

(b) See notes to sec. 17 (1878).

(c) Grindell v. Brendon, 6 C. B. N. S. 698; 28 L. J. C. P. 333 ; 7 W. R. 579.

(d Roe v. Bradshaw, L. R. 1 Ex. 106; 35 L. J. Ex. 71 ; 14 W. R. 284 ; 14 L. T.
641.

(e) Brown v. London & County Advance Co., 5 T. L. R. 199.

(f) Ford v. Kettle, 9 Q. B. D. 139 ; 30 W. R. 741; 46 L. T. 667; 51 L. J. Q. B.
558; Sharpe v. Birch, 8 Q. B. D. 111 ; 51 L. J. Q. B. 64; 45 L. T. 780; 30 W. R. 428.

(g) Exp. Knightley, re Moulson, 30 W. R. 844; 46 L. T. 776; 51 L. J. Ch. 823.

(h) Yates v. Ashcroft, 47 L. T. 337; 31 W. R. 156.

whole affidavit might be read together, in order to collect proof of due execution and attestation; thus although an affidavit of execution did not in terms state that the attesting solicitor was present when the bill of sale was executed, but did state that the deponent was present, and that the bill of sale was duly attested, and that he and the attesting solicitor were the only attesting witnesses, verifying the handwriting and giving the proper description of the parties, it was held sufficient. [a]

In one of the first cases under the principal Act, it was held sufficient to depose to an attestation clause stating that the bill of sale had been explained to the grantor without repeating the statement in the affidavit; [b] and subsequently it was decided that the affidavit need not state that any explanation had been given. [c]

An affidavit of execution by the attesting solicitor under the principal Act was not invalid because sworn before his partner; [d] but now no affidavit is sufficient if sworn before the solicitor acting for the party on whose behalf the affidavit is to be used, or any agent or correspondent of such solicitor; and any affidavit which would be insufficient if sworn before the solicitor himself, will be insufficient if sworn before his clerk or partner. [e] Unless it is shewn that the person before whom the affidavit purports to be sworn had not jurisdiction, the Court will presume that he had; [f] thus, where the person before whom the affidavit was sworn, omitted in the jurat to describe himself as a commissioner, the Court of Appeal, in the absence of proof that he was not a commissioner, admitted the affidavit notwithstanding the omission. [g]

(2) The affidavit must contain such a description of the residence and occupation of the grantor at the time of registering the bill of sale, [h] that creditors and others interested may know that the person giving the bill of sale is the person with whom they have been dealing; in fact, the description must be such as to enable the party to make such investiga-

Description of grantor and attesting witness.

(a) Cooper c. Zeffert, 32 W. R. 402.
(b) Exp. Carter, re Threappleton, 12 Ch. D. 908.
(c) Exp. Bolland, re Roper, 21 Ch. D. 543.
(d) Vernon c. Cooke, 49 L. J. C. P. 767.
(e) R. S. C., 1883, O. xxxviii, 16, 17.
(f) Cheney c. Courtois 32 L. J. C. P. 116; 13 C. B. N. S. 634; 9 Jur. N. S. 1057; 7 L. T. N. S. 680.
(g) Exp. Johnson, re Chapman, 26 Cb. D. 338.
(h) Button v. O'Neill, 4 C. P. D. 354; 48 L. J. C. P. 368; 27 W. R. 502; 40 L. T. 709. This case overrules on this point London & Westminster Loan Co. v. Chase, 10 W. R. 698; 12 C. B. N. S. 730; and the authorities deciding that the description required is that at the time of making or giving the bill of sale.

tions as would be necessary for his protection before he either advanced money or supplied goods on credit.[a] When between the execution of the bill of sale and the date of registration the grantor absconded, it was held to be sufficient to describe his residence as given in the bill of sale.[b]

The object in requiring a description of the residence and occupation of the attesting witness is, that any person having an interest in making inquiries as to the goods of another with whom he is about to deal, or to issue or act upon process of execution against them, should be able to apply to the attesting witness for information for the purpose of making any necessary inquiries to guide his conduct;[c] and that information, it is intended, should be furnished to him by the affidavit, coupled, in case of any ambiguity, with the copy bill of sale, to which the inquirer also has access. A description ought to be held sufficient if an ordinary person, by ordinary inquiry and the exercise of ordinary intelligence, can ascertain where he will find the object of his search.[d]

Description in the affidavit. Such description of the residence and occupation of the grantor and attesting witness must be given in the affidavit either expressly or by direct reference to the bill of sale verifying the description there given; nor did the principal Act require that the bill of sale itself should contain any description, though it has been decided under the amendment Act that a bill of sale to be in accordance with the form in the schedule, must state in the attestation clause on the face the instrument the name, address, and description of the attesting witness or witnesses.

The section it will be observed requires that an affidavit of the description of the residence and occupation of the person making or giving the bill of sale, and of every attesting witness, should be filed together with the bill of sale; and where with a bill of sale containing a proper description was filed an affidavit stating the time when the bill of sale was made, but silent as to any description of the grantor or attesting witness, it was held that the section was not complied with;[f] although if the affidavit states the bill of sale

(a) Jones v. Harris, L. R. 7 Q. B. 157; 41 L. J. Q. B. 6; 20 W. R. 143. 25 L. T. 702; Murray v. Mackenzie, L. R. 10 C. P. 625; 23 W. R. 595; 32 L. T. 777.

(b) Exp. Kahen, re Hewer, 46 L. T. 856.

(c) Lamb v. Bruce, 45 L. J. Q. B. 538; 24 W. R. 645; 35 L. T. 425.

(d) Blount v. Harris, 48 L. J. Q. B. 159; 27 W. R. 202; 39 L. T. 465; 4 Q. B. D. 603.

(e) Parsons v. Brand, 25 Q. B. D. 110.

(f) Hatton v. English, 26 L. J. Q. B. 161; 7 E. & B. 94; 3 Jur. N. S. 294.

to have been made between the parties residing at the places
and of the occupations mentioned in it, or if it recites the
bill of sale, following the description of the parties given
therein, although not in terms verifying them, it will be
sufficient.[a]

If the affidavit contains no description, or if the bill of sale
and affidavit differ, the bill of sale cannot be used to supply
the defect,[b] but where the description given in the affidavit
is merely ambiguous, and the identity of the party is
not fixed by reason of such ambiguity, the bill of sale
may be referred to in order to explain and supplement the
description in the affidavit. Thus, where the affidavit described the grantor as residing at "Dynevor Lodge," and
deposed that the paper writing thereto annexed was a true
copy of the bill of sale, in which a full and proper description
was given, it was held that although the description in the
affidavit, if taken alone, was clearly insufficient, the defect
might be cured by reference to the bill of sale;[c] and so,
where an attesting witness was insufficiently described in his
affidavit, the description was allowed to be supplemented by
that contained in the attestation clause of the bill of sale
which had been verified by the affidavit;[d] indeed it would
seem that under the Act of 1854 the affidavit was sufficient if,
on comparison with the bill of sale, it appeared to have been
made by the attesting witness, although not expressly stating
that the deponent was the attesting witness.[e]

Where the affidavit gave a sufficient description of the
witness in the introductory part, but the description was left
blank in the body of the affidavit, registration was supported
by the Queen's Bench Division; North, J., holding that a
description in the introductory part was sufficient, and
Manisty, J., deciding on the ground that the attestation
clause, which properly described the witness, was incorporated
with the affidavit by which it was verified.[f]

If, however, the description in the affidavit is not merely
insufficient, but untrue or mis-stated, the defect cannot be

Margin note: Description in the affidavit.

(a) Foulger v. Taylor, 5 H. & N. 202; 29 L. J. Ex. 151; 1 L. T. N. S. 57; Banbury v. White, 2 H. & C. 300; Shadden v. Serjeant, 1 F. & F. 323.

(b) Pickard v. Bretz, 5 H. & N. 9; 20 L. J. Ex. 18; 8 W. R. 90; 1 L. T. N. S. 45.

(c) Jones v. Harris, L. R. 7 Q. B. 157; Thorpe v. Brown, L. R. 2 H. L. 220; 15
W. R. 1146.

(d) Exp. Mackenzie, re Bent, 12 L. J. Bank 25; 28 L. T. 480.

(e) Routh v. Roublot, 1 E. & E. 850; 28 L. J. Q. B. 240.

(f) Blaiberg v. Parke, 10 Q. B. D. 90; 31 W. R. 248; 52 L. J. Q. B. 110; 48 L. T.
311; and see Blackwell v. England, 8 E. & B. 541; 27 L. J. Q. B. 124.

cured by reference to the bill of sale, and so it was held where, in the attestation clause, the witness subscribed himself clerk to a solicitor, but in the affidavit was described as a gentleman.[a]

Residence. The residence to be described is the place where a person resides at the time of registering the bill of sale, which, for the purposes of the section, is the place where he is most likely to be found; thus, it may be his place of business; [b] or, if a clerk, his employer's place of business. [c] If the attesting witness is described as of his employer's address where he is personally employed, where anybody can find him and make inquiries, such address is sufficient, though it would probably be otherwise if he was never to be found there. [d] The particularity required in the description is a question of degree, depending on the circumstances of the case, [e] the object being the identification of the parties; thus, in some cases probably the street and even the number of the house would be necessary; and a mis-statement of the number, calculated to mislead, has been held fatal. [f] The description "of the City of Cork," has been held too general, [g] but where a witness was described as of Hanley, in the County of Stafford, it being proved that hundreds of letters had reached the witness with the address of Hanley alone, it was held that the description was sufficient. [h] So the description " A. B., Clerk to C. D., Aldershot," was upheld, it being proved that letters addressed "A. B., Aldershot," reached him through the post. [i]

Bacon, V.-C., is reported to have held that if a person has two residences, both should be described; but the decision appears to have turned on the facts of the case, in which the grantor was a railway contractor, engaged at the time in the construction of a railway at Bury, in Lancashire, with business chambers at Westminster, and a private residence at Kilburn. The Vice-Chancellor held insufficient the description of the

(a) Brodrick *r.* Scale, L. R. 6 C. P. 98; 40 L. J. C. P. 130   19 W. R. 366; 23 L. T. 864; Murray *r.* Mackenzie, L. R. 10 C. P. 625.

(b) Hewer *v.* Cox, 30 L. J. Q. B. 73; 9 W. R. 143; 6 Jur. N. S. 1339; 3 L. T. 508.

(c) Attenborough *r.* Thompson, 2 H. & N. 559; 27 L. J. Ex. 23; Blackwell *r.* England, 8 E. & B. 541.

(d) Simmons *r.* Woodward (1892), A. C. 100.

(e) Briggs *v.* Boss, L. R. 3 Q. B. 270; 37 L. J. Q. B. 101; 16 W. R. 480; Gardner *r.* Smart, 1 Cab. & El. 14.

(f) Murray *r.* Mackenzie, L. R. 10 C. P. 625.

(g) *Re* Hams, 10 Ir. Ch. 100; 1 L. T. N. S. 467.

(h) Briggs *r.* Boss, L. R. 3 Q. B. 270.

(i) Hickley *c.* Greenwood, 59 L. T. 137.

grantor as "residing at No. 1, Westminster Chambers, Victoria Street, in the County of Middlesex, Railway Contractor."[a]

In another case, in which the description was upheld, the Residence. proprietor of a travelling circus, then at Southampton, gave a bill of sale over his circus property, describing himself as of a London address, "now carrying on business at Southampton," he not having resided at the London address for six years, but being the owner of the house, which he permitted a relative to occupy;[b] and so where the grantor was described as of his residence, "stone merchant and quarry owner," it was held sufficient, although he carried on business as lessee of stone quarries at other places.[c] Indeed, where the grantor of a bill of sale is otherwise rightly described, the omission of some other description, unless proved to have been intended or calculated to deceive, or which did in fact deceive, will not invalidate the bill of sale;[d] thus in most cases it would seem sufficient, when a person has two or more addresses, to describe him as of the principal one, for if the bill of sale contains a description of the residence of the grantor, the Act is literally complied with, and the Court has no power to enlarge it. So where a bill of sale described the grantor as of three places, at which were the goods assigned, but the affidavit mentioned as his residence one place only where he lived and carried on his chief business, the others being branch establishments, the description of residence in the affidavit was held sufficient;[e] nor is a bill of sale void for omitting to describe the place where the goods assigned are situate.[f]

When a bill of sale is executed by two grantors, one only of whom is in possession of the goods, it is not sufficient that the affidavit contains a description of such one only who is so in possession.[g]

In another case, however, a bill of sale described the grantors, father and son, by their true addresses, adding that they were both mantle manufacturers, carrying on business together under a specified style. They had formerly carried

(a) Wallis v. Smith, W. N. 1882, p. 77; cf. re Fitzpatrick, 10 L. R. Ir. 206.
(b) Cooper v. Ibberson, 20 W. R. 566; 41 L. T. 309.
(c) Exp. Knightly, re Moulson, 51 L. J. Ch. 823.
(d) Throssell v. Marsh, 53 L. T. 321.
(e) Greenham v. Child, 24 Q. B. D. 29. 59 L. J. Q. B. 47; 38 W. R. 91, 61 L. T. 563.
(f) Exp. Hull, re Lane, 17 Q. B. D. 71; 3 Mor. 148
(g) Hooper v. Parmenter, 10 W. R. 648.

on that business, but at the time of the execution of the bill of sale the partnership had been dissolved, and the business was carried on by the father alone, the son being in his employment as clerk. The property comprised in the deed belonged to the father alone, though both father and son joined in the assignment ; and as against the trustee in the father's bankruptcy, it was held that there was no misdescription—firstly, because the son, not being a bankrupt, any misdescription of him was immaterial ; and, secondly, the statement that the father carried on business with his son was not misleading and might be rejected as mere surplusage.[a] A Company is sufficiently described by its incorporated name as of its principal office.[b]

Occupation. Occupation means the principal business of one's life, vocation. trade, calling ; the business which a man follows to procure a living or obtain wealth : [c] thus, if a man has any office or occupation, "esquire" or "gentleman" is not a sufficient description ; [d] and such a description has been held improper of the lessee and manager of a theatre,[e] or of a person who obtained orders on commission, and was a commercial traveller ; [f] and to describe a spirit retailer as a "trader" has been held too general,[g] but the description in a petition for liquidation of a farmer as a "cattle dealer" has been held sufficient.[h] A merchant, [i] which term has been held to include a person who was a shipbroker and coal merchant,[j] a contractor and financial agent,[k] a government clerk, an insurance clerk,[l] a silk buyer,[m] a law clerk,[n] a schoolmaster,[o] a solicitor,[p] or his clerk,[q] must be

(a) *Exp.* Popplewell, *re* Storey, 21 Ch. D. 73.

(b) Shears *v.* Jacob, L. R. 1 C. P. 513 ; 35 L. J. C. P. 241 ; 14 W. R. 609 ; 14 L. T. 264.

(c) Tuton *v.* Sanoner, 3 H. & N. 263 ; 27 L. J. Ex. 293 ; 6 W. R. 545.

(d) Brodrick *v.* Scalè, L. R. 6 C. P. 98 ; Allen *v.* Thompson, 25 L. J. Ex. 249 ; 1 H. & N. 15 ; 4 W. R. 506 ; 2 Jur. N. S. 451 ; Adams *v.* Graham, 33 L. J. Q. B. 71. 12 W. R. 282 ; 9 L. T. 606 ; 10 Jur. N. S. 356.

(e) *Exp.* Hooman, *re* Vining, L. R. 10 Eq. 63 ; 39 L. J. Bank, 4 ; 18 W. R. 150.

(f) Matthews *v.* Buchanan, 5 T. L. R. 373.

(g) James *v.* Macken, L. T. J. 1879, p. 139.

(h) *Exp.* Kirkwood, *re* Mason, 27 W. R. 806 ; 11 Ch. D. 724 ; 40 L. T. 566.

(i) *Re* O'Connor, 27 L. T. O. S. 27.

(j) Gugen *v.* Sampson, 4 F. & F. 974.

(k) Sharp *v.* McHenry, 38 Ch. D. 427.

(l) Grant *v.* Shaw, L. R. 7 Q. B. 700 ; 41 L. J. Q. B. 305 ; 27 L. T. 602.

(m) Adams *v.* Graham, 33 L. J. Q. B. 71.

(n) M'Cue *v.* James, 19 W. R. 158.

(o) Lee *v.* Turner, 20 Q. B. D. 773.

(p) Tuton *v.* Sanoner, 27 L. J. Ex. 293.

(q) Dryden *v.* Hope, 9 W. R. 18 ; Brodrick *v.* Scalè, L. R. 6 C. P. 98 ; Beales *v.* Tennant, 29 L. J. Q. B. 188 ; 1 L. T. 295 : 6 Jur. N. S. 628.

described as such, but in describing a clerk it is unnecessary to state his master's occupation. *   When in an affidavit
of execution the attesting witness was described as an
accountant, being in fact clerk to an accountant, the business
being managed by the deponent, who was allowed occasionally to do accountant's business on his own account, the
name of the principal being over the door, it was held that
the affidavit contained a sufficient description of the
witness's occupation,[b] but where the grantor of a bill of sale,
described as an accountant, was a clerk in the accountant's department at the Euston Station of the London and North-
Western Railway, and in his leisure time was occasionally
employed to balance tradesmen's books, the description was
held insufficient.[c]

But the Act does not require that in the description of Occupation.
occupation details should be given of every way in which the
grantor may occupy himself, or of every undertaking
involving a liability in which he is interested; thus a grantor,
who led the life of a country gentleman, occupying himself in
the ordinary avocations of country life, and was a sleeping
partner in several businesses, in none of which he took an
active part, though his name appeared in connection with
some of them, was held sufficiently described as of Kings-
down House, Sittingbourne, in the county of Kent, a gentleman, of no occupation.[d]   And so a woman who carried on a
farm which had belonged to her deceased husband, merely as
his executrix, and not with a view to taking permanently
to it, and had no other occupation, was held sufficiently
described as a widow.[e]   And it was held unnecessary to
describe as of any occupation a married woman who was
the leaseholder of a public house, the licence for which was
taken out in her husband's name, he conducting the
business.[f]   In another case, the grantor was described
as a widow, about to remove to a hotel named in the
bill of sale.   It appeared that she had been a licensed
victualler for several years until about a month previous,

(a) Lamb v. Bruce, 45 L. J. Q. B. 53s.
(b) Briggs v. Boss, L. R. 3 Q. B. 268.
(c) Larchin v. North-Western Deposit Bank, L. R. 10 Ex. 64; 42 L. J. Ex. 134
23 W. R. 325 ; 28 L. T. 350.
(d) Feast v. Robinson, 70 L. T. 108; 63 L. J. Ch. 321 ; 8 Rep. 191.
(e) Luckin v. Hamlyn, 21 L. T. 366 ; 18 W. R. 43.
(f) Usher v. Martin, 61 L. T. 778.

and intended to, and shortly afterwards did resume that occupation, but the Court of Appeal held that her description as a widow was sufficient, and that it is unnecessary to state any former or future occupation.[a]

If the principal occupation is stated, it would seem the section is satisfied: thus, where a grantor carried on two distinct occupations, of which only one was described, it was held that the grantor being otherwise rightly described, the omission of some other description which was not intended or likely, nor in fact did deceive, would not invalidate the deed.[b] So when a foreman tailor's cutter, who took in lodgers at his house, where his wife also kept a boarding school, was described as a foreman tailor's cutter, the description was held sufficient, that being his substantive occupation; [c] and a farmer who had been in the habit of discounting bills was held sufficiently described as a farmer, without adding bill discounter to his description; but if farming had not been his substantive occupation, as, for instance, if he merely farmed for amusement, it seems it would have been otherwise.[d] It has, however, been decided in the Irish Courts that all businesses must be described, and a widow possessed of a farm, and also trading as a grocer and licensed vintner, was held insufficiently described as widow and farmer.[e]

Occupation.

A peer may be described by his title,[f] and "gentleman" will be a sufficient description of one who was of no occupation at the time of registering the bill of sale, or who had never been engaged in any regular occupation,[g] if such an addition is not so far inapplicable to the rank of society in which he moves as to mislead; for all that the Act means is, that if the party has an occupation he must state it; it does not mean that if he has none he must expressly say so; thus an attesting witness, who had been a proctor's managing clerk, but had ceased to be so for six years, since which time he had, on a few occasions, collected debts and written letters for other persons and had drawn bills of sale, but had no regular occupation

(a) *Exp.* Chapman, *re* Davey, 45 L. T. 268.
(b) Throssell *v.* Marsh, 53 L. T. 321.
(c) *Exp.* National Deposit Bank, *re* Wills, 26 W. R. 624.
(d) *Exp.* National Mercantile Bank, *re* Haynes, 28 W. R. 848.
(e) *Re* Fitzpatrick, 19 L. R. Ir. 206.
(f) *Re* Earl of Limerick, 7 Ir. Jur. N. S. 65.
(g) Gray *v.* Jones, 14 C. B. N. S. 743.

was held properly described as gentleman;[a] and so was a
medical student who had only temporarily acted as sur-
geon's assistant;[b] and where in the affidavit a blank was left
for the description of the occupation of the attesting witness,
which had not been filled in, but it appeared he had been without
occupation for some years past, the registration was supported.[c]

There is nothing in the Act which requires a son, bearing Names of grantor and grantee.
the same name as his father, to describe himself as the
" younger " in a bill of sale and affidavit;[d] indeed, under the
principal Act a mistake as to the grantor's name was immaterial, as the section makes no provision for the name,
merely requiring a description of the residence and occupation;[e] and a description by an assumed name by which the
party is known is sufficient; though if a grantee, in order to
mislead creditors, knowingly takes a bill of sale in a name by
which the grantor is not generally known, the deed would it
seems be fraudulent and void.[f]   It is now necessary that
the grantee's name and description should be given in the
bill of sale, but the Act does not avoid a bill of sale because
of ambiguity in the grantee's name, [g] and a bill of sale
given to a grantee in his trade name is valid.[h]   It would
seem that the statement of the grantor's name, also, may be
of importance, having regard to the scheduled form.

In an affidavit of registration of a bill of sale by husband
and wife, the grantors were described as Alfred Salmon and
Edith Campbell Salmon, his wife. The husband's true name was
George Henry Arthur Salmon, and the misdescription was
purposely made by both grantors in order to conceal the fact
that they had given a bill of sale, but the registration was
upheld.   In giving judgment, Field, J., observed that it
would be giving too broad a construction to hold that the
provisions of the section were meant to include a correct

(a) Smith v. Cheese, 45 L. J. C. P. 156; 1 C. P. D. 60; 24 W. R. 368; 33 L. T. 670

(b) Sutton v. Bath, 1 F. & F. 152.

(c) Exp. Young, re Symonds, 42 L. T. 744; 28 W. R. 021.

(d) Foulger v. Taylor, 1 L. T. N. S. 57.

(e) Exp. M'Hattie, re Wood, 10 Ch. D. 398; 39 L. T. 373; 27 W. R. 327; 48 L. J. Bank. 26.

(f) Central Bank v. Hawkins, 62 L. T. 901.

(g) Simmons v. Woodward [1892], A. C. 100.

(h) Monson v. Milner, 8 T. L. R. 447.

statement of the grantor's christian name.[a]   But it is otherwise if a mis-statement of christian name is coupled with
misdescription of occupation; and when the grantor of a
bill of sale was described as Kendrick Turner, tutor, his
name, in fact, being Frederick Henry Turner, and his occupation that of a schoolmaster, registration was held to be
avoided.[b]

Occupation.

Care should be taken to describe the occupation followed
at the time of registering the bill of sale; [c] for though no
former or proposed occupation need, it seems, be stated, [d]
where the grantor was described as " until lately a commercial
town traveller and agent," it was held that his occupation at
the time of registration was not sufficiently described; [e] and
so where the grantor, who had formerly carried on a wine, spirit
and general business as sole owner under the style of a Supply
Association, was described as so carrying on business under
such style—he in fact for some months having ceased to
be owner, or to have any share in the business, where he
remained only as paid manager under the supervision of the
person whose property the business had become— the occupation was held mis-described, although the licences were taken
out in the grantor's name, which still appeared over the shop.[f]
But if the description gives a true indication of the grantor's
calling, by which he can be identified, that is a sufficient
compliance, though he may not be actively following that
calling at the time of registration, as, for example, the
description of the grantor as contractor and financial agent, he
for five years having ceased to actively carry on business;[g]
or as a commercial clerk, he having for some weeks been out
of employ; for the Act requires the grantor's ordinary occupation to be stated, though at the moment he may be out of
employ.[h]

What
misdescription
invalidates.

In every case the test will be, is the misdescription one
that is calculated to deceive creditors, [i] and the burden of

(a) Downs v. Salmon, 20 Q.B.D. 775; 36 W. R. 810; 57 L. J. Ch. 454; 59 L. T. 375.
(b) Lee v. Turner, 20 Q. B. D. 773; 59 L.T. 320.
(c) Button v. O'Neill, 4 C. P. D. 354.
(d) Exp. Chapman, re Davey, 45 L. T. 268.
(e) Castle v. Downton, 5 C. P. D. 56; 41 L. T. 528; 49 L. J. C. P. 6.
(f) Cooper v. Davis, 48 L. T. 831; (C.A.) 32 W. R. 329.
(g) Sharp v. McHenry 38 Ch. D. 427.
(h) Martinson v. Consolidated, &c., Co., 5 T. L. R. 353.
(i) Exp. M'Hattie, re Wood, 10 Ch. D. 308; 39 L. T. 373; 48 L. J. Bank. 26.

proof is on the person seeking to shew that the residence or
occupation of the grantor or witness is other than described.[a]
If the description is substantially correct, so that creditors
would not be misled, an erroneous addition, as of a wrong
county, will not vitiate the bill of sale,[b] and the sufficiency
of the description must depend on the circumstances of each
case, and is a question for the judge and not for the jury.[c]

When there are two attesting witnesses, the bill of sale
will be invalid unless both are described in the affidavit;[d]
but where a bill of sale was executed under the common seal
of a trading Company, and opposite the seal were set the
names of two of the Directors, who purported to sign as
Directors, and the document was countersigned by the Secretary, who in the affidavit of execution stated that he saw the
bill of sale sealed with the seal of the Company, and countersigned by two of the Directors whose signatures appeared
subscribed thereto, the affidavit was held sufficient without
giving a description of the Directors whose names appeared
on the bill of sale.[e]

If the affidavit is defective, application was under the
former practice made to remove the bill of sale from the file,
and for leave to file a fresh copy with amended affidavit;[f]
and under the provisions of sec. 14, any Judge of the High
Court, on being satisfied that the omission or mis-statement
of the name, residence or occupation of any person was
accidental or due to inadvertence, may, in his discretion,
order such omission or mis-statement to be rectified in the
manner prescribed.

(3) Under the Bills of Sale Act, 1854, it was optional to file Registration.
the original bill of sale or a copy, and the officer could not
refuse to receive the original, but by the section the copy, and
not the original, is to be filed with the registrar. It was held
that the alteration or destruction of the original schedule
before registration did not affect the registration of a copy,

(a) Sutton c. Bath, 27 L. J. Ex. 388; 3 H. & N. 382; Grant c. Shaw, L. R. 7 Q.
B. 700.
(b) Hewer c. Cox, 30 L. J. Q. B. 73; exp. McHattie, re Wood, 39 L. T. 137.
(c) Phillips c. Burt, 2 F. & F. 802.
(d) Pickard c. Marriage, 1 Ex. D. 364; Fonblanque c. Lee, L. R. 7 Ir. C. L.
550; 3 Ir. Jur. N. S. 224.
(e) Shears c. Jacob, L. R. 1. C. P. 513; Deffell c. White, L. R. 2 C. P. 144 3
L. J. C. P. 25; 15 W. R. 68; 15 L. T. 211.
(f) Re Wright, 27 L. T. 192; re O'Brien, 10 Ir. C. L. App. 33.

L 2

the property in the goods passing on the execution of the bill of sale.[a]

It is not the registrar's province to inquire whether the bill of sale and affidavit comply with the provisions of the Act, his duties being purely ministerial.[b]

By sec. 41 of the Stamp Act, 1891, a bill of sale is not to be registered under any Act for the time being in force relating to the registration of bills of sale unless the original, duly stamped, is produced to the proper officer. The absence of a proper stamp would not, however, invalidate the registration; as under sec. 15, Stamp Act, 1891, the instrument may be stamped on payment of the unpaid duty, and the penalty therein mentioned.

As by the section, coupled with sec. 8 of the amendment Act, a bill of sale shall be filed with the registrar within seven clear days after the execution thereof, it would seem that a bill of sale made or given on the first of the month will be in time if registered on the eighth, unless that day happens to be a Sunday, or other day on which the registrar's office is closed, when registration will be valid if made the following day on which the office is open.[e]   A bill of sale executed in any place out of England shall be registered within seven clear days after the time at which it would, in the ordinary course of post, arrive in England, if posted immediately after the execution thereof.[d]

Defeasance, condition, or declaration of trust to be deemed part of bill of sale.

(3.) If the bill of sale is made or given subject to any defeasance or condition, or declaration of trust not contained in the body thereof, such defeasance, condition, or declaration shall be deemed to be part of the bill, and shall be written on the same paper or parchment therewith before the registration, and shall be truly set forth in the copy filed under this Act therewith and as part thereof, otherwise the registration shall be void.

(a) Green v. Attenborough, 3 H. & C. 468; 34 L. J. Ex. 88; 13 W. R. 185; 11 L. T. 513.

(b) Needham v. Johnson, 8 B. & S. 190; 15 W. R. 346; 15 L. T. 467.

(c) Sec. 22 (1878); Williams v. Burgess, 12 Ad. & E. 635.

(d) Sec. 8 (1882).

A defeasance is an instrument which defeats the force or
operation of some other deed or estate, and that which in the
same deed is called a condition, when in a separate deed is a
defeasance.[a]

Conditions may be either precedent, subsequent, or inherent; a condition is precedent where, unless it is complied
with, the estate does not arise; it is subsequent where, if it is
broken, the estate is defeated; it is inherent where the estate
is qualified, restrained or charged; in every case it denotes
something which prejudicially affects the interest of the
donee.[b]

But the meaning of the defeasance or condition mentioned
in the sub-section is not, it seems, so limited, and the sub-
section applies to any defeasance or condition in favour of
either party; the object being to avoid a bill of sale, in respect
of the chattels comprised therein, if given subject to a
defeasance or condition not expressed on the face of it,
whether in favour of the grantor or grantee, and thus not
stating the true contract between the parties, or the terms on
which the chattels are redeemable [c]

Before this decision it had been held, under sec. 2 of the
Bills of Sale Act, 1854, that the defeasance, condition or
declaration of trust contemplated by the section was such as
is usually found appended to a bill of sale, affecting its
operation as between the grantor and grantee, by diminishing
the rights of the grantee in the estate purported to be granted,
or affecting them prejudicially in favour of the grantor, and did
not include an independent agreement not qualifying the rights
of the grantee; and that the object of the provision was to prevent creditors being defrauded by sham bills of sale, by which
the whole interest of the grantor is apparently transferred,
whereas in reality he retains some interest in the subject
of the transfer.[d] So when with a registered bill of sale
expressed to be made in consideration of £130 to be repaid
by certain instalments without interest, the whole to
become payable on default in any instalment, the sum in
fact advanced being only £100, the £30 being charged by

Defeasance or condition.

(a) Com. Dig. Defeasance.
(b) Co. Litt. 201 a.
(c) Edwards v. Marcus [1894], 1 Q. B. 587; 70 L. T. 182; 1 Mans. 70; 63 L. J.
Q. B. 363.
(d) Robinson v. Collingwood, 17 C. B. N. S. 777; 34 L. J. C. P. 18; 13 W. R. 81;
10 Jur. N. S. 1060; 11 L. T. N. S. 313.

way of bonus and interest, a written memorandum was
signed by the mortgagor at the same time as the bill
of sale, which stated that the £30 was to be paid in full,
notwithstanding that the money secured by the bill of sale
might be repaid, or the mortgagee's right under it enforced
before the expiration of the time limited for payment, want
of registration of the memorandum securing a bonus to the
grantee was held not to be such a defeasance or condition
within the section as to affect the validity of the bill of sale.[a]
The memorandum in that case was not in fact a condition, and
the observations of James, L.J., to the effect that a condition
to be within the sub-section must be something prejudicially
affecting the position of the donee, are now stated to have
been *obiter*, and unnecessary to the decision.[b]

Defeasance or
condition.

But a collateral arrangement respecting the application of
the consideration money is not necessarily a condition or
declaration of trust ; as where a grantor borrowed £290 on
the understanding, which he kept, that he was thereout to
pay to the lender £235 due to him on an old bill of sale of the
same chattels.[c]   Nor does the deposit by the grantor of a
policy of insurance at the time of executing a bill of sale, by
way of collateral security for the same debt, operate as a
defeasance ;[d] and as a debt is not defeated by being paid, a
collateral agreement that the grantee would first resort to
securities other than the bill of sale, was held not to be a
defeasance, though admitted in evidence to prevent the
grantee recovering on the bill of sale.[e]

But when a bill of sale does not, on the face of it, express
the true contract between the parties, any collateral agreement
by way of defeasance, condition, or declaration of trust,
whether in favour of one party or the other, will be within the
sub-section.   So where husband and wife, by a bill of sale,
assigned to the claimant chattels in their dwelling-house to
secure £300 with simple interest, payable by instalments ; the
wife, by contemporaneous deed mortgaging to the claimant
her reversionary interest under a will, to secure the same

(a) Exp. Collins, re Lees ; L. R. 10 Ch. 367 ; 44 L. J. Bank. 78 ; 32 L. T. 108;
23 W. R. 862.
(b Edwards v. Marcus [1894], 1 Q. B. 587.
(c) Thomas v. Searles [1891], 2 Q. B. 408.
(d) Carpenter v. Deen, 23 Q. B. D. 566.
(e) Heseltine v. Simmons [1892], 2 Q. B. 547.

debt, with compound interest, payable by instalments on the same days as mentioned in the bill of sale, both securities being given as part of the same transaction; it was held that the agreement in the mortgage to pay compound interest was a condition under the sub-section, which being unregistered avoided the registration of the bill of sale.[a]

It was formerly doubted whether a collateral parol agreement could be a defeasance.[b]　But where a person purchased household furniture, and being unable to pay for it at the time, offered to do so by weekly instalments, which the vendor consented to accept, a bill of sale being given to secure the purchase-money, which was made payable in one sum, it was held that the antecedent parol arrangement to pay by instalments was a condition within the section, and as such should have been reduced into writing and have appeared on the registered copy of the bill of sale.[c]

And where with a bill of sale repayable by instalments the grantor contemporaneously, in respect of the same loan and as part of the same transaction, gave the grantee a promissory note for the total amount of the loan and interest payable by the same instalments as in the bill of sale, the whole sum remaining unpaid to become due on default in payment of one instalment, it was held, having regard to the identity of dates and figures, that there was only one contract embodied in the bill of sale and promissory note, and as if the amount of the latter were paid, either to the grantee or a third person, who might discount it, the former would have no further effect and would be defeated, the note therefore operated as a defeasance of the bill of sale and ought to have been registered.[d]　Nor will the fact that persons other than the grantor join in the promissory note alter its operation as a defeasance.[e]　But the promissory note itself is not avoided, and the amount secured by it may be recovered.[f]

An agreement was entered into providing that a deed of covenant and bill of sale should be given to secure

(marginal note:) Defeasance or condition

(a) Edwards v. Marcus [1894], 1 Q. B. 587.
(b) *Exp.* Popplewell *re* Storey, 21 Ch. D. 61.
(c) *Exp.* Southam, 44 L. J. Bank. 39; 17 Eq. 578; 22 W. R. 456; 30 L. T. 132.
(d) Counsell v. London & Westminster Loan Co., 19 Q. B. D. 512.
(e) Onn v. Fisher, 5 T. L. R. 504.
(f) Monetary Advance Co. v. Cater, 20 Q. B. D. 785.

principal and capitalized interest accrued due on an existing mortgage, together with compound interest on the sum secured. The bill of sale was given, but omitted the stipulated provisions for compound interest which, however, were inserted in a deed of covenant subsequently executed in pursuance of the agreement. The registration of the bill of sale was held void on the ground that the true agreement between the parties was not set forth, for a bill of sale must not be dependent for its real effect on some other document.[a]

On the other hand, it was unnecessary to state in the bill the name of the person really advancing the money, unless there be some trust in favour of the grantor; and where on an execution, the plaintiff paid the sheriff the amount of levy and bought the goods by bill of sale, but, as a fact, he was merely solicitor for the person finding the money the transaction was held valid against a subsequent execution creditor.[b]

A verbal agreement not to register a bill of sale, in consideration of which a larger bonus is given, need not appear on the filed copy, and is not a condition or defeasance; [c] nor is a hiring agreement entered into subsequently to an absolute bill of sale, and forming a separate and distinct transaction.[d]

Defeasance or condition. It may be laid down generally, that if there is a trust between the grantor and grantee rendering the deed a contrivance to secure the property for the grantor's benefit, or a device against the general body of his creditors, as for instance, a contract to obtain some additional advantage in the event of bankruptcy, which prevents the debtor's property being equally distributed, it will be void both at common law and as against the policy of the bankruptcy laws; [e] and a power of revocation has always been deemed a strong mark of fraud, for it virtually leaves the property in the settlor's hands: and so it has been held where an unlimited power of sale or mortgage is reserved, as shewing that the settlor did not *bonâ fide* intend to put the property out of his reach.[f]

(a) Sharp v. McHenry, 38 Ch. D. 427.

(b) Robinson v. Collingwood, 17 C. B. N. S. 777.

(c) Exp. Popplewell, re Storey, 21 Ch. D. 73.

(d) Exp. Shane, re McGinity, 29 S. J. 70.

(e) Exp. Mackay, re Jeavons, L. R. 8 Ch. 643 ; 42 L. J. Bank. 68; 28 L. T. 828 ; 1 W. R. 664.

(f) Tarback v. Marbury, 2 Vern, 510.

Under 3 Geo. IV. c. 39, sec. 4, in which the words are some-what the same as in the present section, it has been held not to be an objection to a warrant of attorney that part of the defeasance was written on a separate sheet of paper annexed.[a]

In case two or more bills of sale are given, com- Priority of title. prising in whole or in part any of the same chattels, they shall have priority in the order of date of their registration respectively as regards such chattels.

The provisions of the section are applicable to all bills of sale whether absolute or by way of security for the payment of money.[b]

Before the amendment Act it was decided that where there are conflicting bills of sale the date of registration determines their priority ; and if one of them is unregistered, the registered document will prevail, for the sub-section is of general application, and does not confer priority only as against the persons named in sec. 8 of the principal Act; thus the title of the holder of a prior unregistered bill of sale is postponed to that of a mort-gagee claiming under a subsequent duly registered bill of sale over the same chattels;[c] and it is immaterial whether the grantee under the registered or unregistered instrument is in possession of the goods.[d]

This rule is now modified in cases of conflict between absolute bills of sale governed by the principal Act and securities to which the amendment Act applies. For as by an absolute bill of sale the grantor parts with his whole interest in the goods, he is not the true owner at the time of giving a subsequent security over them. In such a case, sec. 5 of the amendment Act avoids the subsequent bill of sale except as against the grantor, and it does not take priority of the first deed. Thus an absolute unregistered bill of sale executed in 1885 was held not to be postponed to a bill of sale given in 1888 to secure payment of money, and duly registered under the amendment Act.[e]   But this is not

(a) Burdekin c. Potter, 1 Dowl. N. S. 134.
(b) Tuck c. Southern Counties Deposit Bank, 42 C. D. 471.
(c) Conelly c. Steer, 7 Q. B. D. 520 ; 45 L. T. 402 ; 29 W. R. 529 ; 50 L. J. Q. B. 326.
(d) Lyons c. Tucker, 7 Q. B. D. 523 ; 45 L. T. 449, reversing s. c. 6 Q. B. D. 660.
(e) Tuck c. Southern Counties Deposit Bank, 42 C. D. 471.

so if both bills of sale are given to secure the payment
of money, for the grantor has an equity of redemption, and
is the true owner of the goods, subject to the security he
has created.[a]   Consequently such bills of sale would seem
to take priority in the order of date of their registration,
and the rule would probably be the same if both bills of
sale are absolute, or given before the commencement of the
amendment Act.

Formerly registration conferred no priority against
claimants other than execution creditors or a trustee in bankruptcy;[b] nor did a subsequent bill of sale holder obtain any
priority by taking possession; and where a non-trader gave
on the 10th February, a bill of sale to A. as security for
advances, and on the 28th February a second bill of sale of
the same goods to B., who had no notice of A.'s bill, both bills
being duly registered; on B. taking possession and selling the
goods after notice of A.'s claim, the debtor having become
bankrupt between the seizure and sale, it was held that B. had
not acquired any priority over A., since A.'s legal title to the
goods was complete against B. without taking possession.[c]

Priority of title.   When, however, execution was levied, an unregistered
security was displaced altogether, and the title of a registered
bill of sale holder prevailed;[d] nor could the holder of a
prior unregistered bill of sale set up a duly registered later
bill of sale against a trustee in bankruptcy,[e] and a
registered mortgagee was entitled, as against the debtor's
trustee and a prior unregistered mortgagee, to such goods
as had not been seized by the latter before an act of bankruptcy.[f]   But on an interpleader between the grantee of a
bill of sale and an execution creditor, the latter was permitted
to defeat the title of the former by setting up a prior bill of sale
to a third party, or to shew that the claimant had no title at
the time of seizure.[g]   And the fact that a bill of sale is set
aside as void against the trustee in bankruptcy of the grantor

(a) Thomas v. Searles [1891], 2 Q. B. 408.

(b) Hills v. Shepherd, 1 F. & F. 191.

(c) Exp. Allen, re Middleton, 40 L. J. Bank. 17; 11 Eq. 209; 19 W. R. 274;
Payne v. Cales, 38 L. T. 355.

(d) Richards v. James, 36 L. J. Q. B. 116.

(e) Nicholson v. Cooper, 27 L. J. Ex. 393; Hunter v. Turner, 32 L. T. 556; 23
W. R. 792.

(f) Exp. Leman, re Barraud, 4 Ch. D. 23; 46 L. J. Bank. 38; 25 W. R. 65; 35
L. T. 422.

(g) Gadsden v. Barrow, 23 L. J. Ex. 134; 9 Ex. 514; Richards v. Jenkins, 18
Q. B. D. 451.

does not entitle the trustee to stand in the place of the grantee, and thus acquire priority over the grantee under a valid bill of sale subsequently executed by the grantor;[a] nor could a trustee take advantage of an execution void against himself, to invalidate a bill of sale comprising chattels which were not in the apparent possession of the grantor when the petition for bankruptcy or liquidation was filed.[b]

As registration is now essential to the validity of bills of sale, which, by sec. 8 of the amendment Act, are void in respect of the personal chattels comprised therein, unless registered, the clause would seem to apply and confer priority, although the second mortgagee takes his security with notice of a prior mortgage, at all events where the time for registering the first bill of sale has elapsed without registration; and it would therefore appear that the rule laid down by Lord Hardwicke in Le Neve v. Le Neve,[c] will not be applicable. By that rule, a purchaser with notice of a right in another is liable to the same extent and in the same manner as the person from whom he made the purchase, and an estate in the hands of a subsequent purchaser or mortgagee, with notice of a prior defective mortgage, will be bound by it. It is only when the notice is so clearly proved as to make it fraudulent in the purchaser to take and register a conveyance in prejudice of the known title of another, that the registered deed will be affected,[d] for a purchaser or mortgagee is not bound to make inquiries with a view to the discovery of unregistered instruments, though he may be bound by actual knowledge of them.[e]

Subject, it may be, to sec. 5 of the amendment Act, *Priority of title.* if the grantee permits the grantor to have possession of the goods, and thus enables him to hold himself forth to the world as having not only the possession but the property in them, as when he is permitted to carry on his trade, a purchaser, in the ordinary course of business, without notice of the bill of sale, has been held to obtain a good title; thus, where a farmer and dealer granted a bill of sale over all his growing crops, goods, chattels and effects, which then or thereafter should be on or about his farm and premises, and was allowed to remain

(a) *Exp.* Payne, *re* Cross, 11 Ch. D, 539 ; 49 L. T. 204 ; 27 W. R. 368.
(b) *Exp.* Blaiberg, *re* Toomer, 23 Ch. D. 254.
(c) Amb. 436 ; 2 W. & T. L. Cases, 6th ed. 26.
(d) Wyatt v. Barwell, 19 Ves. 439.
(e) Lee v. Clutton, 46 L. J. Ch. 48 ; 24 W. R. 942 ; 35 L. T. 84.

in possession and carry on his farm, it was held that he had
implied authority to sell the farm produce in the ordinary
course of his business, and that the bill of sale holder had no
cause of action against a purchaser in good faith, and without
notice;[a] and so where the grantor of a bill of sale, being a horse
dealer was by the deed authorized to hold, make use of and
possess the goods comprised in it, he covenanting not to dispose of them without the grantee's consent in writing, a
purchaser, without notice of the bill of sale, was held to have
acquired a good title to a horse, included in the deed, sent by
the grantor to a repository for sale by auction, in the ordinary
course of his business.[b]

Priority of title.   But if the sale is not in the ordinary course of the grantor's
business, a purchaser or person dealing with the goods, though
without notice of the bill of sale, will be liable in an action of
trover at the suit of the grantee—thus the auctioneer who sells
them has been held responsible.[c]   A grantor having given a
bill of sale of her furniture to the plaintiffs, without their
consent employed the defendants, a firm of auctioneers, to
sell it on her behalf; and they, without notice of the
bill of sale, having sold the furniture and delivered
it to the purchasers, were held responsible to the plaintiffs in trover.[d]   But where the grantor, without the
mortgagee's knowledge, took to the defendant's repository
certain horses and harness included in the bill of sale, and
entered them for sale by auction, but before they were
put up sold them privately in the defendant's yard, the
purchase-money being paid to the defendants, who deducted
their commission, handing the balance to the grantor, they
were held not guilty of a conversion.[e]   In another case, where
the purchaser of goods by bill of sale from the sheriff permitted the execution debtor to continue in possession, who
afterwards executed another bill of sale to another person, it
was held that the first bill of sale holder was entitled to
recover from the latter;[f] and where the jury found that the
grantor sold the goods fraudulently and not in the ordinary
way of his business, but that the defendants did not know this

(a) National Mercantile Bank v. Hampson, 5 Q. B. D. 177 ; 49 L. J. Q. B. 480;
28 W. R. 424.

(b) Walker v. Clay, 42 L. T. 369 ; 49 L. J. C. P. 560.

(c) Cochrane v. Rymill, 27 W. R. 776 ; 40 L. T. 744 : cf. Turner v. Hockey,
56 L. J. Q. B. 301.

(d) Consolidated Co. v. Curtis [1892], 1 Q. B. 495.

(e) National Mercantile Bank v. Rymill, 44 L. T. 767.

(f) Kidd v. Rawlinson, 2 B. & P. 59 ; Jezeph v. Ingram, 1 Moo. 189.

and bought the goods *bonâ fide*, judgment was entered for the plaintiffs.[a]   So where a landlord who had distrained, allowed the tenant to sell a crop of wheat included in a bill of sale given by the tenant, in order to pay the incoming valuation due to the landlord who received the proceeds, the sale was held bad against the mortgagee, as not being in the ordinary course of business, and the landlord had to refund.[b]

Again, a pledge of goods comprised in a bill of sale, not being in the ordinary course of business, was held not to prevail against the bill of sale holder ; who it was said did not make the grantor his agent within the Factors Acts by leaving him in possession of the goods.[c]   The absence of a covenant by the grantor not to sell or dispose of the mortgaged property does not affect the mortgagee's rights against purchasers from the grantor.[d]

But as a bill of sale only conferred an equitable title to after-acquired property, a pledgee or mortgagee of after-acquired property, who obtained the legal title without notice of the bill of sale, was held to take in priority.[e]

So, where a grantor assigned by bill of sale all chattels **Priority of title.** then being, or which might thereafter be on certain premises, and afterwards gave the plaintiff, who had no notice of the prior security, a bill of sale over the chattels then on the same premises.   The plaintiff attempted to seize under his security, but found that possession of the chattels had been taken by the defendant, who claimed under an assignment of the first bill of sale ; and on the defendant refusing to give up certain chattels which had been brought on the premises after the date of the first bill of sale, it was held that his interest in chattels acquired since the bill of sale was equitable only, and that the legal title to such chattels being in the plaintiff, prevailed over the defendant's equitable title, notwithstanding he had first taken possession.[f]

If a person induces another to advance him money on a bill of sale of chattels by representing that they are unincumbered,

(a) Taylor v. McKeand, 24 W. R. 024;   49 L. J. C. P. 564;   42 L. T. 833;
C. P. D. 358.
(b) Musgrave v. Stevens, 1 Cab. & E. 34 ; 47 J. P. 295.
(c) Joseph v. Webb, 1 Cab. & E. 262.
(d) Payne v. Fern, 29 W. R. 441 ; 6 Q. B. D. 620 ; 50 L. J. Q. B. 446.
(e) Joseph v. Lyons, 15 Q. B. D. 280.
(f) Hallas v. Robinson, 15 Q. B. D. 288.

he having in fact included them in a subsisting prior bill of sale, he is guilty of an indictable false pretence.[a] And where the tenant of a farm sold, otherwise than in the ordinary course of business, property over which he had previously given a bill of sale, but said nothing as to the ownership of the property or existence of the bill of sale, it was held that by the act of selling he represented himself as being absolute owner, and that as the purchaser had paid for the property under the belief that the grantor had authority to sell, the grantor was guilty of obtaining money by false pretences, unless he had the mortgagee's authority to sell, which it was for him to prove.[b]

A bill of sale to secure future advances to a specified amount gave the mortgagee no priority in respect of further advances, after notice of a second mortgage, over advances made by the second mortgagee with notice of the bill of sale ; [c] but a second mortgagee in possession of the mortgaged property, who expends money in permanently improving or preserving it, is not entitled, as against a first mortgagee, to any charge on the property for money so expended.[d]

Consolidation.   The doctrine of consolidation does not extend to bills of sale, at least against the parties named in sec. 8 of the principal Act; and the grantee of a bill of sale of chattels seized under an execution is not entitled to tack a previous mortgage of other property of the grantor, and claim that the surplus proceeds of the chattels, after discharging the sum due under the bill of sale, shall be applied in satisfaction of the prior mortgage, so as to defeat the right of the execution creditor to such surplus.[e]

As between grantor and grantee, the former may, where the bill of sale is made on or after the 1st of January, 1882, if sections 2 (vi.), 17, Conveyancing Act, 1881, apply, redeem it without paying any money due under any separate bill of sale or mortgage on property other than that comprised in the security sought to be redeemed, unless the bills of sale or mortgages, or one of them, shew a contrary intention.

(a) R. v. Meakin, 11 Cox, 270. Form of declaration against incumbrances, p. 272.

(b) R. v. Sampson, 52 L. T. 772 ; distinguishing R. v. Hazlewood, 48 J. P. 151.

(c) Hopkinson v. Rolt, 9 H. L. Ca. 514; 7 Jur. N. S. 1200.

(d) Landowners, &c. Co. v. Ashford, 16 Ch. D. 411.

(e) Chesworth v. Hunt, 5 C. P. D. 266; 28 W. R. 815; 49 L. J. C. P. 507; 12 L. T. 774.

A transfer or assignment of a registered bill of sale need not be registered.

By sec. 11 of the principal Act it is enacted that a renewal of registration shall not become necessary by reason only of a transfer or assignment of a bill of sale; but it would seem that if there is a further advance upon the transfer, registration will be necessary, for the transfer would be an assurance of chattels to secure the additional debt ;[a] and for the purposes of the Stamp Act would appear to be a transfer as to the amount of the original debt, and a new bill of sale to the extent of the further advance.

But if part of the amount secured by a duly registered bill of sale has been paid off, and on a transfer of the security the transferee makes a fresh advance to the mortgagor, not, with the sum remaining due, in excess of the sum originally secured, the transfer does not become a bill of sale, and is a good security, without registration, for the amount remaining due on the bill of sale at the time of transfer; but the Court of Appeal declined to express their opinion whether it was a good security for the further advance, as against the persons named in sec. 8 of the principal Act, without registration.[b]

A deposit of a bill of sale, by way of sub-mortgage, by a transferee of such bill of sale, has been held within the protection of the sub-section, even though the transferee subsequently acquired the equity of redemption under the original bill of sale.[c]

It was decided that a transfer made subsequently to 1854, by a mortgagee alone, without the concurrence of the mortgagor, of a bill of sale made before the passing of the Bills of Sale Act, 1854, did not require registration under that Act, or under the repealed Act of 1866, as against the trustee under the bankruptcy of the original mortgagor.[d] Where goods comprised in a duly registered bill of sale were assigned *bonâ fide*, but the transfer was not registered, nor was any re-registration of

(a) Wale e. Commissioners of Inland Revenue, 4 Ex. D. 270; 48 L. J. Ex. 574 ; 27 W. R. 916 ; 41 L. T. 165.

(b) Horne c. Hughes, 29 W. R. 576 44 L. T. 678 ; 6 Q. B. D. 676.

(c) *Exp.* Turquand, *re* Parker, 14 Q. B. D. 636 ; 43 W. R. 147 ; 54 L. J. Q. B. 242 ; 53 L. T. 570.

(d) *Exp.* Shaw, 25 W. R. 686; 36 L. T. 805 ; 46 L. J. Bank. 114.

the bill of sale effected, it was held, under the repealed Act of 1866, that after the expiration of five years the registration of the original bill of sale became absolutely void.[a]

Transfer or assignment of bill of sale.

The assignee of a mortgagee cannot stand in a better position than the mortgagee himself, for every mortgagor has a right to have a reconveyance of the mortgaged property upon payment of the amount due on the mortgage, and the mortgagee is charged with the duty of reconveying upon such payment being made. Where, therefore, a mortgagee, having besides the property mortgaged, promissory notes made by the mortgagor as collateral security for the debt, transferred the mortgage without assigning the collateral securities, it was held he was not entitled to sever the debt from the security, and an injunction was granted against his proceeding to recover one of the notes pending an action instituted by the mortgagor to redeem and to settle the equities of the parties.[b] Nor can a bill of sale holder, by transferring his interest to a third party, confer a better title than he himself possesses; [c] thus, where the goods of an execution debtor were assigned by inventory and receipt to a person who again assigned them, neither transaction being registered, and were then again granted by a bill of sale duly registered, remaining all the time in the apparent possession of the execution debtor, it was held by Grove, J. (Lopes, J., *diss.*), that the want of registration of the two prior assignments invalidated the title of the third assignee under the registered bill of sale.[d] But it was decided under the Act of 1854 that the purchaser from a bill of sale holder, whose security was defective, had a good title against an execution creditor of the original mortgagor ; for the exercise of the power of sale when there was no person entitled as against the mortgagee, put an end to the bill of sale, and the Act did not apply.[e]

An assignment to trustees of debts secured by bills of sale with a direction to collect, has been said to empower the trustees to put in force in the name of the settlor, or perhaps in their own names, the powers contained in the bills of sale,

(a) Karet *v.* Kosher Meat Supply Association, 2 Q. B. D. 361 ; 46 L. J. Q. B. 548 ; 25 W. R. 691 ; 36 L. T. 694.

(b) Walker *v.* Jones L. R. 1 P. C. 50 ; 35 L. J. P. C. 30 ; 14 W. R. 484 ; 14 L. T. 686 ; 12 Jur. N. S. 381

(c) *Exp.* Odell, *re* Walden, 39 L. T. 333 ; 48 L. J. Bank. 1.

(d) Chapman *v.* Knight, 49 L. J. C. P. 425.

(e) Cookson *v.* Swire, 9 App. Ca. 653.

though the securities for the debts were not expressly assigned.[a]

Where a person bought of the grantor goods comprised in a bill of sale, paying off the mortgagee, and taking the bill of sale with a receipt purporting to assign the goods to him, it was held under the Bills of Sale Act, 1854, that he did not acquire the mortgagee's rights even to the extent of the money paid, and his claim was postponed to that of the holder of a bill of sale, of which he had no notice, given by the grantor subsequent to the mortgage paid off, but prior to his purchase.[b]

11. (1878.) The registration of a bill of sale, *Renewal of registration.* whether executed before or after the commencement of this Act, must be renewed once at least every five years, and if a period of five years elapses from the registration or renewed registration of a bill of sale without a renewal or further renewal (as the case may be), the registration shall become void.

The renewal of a registration shall be effected by filing with the registrar an affidavit stating the date of the bill of sale and of the last registration thereof, and the names, residences, and occupations of the parties thereto as stated therein, and that the bill of sale is still a subsisting security.

Every such affidavit may be in the form set forth in the schedule (A) to this Act annexed.

A renewal of registration shall not become necessary by reason only of a transfer or assignment of a bill of sale.

The repealed Bills of Sale Act, 1866 (29 & 30 Vic. c. 96), formerly regulated the renewal of bills of sale.

The amendment Act does not apply to any bill of sale registered before its commencement so long as registration is not avoided by non-renewal or otherwise; nor does it invalidate as between grantor and grantee a bill of sale registered under the repealed Acts, the registration of which has become void for want of renewal.[c]

(a) *Re* Patrick, 30 W. R. 113; [1891] 1 Ch. 82; 60 L. J. Ch. 111; 63 L. T. 722.
(b) Cooper *v.* Braham, 15 L. T. N. S. 610.
(c) Sec. 3 [1882]. Swire *v.* Cookson, 48 L. T. 877; Cookson *v.* Swire, 9 App. Cases, 653.

Bills of sale registered after the 31st October, 1882, will require renewal every five years under the principal Act ; and a bill of sale to which the amendment Act applies, if not duly re-registered, will become void even as between the parties.[a]

Renewal of registration.

By sec. 23 of the principal Act, any renewal after the commencement of the Act of the registration of a bill of sale executed before the commencement of the Act and registered under the Bills of Sale Acts, 1854, 1866, shall be made under the principal Act in the same manner as the renewal of a registration made under that Act. But a bill of sale, the registration of which was void for want of renewal at the commencement of the principal Act, cannot be renewed under that Act.[b]

By sec. 14 of the principal Act, any Judge of the High Court of Justice, on being satisfied that the omission to file an affidavit of renewal within the prescribed time was accidental or due to inadvertence, may extend the time for renewal on such terms as he thinks fit to direct.

When a bill of sale has been re-registered since the 31st October, 1882, an abstract of the re-registration, sealed and dated, shall be transmitted by post to the registrar of the County Court to which such abstract should have been transmitted had the bill of sale been registered under the amendment Act.[c]

The affidavit should state the names, residences, and occupations of the parties as given in the bill of sale, although such description may be erroneous ; thus, where the mortgagee was, in the bill of sale, described as of a wrong county, and in the affidavit her right address was given, which did not appear in the bill of sale, it was held that the affidavit did not comply with the provisions of the section, and therefore the renewal of registration was invalid. In such a case the description should have been stated as in the bill of sale, followed by a description of the true residence.[d]

A transfer or assignment of a registered bill of sale does not require registration.[e]   Under the Bills of Sale Act, 1866,

---

(a) Fenton v. Blythe, 25 Q. B. D. 417.

(b) Re Emery, 21 Q. B. D. 405 ; 37 W. R. 21.

(c) R. S. C., Bills of Sale Acts, 1878 and 1882, Rule 5.

(d) Exp. Webster, re Morris, 31 W. R. 111 ; 22 Ch. D. 136 ; 48 L. T. 295 ; 52 L. J. Ch. 375.

(e) Sec. 10, cl. 5 [1878].

which required the registration of a bill of sale to be renewed
once in every five years, where the goods under a bill of sale
originally duly registered, were within five years assigned
bonâ fide, but the assignment was not registered, nor was any
re-registration of the bill of sale effected, it was held that
after the expiration of the five years the registration of the
bill of sale became absolutely void, and the goods, being in
the possession of the grantor, were not protected against his
creditors.[a]

11. (1882.) Where the affidavit (which under *Local registration of contents of bill of sale.* section ten of the principal Act is required to accompany a bill of sale when presented for registration) describes the residence of the person making or giving the same, or of the person against whom the process is issued to be in some place outside the London bankruptcy district as defined by the Bankruptcy Act, 1869, or where the bill of sale describes the chattels enumerated therein as being in some place outside the said London bankruptcy district, the registrar under the principal Act shall forthwith and within three clear days after registration in the principal registry, and in accordance with the prescribed directions, transmit an abstract in the prescribed form of the contents of such bill of sale to the county court registrar in whose district such places are situate, and if such places are in the districts of different registrars, to each such registrar.

Every abstract so transmitted shall be filed, kept, and indexed by the registrar of the county court in the prescribed manner, and any person may search, inspect, make extracts from, and obtain copies of the abstract so registered in the like manner and upon the like terms as to payment or otherwise as near as may be as in the case of bills of sale registered by the registrar under the principal Act.

(a) Karet v. Kosher Meat Supply Association, 2 Q. B. D. 361.

M 2

Local
registration.

This provision for local registration is a new one, and will afford additional facilities to creditors for ascertaining the position of persons with whom they are about to deal; but the omission of the registrar to transmit the abstract to the County Court Registry does not invalidate registration.[a]

By sec. 96, with schedule 3 of the Bankruptcy Act, 1883, the London bankruptcy district comprises the City of London and the liberties thereof, and all such parts of the metropolis and other places as are situated within the districts of the Metropolitan County Courts of Bloomsbury, Bow, Brompton, Clerkenwell, Lambeth, Marylebone, Shoreditch, Southwark, Westminster, and Whitechapel.

By the rules of the Supreme Court, Bills of Sale Acts. 1878 & 1882,[b] it is directed that the abstract of the contents of a bill of sale shall be in the form given in the Appendix thereto.[c] The abstract shall be sealed with the seal of the Bills of Sale Department of the Central Office, and dated on the day on which it is transmitted by post to the registrar of the County Court named therein.[d] Where a bill of sale is re-registered since the amendment Act, an abstract of the re-registration, sealed and dated, shall be transmitted by post to the registrar of the County Court to which such abstract should have been transmitted had the bill of sale been registered under the amendment Act.[e] When a memorandum of satisfaction is written upon any registered or re-registered bill of sale, an abstract of which has been so transmitted, a notice of such satisfaction, in the form in the appendix, duly sealed and dated, shall be transmitted to each of the registrars to whom an abstract of such bill of sale shall have been transmitted.[f] The registrar shall number the abstracts and notices of satisfaction in the order in which they shall respectively be received by him, and shall file and keep them in his office.[g]

The registrar shall keep an index, alphabetically arranged. in which he shall enter under the first letters of the surname of the mortgagor or assignor, such surname, with his Christian name or names, address, and description, and the number which he has affixed to the abstract.[h]

(a) Trinder v. Raynor, 56 L. J. Q. B. 422.
(b) P. 265.
(c) Rule 3, Form, p. 276.
(d) Rule 4.
(e) Rule 5.
(f) Rule 6, Form, p. 277.
(g) Rule 7.
(h) Rule 8.

Upon receipt of a notice of satisfaction, the registrar shall enter it in the abstract of the bill to which it relates, and shall note in the index against the name of the mortgagor or assignor the fact of the satisfaction having been entered." [a]

The regulations for searches in local registries differ in some respect from those prescribed by sec. 16 of the principal and amendment Acts, and are as follows:—The registrar shall allow any person to search the index at any time during which he is required by the County Court Rules, for the time being, to keep his office open, upon payment by such person of one shilling; and to make extracts from the abstract or notice of satisfaction upon payment of one shilling for each abstract or notice of satisfaction inspected.[b] He shall also, if required, cause an office copy to be made of any abstract or notice of satisfaction, at a fee for making, marking and sealing the same, of sixpence per folio.[c]

12. (1878.) The registrar shall keep a book (in this Act called "the register") for the purposes of this Act, and shall, upon the filing of any bill of sale or copy under this Act, enter therein in the form set forth in the second schedule (B) to this Act annexed, or in any other prescribed form, the name, residence, and occupation of the person by whom the bill was made or given (or in case the same was made or given by any person under or in the execution of process, then the name, residence and occupation of the person against whom such process was issued, and also the name of the person or persons to whom or in whose favour the bill was given), and the other particulars shewn in the said schedule or to be prescribed under this Act, and shall number all such bills registered in each year consecutively, according to the respective dates of their registration.

Form of register.

Upon the registration of any affidavit of renewal the like entry shall be made, with the addition of the ·date and number of the last previous entry relating

(a) Rule 9.　　　　(b) Rule 10.　　　　(c) Rule 11.

to the same bill, and the bill of sale or copy originally
filed shall be thereupon marked with the number
affixed to such affidavit of renewal.

The registrar shall also keep an index of the
names of the grantors of registered bills of sale with
reference to entries in the register of the bills of sale
given by each such grantor.

Such index shall be arranged in divisions corresponding with the letters of the alphabet, so that
all grantors whose surnames begin with the same
letter (and no others) shall be comprised in one
division, but the arrangement within each such
division need not be strictly alphabetical.

The register.   By Rules of the Supreme Court, 1883 (Order LXI., Rule 18),
there shall be entered in proper books kept for the purpose,
the time of delivery of every document filed at the Central
Office ; and such book shall, at all times during office hours,
be accessible to the public on payment of the usual fee.

It would seem that publication, in good faith and without
malice, of a mere copy of the register, which under section 16.
amendment Act, the public have a right to inspect, is privileged ;[a] though publication of a copy register of judgments
untruly representing them as still unsatisfied has been held
libellous.[b]

The proprietors of a list of registered bills of sale, compiled on the terms that the copyright is to belong to them,
and registered under the Copyright Act, the compilation requiring skill, and involving labour and expense, are entitled
to restrain infringement of their list, or any material part of
it, as, for instance, so much of the list as relates to a particular
neighbourhood, nor are they disentitled because the list is
not compiled on the terms of the copyright belonging to any
one of the proprietors alone.[c]

(a) Searles v. Scarlett [1892], 2 Q. B. 56; 61 L. J. Q. B. 573; 66 L. T. 837; 40
W. R. 696.
(b) Williams v. Smith, 22 Q. B. D. 134; 58 L. J. Q. B. 21; 59 L. T. 757; 37 W.
R. 93.
(c) Trade Auxiliary Co. v. Middlesbrough Tradesmen's Association, 40 C. D.
425; 58 L. J. Ch. 293; 60 L. T. 681; 37 W. R. 337.

12. (1882.) Every bill of sale made or given in consideration of any sum under thirty pounds shall be void.

Bill of sale under £30 to be void.

The proposed limit was originally £50, and the amount named in the section is the result of a compromise. A bill of sale given in consideration of £30 would not be within the section; and it will be observed that the test is the amount of the consideration, and not the sum secured by the bill of sale; thus, a bill of sale given to secure £25 lent and £10 bonus on the loan would seem void within the section; but if given to secure a pre-existing debt of £25, and £5 then paid, or a pre-existing debt of £30, would be good.

A grantor having applied for a loan of £15, the lender offered £30 if the grantor would agree to repay £15 on demand and the balance by instalments, to which the grantor assented, and £30 without deduction was paid to him, and stated, in a bill of sale then given, to be the consideration. Immediately after executing the bill of sale, the grantor asked the mortgagee to demand the £15 at once, as he did not want it. This the mortgagee did, and the £15 was repaid, a receipt being given. On default in payment of the instalments of the remaining £15, seizure was effected, when payment was made under protest, and an action for damages brought; but it was held that the bill of sale was valid and not an evasion of the section, for it did not appear that before the bill of sale was executed there was any understanding that the £15 should be at once repaid, or that the transaction was a sham.[a]

13. (1882.) All personal chattels seized or of which possession is taken after the commencement of this Act, under or by virtue of any bill of sale (whether registered before or after the commencement of this Act), shall remain on the premises where they were so seized or so taken possession of, and shall not be removed or sold until after the expiration of five clear days from the day they were so seized or so taken possession of.

When chattels may be removed or sold.

(a) Davies v. Usher, 12 Q. B. D. 490; 32 W. R. 832; 53 L. J. Q. B. 422; 51 L. T. 207.

Sec. 13.
[1878.]

When chattels
may be re-
moved or sold.

The section will, in a great measure, prevent the extortion too often practised upon borrowers of money who had made default in strict observance of the stipulations of the deed, and by sec. 7 of the amendment Act, which limits seizure to certain cases of default, it is provided that the grantor may, within five days from seizure, apply to the Court or a Judge, who, if satisfied that by payment of money or otherwise the cause of seizure no longer exists, may restrain the grantee from removing or selling the chattels seized, or may make such other order as may seem just.

The section will, however, increase the danger of distraint upon the chattels for rent, rates and taxes; though as the protection it affords is for the benefit of grantors and not of landlords, a bill of sale holder may with the grantor's consent remove the goods, even within the period of five days, in order to avoid a distress, and will not be responsible to the landlord for loss of rent occasioned by the removal, or to an action for double value under 2 Geo. II. c. 19.[a]

Actual seizure of the goods without removal will, it would seem, prevent the operation of the reputed ownership clause.

Where, after default, a bill of sale holder seized a horse and cab, comprised in his security, while plying for hire, and removed them to a private yard, where he kept them for five days, on the grantor, who had notice where they were, suing for damages for wrongful seizure, it was held that the section had been reasonably complied with[b]

The five clear days during which the goods are to remain on the premises are, it would seem, to be reckoned exclusive of the days of seizure and removal.

The registrar.

13. (1878.) The Masters of the Supreme Court of Judicature attached to the Queen's Bench Division of the High Court of Justice, or such other officers as may for the time being be assigned for this purpose under the provisions of the Supreme Court of Judicature Acts, 1873 and 1875, shall be the registrar for the purposes of this Act, and any one of

(a) Tomlinson, c. Consolidated Credit Corporation, 24 Q. B. D. 135; Lane c. Tyler, 56 L. J. Q. B. 461.

(b) O'Neill r. City Finance Co., 17 Q. B. D. 234; 34 W. R. 545; 55 L. T. 408.

the said masters may perform all or any of the duties
of the registrar.

By Order LXI., Rule 25, Rules of the Supreme Court, 1883,
the Masters shall execute the office of registrar for the purposes
of the Acts, and any one of the Masters may perform all or
any of the duties of the registrar.

14. (1878.) Any judge of the High Court of Rectification of register. Justice, on being satisfied that the omission to register
a bill of sale or an affidavit of renewal thereof within
the time prescribed by this Act, or the omission or
mis-statement of the name, residence or occupation
of any person, was accidental or due to inadvertence,
may, in his discretion, order such omission or mis-
statement to be rectified by the insertion in the
register of the true name, residence, or occupation,
or by extending the time for such registration on
such terms and conditions (if any) as to security,
notice by advertisement or otherwise, or as to any
other matter, as he thinks fit to direct.

Orders under the section are usually made without prejudice to the rights of parties acquired when the bill is
actually registered; but it was formerly held that the section
gave the judge discretionary power to order rectification after
the rights of third parties had accrued.[a] But even if the
Court has discretionary power to order rectification after
some third person has acquired a vested interest adverse to
the bill of sale holder, which seems doubtful, such discretion
should not be exercised to extend the time for registration
after an execution creditor has seized, and has thus acquired
an interest in the goods.[b]

And where after the time had expired for renewing registration of a bill of sale, the grantor was adjudged bankrupt
before any application to rectify, the Court of Appeal held
that the time for renewal of registration could not be
extended so as to defeat the rights of the trustee in bankruptcy, in whom the grantor's property had vested; and that

(a) *Re* Dobbin, 50 L. J. Q. B. 205; 57 L. T. 277; Form, p. 277.
(b) Crew *v.* Cummings, 21 Q. B. D. 120; 36 W. R. 908; 57 L. J. Q. B. 641;
59 L. T. 886.

the decision of the Queen's Bench Division in *re* Dobbin must be treated as overruled.[a]

The application for rectification or extension of time must be to a judge of the High Court, and the Court of Appeal has no jurisdiction to rectify the register.[b] The judge has no power to allow an affidavit to be filed supplying the residence and occupation of an attesting witness inadvertently omitted in the affidavit filed on registration, his powers being limited to rectification of the register;[c] but he might, it would seem, cure any defect by extending the time for registration.

Rectification of register.   The tendency of the cases for some time past has been to relax the severity of the rule that a slight misdescription vitiates a bill of sale; but it will now be safer, in all cases where any doubt exists as to the materiality of the error, to adopt the course pointed out by the section; or to prepare and register a new bill of sale, stating that it is given for the purpose of correcting a material error in the prior security.

A bill of sale given in November, through inadvertence not being registered, leave was given on the mortgagee's *ex parte* application in the following January, to register within three days, the order providing that " the time for registration be enlarged for three days from this date, notwithstanding that the time for registration has elapsed." The bill of sale was not registered until the fourth day from the order, reckoning an intervening Sunday, and prior to the *ex parte* application the grantor had executed an assignment for the benefit of creditors, which constituted an act of bankruptcy, on which he was afterwards adjudicated a bankrupt, but it was held against the trustee in bankruptcy that registration was in time, the practice of the High Court where the order was made not reckoning Sundays, and that the validity of the order could only be questioned in the Court by which it was made.[d]

It has been held that the section is not retrospective and there is no power to enlarge the time for renewal of registration of a bill of sale void for want of renewal of registration at the time of the commencement of the principal Act.[e]

(a) *Exp.* Furber, *re* Parsons [1893], 2 Q. B. 122; 62 L. J. Q. B. 365; 41 W. R. 468; 68 L. T. 777.
(b) *Exp.* Webster, *re* Morris, 48 L. T. 295.
(c) Crew *v.* Cummings, 21 Q. B. D. 120; 30 W. R. 908; 57 L. J. Q. B. 641; 59 L. T. 886.
(d) *Re* Parke, 13 L. R. Ir. 85.
(e) Askew *v.* Lewis, 48 L. T. 531; 31 W. R. 567; 10 Q. B. D. 477; 1 Cab. & E. 34; J. P. 312; *re* Emery, 21 Q. B. D. 405.

Bill of sale not to protect chattels against taxes, poor and parochial rates.

14. (1882.) A bill of sale to which this Act applies shall be no protection in respect of personal chattels included in such bill of sale, which but for such bill of sale would have been liable to distress under a warrant for the recovery of taxes and poor and other parochial rates.

Before the section, by the statutes authorizing distress for rates, only the goods of the person assessed could be levied, this being the usual rule with regard to distress for fines or amerciaments, as distinguished from distraint for rent, to which, with some few exceptions, all goods on the premises are subject, whether of the tenant or a stranger; thus, where by bill of sale the grantor had parted with his property in the goods, they were not subject to distress for rates, although liable to the landlord's claim for rent.

The levy may be upon the goods of the person assessed, not only in the place for which assessment is made, but in any other place in the same county, or if no sufficient distress is there found, then in any other county on oath made before justices.[a] Wearing apparel and bedding of the person assessed and his family, and, to the value of £5, the tools and implements of his trade, are not to be levied under a distress for rates.

The section only deprives the bill of sale holder of protection where a distress warrant has been, or could be, issued for the taxes or rates; thus he is protected against an execution for rates, and where a local authority proceeded for rates in the County Court, under section 261 of the Public Health Act, 1875, recovering judgment, on which they levied execution, the bill of sale holder was held entitled to the goods against the local authority as execution creditors.[b]

Entry of satisfaction.

15. (1878.) Subject to and in accordance with any rules to be made under and for the purposes of this Act, the registrar may order a memorandum of satisfaction to be written upon any registered copy of a bill of sale, upon the prescribed evidence being given that the debt (if any) for which such bill of sale was made or given has been satisfied or discharged.

(a) Stone's Pr. for JJ.P., 9th ed. 532.
(b) Wimbledon Local Board v. Underwood [1892], 1 Q. B. 836; 40 W. R. 640; 67 L. T. 55; 61 L. J. Q. B. 484; 56 J. P. 631.

Under the repealed Act of 1854, the duty of ordering satisfaction to be entered was discharged by a Judge. The practice was for the debtor to obtain from the creditor a certificate of the satisfaction of his claim, signed in the presence of a solicitor. This certificate, together with payment of the debt, was verified by the affidavit of the solicitor attesting the creditor's consent; and on this evidence an order was made to enter up satisfaction, which was then endorsed on the filed bill of sale at the Queen's Bench Office.

Entry of
satisfaction.

Under the present practice a memorandum of satisfaction may be ordered to be written upon a registered copy of a bill of sale on a consent to the satisfaction, signed by the person entitled to the benefit of the bill of sale, and verified by affidavit, being produced to the registrar, and filed in the Central Office. Where this consent cannot be obtained, the registrar may, on application by summons, and on hearing the person entitled to the benefit of the bill of sale, or on affidavit of service of the summons on that person, and in either case on proof to the satisfaction of the registrar that the debt (if any) for which the bill of sale was made has been satisfied or discharged, order a memorandum of satisfaction to be written upon a registered copy thereof.[a]

A form of summons and affidavit with consent will be found in the Appendix, Part II., pp. 273, 274.

It will be observed that the present rule dispenses with verification by a solicitor; but in practice, some of the Masters had required the consent to be so verified; and by Central Office Practice Rules, settled by the practice masters, March, 1884, if the attesting witness and deponent is a solicitor, and described as such, the entry of satisfaction will be directed by the registrar (the papers being otherwise correct) as of course; but under special circumstances the registrar may accept any other deponent, if satisfied that he is a proper person to attest and verify the signature and consent. The mere fact that the deponent to the affidavit is not a solicitor is not sufficient reason for refusing to enter satisfaction.[b]

The fee on filing a fiat of satisfaction is 5s.

Where a memorandum of satisfaction is written upon any registered or re-registered copy of a bill of sale, an abstract of which has, under sec. 11 of the amendment Act, been transmitted to any registrar of a County Court, a notice of such satisfaction, duly sealed and dated, shall be transmitted to each of the registrars to whom an abstract of such bill of sale

(a) R. S. C., 1883, O. lxi., 26, 27.   (b) White v. Rubery, [1891] 2 Q. B. 923.

shall have been transmitted; and upon receipt of such notice
the registrar shall enter it on the abstract of the bill to which
it relates, and shall note in the Index against the name of the
mortgagor or assignor, the fact of the satisfaction having
been entered. *)

Although satisfaction has not been entered, the holder of
a bill of sale which has been actually satisfied cannot set up
the bare legal property vested in him against an execution
creditor. b) The release of the grantor of a bill of sale by
discharge under the bankruptcy laws is a satisfaction of the
debt, but the security is preserved so far as it operates
as an actual assignment of chattels; for although the Bankruptcy Act discharges the bankrupt, it does not discharge
the property which he has made liable to the demand; c)
but if the security is a mere licence to seize after-acquired
property, it will be avoided by the bankruptcy. d)

As an assignment of general future property operates
merely as a contract to assign, if and when the property is
acquired, an order of discharge in bankruptcy relieves the
grantor from all liability under such a contract, and the
mortgagee's remedy is by proof. Thus, when a bill of sale
purported to assign all chattels which should subsequently be
brought upon the grantor's premises, on his becoming bankrupt and obtaining his order of discharge, it was held that
chattels afterwards brought by him upon the premises were
not subject to the bill of sale, and that, so far, the security
was avoided by the order of discharge, the contract to assign
being a proveable liability under the Bankruptcy Act. It
seems doubtful, however, whether an order of discharge would
bar an agreement to assign chattels specified so as to be
identified. e)

15. (1882.) The eighth and the twentieth sections
of the principal Act, and also all other enactments
contained in the principal Act which are inconsistent
with this Act are repealed, but this repeal shall not
affect the validity of anything done or suffered
under the principal Act before the commencement
of this Act.

Repeal of part
of Bills of Sale
Act, 1878

(a) R. S. C., Bills of Sale Acts, 1878 & 1882, Rules 8, 9, Form, p. 276.
(b) Waterton r. Baker, 17 L. T. 494.
(c) Lyde r. Mann, 4 Sim. 505; 1 My. & K. 683.
(d) Thompson r. Cohen, L. R. 7 Q. B. 527.
(e) Collyer r. Isaacs 19 Ch. D. 342.

The amendment Act also repeals sec. 10, sub.-sec. 1 [a] and a portion of sec. 16 of the principal Act.[b]   Also the effect of sec. 8 of the amendment Act is practically to repeal sec. 4, clause 4, of the principal Act, so far as affects bills of sale within the amendment Act.

The repeal, however, is by sec. 3 of the amendment Act limited to bills of sale given by way of security for the payment of money, and leaves the repealed sections in full force so far as regards bills of sale by way of absolute transfer, or given for any purpose other than to secure payment of money.[c]

The repeal of sec. 20 is not retrospective, and chattels comprised in a bill of sale duly registered before the commencement of the amendment Act, are not within the reputed ownership clause of the Bankruptcy Act.[d]

The effect of the repeal of sec. 20 will be to bring within the operation of the reputed ownership clause of the Bankruptcy Act, chattels comprised in a bill of sale given to secure the payment of money, and registered under the amendment Act, which, after the 1st of November, 1882, are at the commencement of the bankruptcy, in the possession, order, or disposition of the bankrupt, in his trade or business, by the consent and permission of the true owner, under such circumstances that the bankrupt is the reputed owner thereof; but chattels comprised in bills of sale given by way of absolute transfer, and registered under the principal Act, after the commencement of the amendment Act, appear still to be within the protection of the repealed section.[e]

Office copies.

16. (1878.) Any person shall be entitled to have an office copy or extract of any registered bill of sale, and affidavit of execution filed therewith or copy thereof, and of any affidavit filed therewith, if any, or registered affidavit of renewal, upon paying for the same at the like rate as for office copies of judgments of the High Court of Justice, and any copy of a registered bill of sale and affidavit,[e] purporting

(a) Sec. 10 [1882].   (b) Sec. 16 [1882].
(c) Swift v. Pannell, 24 Ch. D. 210; Heseltine v. Simmons [1892], 2 Q. B. 547.
(d) Exp. Izard, re Chapple, 23 Ch. D. 409; 52 L. J. Ch. 802; 32 W. R. 218; 9 L. T. 230.
(e) In the authorised copy of the statute this is printed, "any copy of a registered bill of sale, and affidavit purporting to be an office copy thereof," but the above would seem to be the correct reading. See the section in Appendix.

to be an office copy thereof, shall in all Courts, and
before all arbitrators or other persons, be admitted
as prima facie evidence thereof, and of the fact and
date of registration as shewn thereon.   Any person *Repealed in*
shall be entitled at all reasonable times to search the *part. sec. 16*
                                                        1882.
register and every registered bill of sale, upon payment of one shilling for every copy of a bill of sale
inspected ; such payment shall be made by a Judicature stamp.

So much of the section as enacts that any person shall
be entitled at all reasonable times to search the register and
every registered bill of sale, upon payment of one shilling for
every copy of a bill of sale inspected, is repealed by sec.
16 of the amendment Act.

The section alters the former practice as to proof of a bill
of sale, and avoids the trouble and expense of calling an officer
of the Queen's Bench Division.

No affidavit or record of the Court shall be taken out of
the Central Office without the order of a judge or master, and
no subpœna for the production of any such document shall be
issued.[a]

Under the repealed Acts, a certificate of registration of a *Proof of bill of
document purporting to be a bill of sale, with the date and   sale.*
endorsement of the names of the parties, was no evidence that
an affidavit satisfying all the requirements of the statute had
been filed with the bill of sale.[b] Neither was a certificate of
registration of "a document purporting to be a copy bill of
sale together with an affidavit," sufficient evidence of the due
filing of the bill of sale, unless there was also proof that
the document registered was a true copy of the original bill
of sale.[c] Nor under the present Acts is production of a bill
of sale and certificate of registration evidence of due registration, but if the objection is taken it seems that the proper
course is to adjourn the hearing for the production of further
evidence. [d]

(a) R. S. C., 1883, O. lxi. 24.
(b) Mason v. Wood, 1 C. P. D. 63 ; 24 W. R. 11 ; 45 L. J. C. P. 76 ; 34 L. T. 571.
(c) Halkett v. Emmott, 38 L. T. 504 ; 3 Q. B. D. 555 ; s. n. Emmott v. Marchant,
26 W. R. 632 ; 47 L. J. Q. B. 436 ; Grindell v. Brendon, 6 C. B. N. S. 698 ; Wad-
dington v. Roberts, L. R. 3 Q. B. 579 ; 37 L. J. Q. B. 253 ; 9 B. & S. 697 ; 16 W. R.
1019 ; 18 L. T. 853.
(d) Turner v. Culpan, 36 W. R. 274.

Under the present system, office copies of all documents filed in the High Court shall be admissible in evidence in all causes and matters, and between all persons or parties, to the same extent as the original would be admissible : [a] and all copies, certificates, and other documents appearing to be sealed with a seal of the Central Office shall be presumed to be office copies or certificates or other documents issued from the Central Office, and if duly stamped may be received in evidence ; and no signature or other formality, except the sealing with a seal of the Central Office, shall be required for the authentication of any such copy, certificate, or other document. [b]

The fee for office copies is sixpence per folio.

By the Common Law Procedure Act, 1854, [c] it is not necessary to prove by the attesting witness any instrument to the validity of which attestation is not requisite. Sec. 8 of the principal Act will, it seems, render it necessary to prove by the attesting witness all unregistered bills of sale where the fact of execution is in issue ; but if the bill of sale has been registered, an office copy of the affidavit by the attesting witness will, under the provisions of the section, be *primâ facie* evidence thereof.

The rule applies to a cancelled or burnt deed, [d] as also to one the execution of which is admitted by the party to it, even in open Court, [e] or in a subsequent agreement, [f] or in a sworn answer to interrogatories, [g] nor will illness excuse the attendance of an attesting witness. [h]

When it is unnecessary to call the attesting witness.

Where the instrument is thirty years old it proves itself ; and if it is in the possession of the adverse party, who refuses to produce it pursuant to notice, or, if producing it, claims an interest under it in the subject-matter of the cause ; [i] or where the document is tendered in evidence against a public officer who is bound by law to have procured its due execution, and who has dealt with it as a document duly executed ; [j]

(a) R. S. C., 1883, O. xxxvii. 4.
(b) R. S. C., 1883, O. lxi. 7.
(c) Sec. 26.
(d) Breton *v.* Cope, Pea. R, 44 ; Gillies *v.* Smither, 2 Stark, 528.
(e) R. *v.* Harringworth, 4 M. & S. 353 ; Johnson *v.* Mason, 1 Esp. 89.
(f) Doe *v.* Penfold, 8 C. & P. 536 ; *contra*, Bringloe *v.* Goodson, 5 Bing. N. 740.
(g) Call *v.* Dunning, 4 East. 53 ; Bowles *v.* Langworthy, 5 T. R. 366.
(h) Harrison *v.* Blades, 3 Camp. 357 ; *contra*, Jones *v.* Brewer, 4 Taunt. 46.
(i) Doe *v.* M. of Cleveland, 9 B. & C. 864.
(j) Plumer *v.* Brisco, 11 Q. B. 46 ; 12 Jur. 351 ; 17 L. J. Q. B. 158 ; Barnes *v.* Lucas, Ry. & M. 264.

it will be unnecessary to call the attesting witness; neither will the rule apply where the party, from physical or legal obstacles, is unable to produce the attesting witness—as, if the witness be dead, or insane, or out of the jurisdiction of the Court, or cannot be found, or if he be absent by collusion with the opposite party,[a] and if the instrument be lost and the name of the witness be unknown, the execution may be proved by other evidence.

Where an instrument, requiring attestation, is subscribed by several witnesses, it is only necessary to call one of them.[b]

16. (1882.) So much of the sixteenth section of the principal Act as enacts that any person shall be entitled at all reasonable times to search the register and every registered bill of sale upon payment of one shilling for every copy of a bill of sale inspected is hereby repealed, and from and after the commencement of this Act any person shall be entitled at all reasonable times to search the register, on payment of a fee of one shilling, or such other fee as may be prescribed, and subject to such regulations as may be prescribed, and shall be entitled at all reasonable times to inspect, examine, and make extracts from any and every registered bill of sale without being required to make a written application, or to specify any particulars in reference thereto, upon payment of one shilling for each bill of sale inspected, and such payment shall be made by a judicature stamp : Provided that the said extracts shall be limited to the dates of execution, registration, renewal of registration, and satisfaction, to the names, addresses, and occupations of the parties, to the amount of the consideration, and to any further prescribed particulars.

Inspection of registered bills of sale.

By Order lxi., Rule 23, R. S. C., 1883, the registrar of bills of sale shall, on a request in writing giving sufficient

(a) Currie r. Child, 3 Camp. 283; R. r. St. Giles, E. & B. 642.

(b) Forster r. Forster, 33 L. J. P. & M. 113; *see* Taylor on Evidence, 8th ed. 1561, *et seq.*

S

particulars, and on payment of the prescribed fee, cause a search to be made in the registers or indexes under his custody, and issue a certificate of the result of the search. Under a former rule it was necessary, before inspecting the register, to satisfy the officer as to the object of the search.

Provision has been made by the Rules of the Supreme Court, Bills of Sale Acts, 1878 & 1882, for search, inspection, and office copies of abstracts filed in local registries.[a]

An official search for bills of sale may also be made under sec. 2 of the Conveyancing Act, 1882, and rules which will be found in Appendix, Part I., p. 267. The fees payable on searches and inspections will be found noted to sec. 18.

The office hours of the bills of sale department of the Central Office are from ten to four, except on Saturday and in vacation, when the offices close at two.

Debentures to which Act not to apply.

17. (1882.) Nothing in this Act shall apply to any debentures issued by any mortgage, loan, or other incorporated Company, and secured upon the capital, stock or goods, chattels and effects of such Company.

The term debenture does not seem to have received a precise legal definition, but as commonly used imports a debt, an acknowledgment of a debt, with an obligation or covenant to pay, in most cases accompanied by a charge or security; and a document which is a debenture in this common acceptation of the term will be within the exception. Thus, a memorandum by a Company in consideration of a loan, which, with other clauses usually found in debentures, contained a covenant to pay each of the lenders the sum advanced with interest, charging as security all the undertaking, property, estate and effects of the Company, was held a debenture within the meaning of the section;[b] as also was an agreement between a Company and a lender whereby the Company agreed to pay the money lent with interest, charging the hereditaments of the Company with payment, and further agreed on request to execute a legal mortgage and to issue debentures to the extent of the loan secured over the capital, stock, goods.

(a) Rules 10, 11.
(b) Edmonds v. Blaina Furnaces Co.; 35 W. R. 798; 57 L. T. 139; 56 L. J. Ch. 815; 36 Ch. D. 215.

chattels and effects of the Company. But it seems doubtful
whether a mere memorandum of deposit of title deeds as
security for a floating balance, not admitting any specific
debt or containing an agreement to pay is within the exception, or whether an instrument which charges specific
property as distinguished from a general charge on assets
is a debenture; thus, a memorandum by a brick making Company given on a deposit of title deeds to beds of coal and fire-
clay, stating that the deposit was made to secure present and
future advances and agreeing to execute on request a proper
mortgage with power of sale or such further security as might
be necessary for effectually passing the legal estate in the
property to which the security related, was held not to be a
debenture. [b]

It has been held that the section does not protect an
assignment of plant, machinery, stock-in-trade, &c., to
a trustee for debenture-holders; [c] so where a limited Company issued debenture bonds, payable to bearer, purporting to
be secured by a mortgage of the property of the Company to
trustees, who executed a declaration of trust for the debenture-
holders, and all the debenture bonds came into the claimant's
hands, his claim to the property, covered by the mortgage,
which was unregistered, and contained no express trust for
debenture-holders, was held ineffectual against an execution
creditor. [d] But the form of debenture may be such as to
equitably charge in favour of debenture-holders the chattels
purported to be assigned by the invalid deed; thus, where
debentures were issued by a Company, with a condition annexed,
that the holders were entitled to the benefit of an indenture
whereby, amongst other things, certain specified chattels of
the Company were vested in trustees to secure payment of all
moneys payable on such debentures, it was held, that even if
the covering deed was void under the Acts, the intention to
give the debenture-holders a valid charge within sec. 17
was manifest on the face of the debentures read in conjunction
with the condition, and amounted to an equitable contract,
which would be carried into effect so as to charge the chattels
in favour of the debenture-holders. [e]

(*margin*) Assignment to secure deben- tures.

(a) Levy c. Abercorris Slate and Slab Co., 37 Ch. D. 260; 36 W. R. 411; 57 L. J. Ch. 202; 58 L. T. 218.
(b) Topham c. Greenside &c. Co., 37 Ch. D. 281.
(c) Brocklehurst c. Railway Printing, &c., Co., W. N., 1884, 70.
(d) Jenkinson c. Brandley Mining Co., 35 W. R. 811; 19 Q. B. D. 568.
(e) Ross c. Army and Navy Hotel Co., 34 Ch. D. 43; 35 W. R. 69; 55 L. T. 476.

The words "other incorporated Company" used in the section, are not limited to an incorporated Company, *ejusdem generis* with mortgage or loan Companies; but even if it were so, any Company authorized to raise money on loan or mortgage would, for the purposes of the sections, be *ejusdem generis.* [a]

Debentures to which Acts not to apply.

Debentures which create a charge on the floating real and personal property of a Company do not require registration under the amendment Act. [a] It was questioned whether debentures, although excluded by the section from the operation of the amendment Act, were bills of sale within the definition contained in the principal Act; [b] but this has now been decided in the negative; and although debentures are agreements by which a right in equity to a charge on personal chattels is conferred, mortgages or charges by an incorporated Company, for the registration of which statutory provision has been made by the Companies Clauses Act, 1845, or the Companies Act, 1862, are not bills of sale within the principal Act. The principal Act, therefore, does not apply to a debenture issued by an incorporated Company; [a] indeed, it has been pointed out that if it did, as the Acts are by sec. 3 of the amendment Act to be construed together, sec. 17 would exclude the necessity for registration. [c]

A transfer, by the mortgagee, of a charge on chattels given by an incorporated Company, does not, it is said, confer a valid charge on the chattels charged or the debt secured, unless the formalities of the Bills of Sale Acts are complied with. [d]

A bill of sale by a Company has been said to be within the Acts, [e] and may be given or taken in the incorporated name of the Company; [f] and where chattels were assigned to a Company, which consisted of two persons only, it was held that the assignment enured for their benefit; [g] so a bill of sale to " The D. Bank of London, of a given address, of which said bank A. B., of the same place, is the sole proprietor," was held sufficient. [h]

(a) *Re* Standard Manufacturing Co., *exp.* Lowe [1891], 1 Ch. 627; 39 W. R. 369; 60 L. J. Ch. 72; 64 L. T. 487.

(b) Welsted *v.* Swansea Bank, Ld., 5 T. L. R. 332.

(c) Read *v.* Joannon, 25 Q. B. D. 300; 38 W. R. 734; 63 L. T. 387 ; 59 L. J. Q. B. 511.

(d) Jarvis *v.* Jarvis, 63 L. T. 412.

(e) *Re* Cunningham, 28 Ch. D. 682.

(f) Shears *v.* Jacob, L. R., 1 C. P., 513.

(g) Maugham *v.* Sharpe, 17 C. B. N. S. 443.

(h) Simmons *v.* Woodward, [1892] A. C. 100.

Under the principal Act, it has been held that want of
registration does not avoid, as against the official liquidator
of a Company, a debenture whereby the Company acknowledged its indebtedness in a principal sum, on which interest
was to be paid, and for payment of principal and interest
pledged to the debenture-holder, rateably with holders of
other debentures, amongst other things, personal chattels of
the Company, which debenture, it was provided, should not
be registered as a bill of sale.[a]

17. (1878.) Every affidavit required by or for the *Affidavit.*
purposes of this Act may be sworn before a Master of
any division of the High Court of Justice, or before
any Commissioner empowered to take affidavits in
the Supreme Court of Judicature.

Whoever wilfully makes or uses any false affidavit
for the purposes of this Act shall be deemed guilty
of wilful and corrupt perjury.

By Rule 12, R. S. C., Bills of Sale Acts. 1878 and 1882
every first and second class clerk in the Bills of Sale Department of the Central Office of the Supreme Court shall, by
virtue of his office, have authority to take oaths and affidavits
in matters relating to that department.

Every affidavit shall be intituled in the cause or matter
in which it is sworn, and shall be confined to such facts as the
witness is able of his own knowledge to prove, except on
interlocutory motions, on which statements as to his
belief, with the grounds thereof, may be admitted. The costs
of every affidavit which shall unnecessarily set forth matters
of hearsay, or argumentative matter, or copies of or extracts
from documents, shall be paid by the party filing the same. [b]
Every commissioner to administer oaths shall express the time
when and the place where he shall take any affidavit, or the
acknowledgment of any deed or recognizance; otherwise the
same shall not be held authentic, nor be admitted to be filed
or enrolled without the leave of the Court or a Judge; and
every such commissioner shall express the time when and the
place where he shall do any other act incident to his office. [c]

(a) Re Asphaltic Wood Pavement Co., 19 L. T. 159; 32 W. R. 6.
(b) R. S. C., 1883, O. xxxviii. 2, 3.
(c) Rule 6.

All affidavits, declarations, affirmations and attestations of honour, in causes or matters depending in the High Court, may be sworn and taken in Scotland or Ireland, or the Channel Islands, or in any colony, island, plantation or place under the dominion of Her Majesty in foreign parts, before any Judge, Court, notary public, or person lawfully authorized to administer oaths in such country, colony, island, plantation or place respectively, or before any of Her Majesty's consuls or vice-consuls in any foreign parts out of Her Majesty's dominions; and the Judges and other officers of the High Court shall take judicial notice of the seal or signature, as the case may be, of any such Court, Judge, notary public, person, consul or vice-consul, attached, appended or subscribed to any such affidavits affirmations, attestations of honour, declarations, or to any other deed or document.[a]   Every affidavit shall be drawn up in the first person, and shall be divided into paragraphs, and every paragraph shall be numbered consecutively, and, as nearly as may be, shall be confined to a distinct portion of the subject.   Every affidavit shall be written or printed bookwise. No costs shall be allowed for any affidavit or part of an affidavit substantially departing from this rule.[b]   Every affidavit shall state the description and true place of abode of the deponent,[c] and if made by two or more deponents, the names of the several persons making the affidavit shall be inserted in the jurat, except that if the affidavit of all the deponents is taken at one time by the same officer, it shall be sufficient to state that it was sworn by both (or all) of the " above-named " deponents.[d]

The Court or a Judge may order to be struck out from any affidavit any matter which is scandalous, and may order the costs of any application to strike out such matter to be paid as between solicitor and client.[e]

Affidavits.   No affidavit having in the jurat or body thereof any interlineation, alteration, or erasure, shall, without leave of the Court or a Judge, be read or made use of in any matter depending in Court, unless the interlineation or alteration (other than by erasure) is authenticated by the initials of the officer taking the affidavit; or, if taken at the Central Office, either by his initials or by the stamp of that office; nor in the case of an erasure, unless the words or figures appearing at

(a) Rule 6   (b) Rule 7.   (c) Rule 8.
(d) Rule 9.   (e) Rule 11.

the time of taking the affidavit to be written on the erasure are re-written and signed or initialled in the margin of the affidavit by the officer taking it.[a]

Where an affidavit is sworn by any person who appears to the officer taking the affidavit to be illiterate or blind, the officer shall certify in the jurat that the affidavit was read in his presence to the deponent, that the deponent seemed perfectly to understand it, and that the deponent made his or her signature in the presence of the officer. No such affidavit shall be used in evidence in the absence of this certificate, unless the Court or a Judge is otherwise satisfied that the affidavit was read over to, and apparently perfectly understood by the deponent.[b]

Every affidavit shall be filed in the Central Office,[c] and there shall be appended to it a note shewing on whose behalf it is filed,[d] and no affidavit shall be filed or used without such note, unless the Court or a Judge shall otherwise direct; but the Court or a Judge may receive any affidavit sworn for the purpose of being used in any cause or matter, notwithstanding any defect by misdescription of parties or otherwise in the title or jurat, or any other irregularity in the form thereof, and may direct a memorandum to be made on the document that it has been so received.[e] Affidavits used on applications in Court or at chambers respecting bills of sale are filed in each case under the name of the party by whom the bill of sale was given.

In cases in which, by the present practice, an original *Affidavits.* affidavit is allowed to be used, it shall, before it is used, be stamped with a proper filing stamp, and shall, at the time when it is used, be delivered to and left with the proper officer in Court or in chambers, who shall send it to be filed. An office copy of an affidavit may in all cases be used, the original affidavit having been previously filed, and the copy duly authenticated with the seal of the office.[f] Where a special time is limited for filing affidavits, no affidavit filed after that time shall be used except by leave of the Court or a Judge.[g]

(a) R. S. C. 1881, O. xxxviii., Rule 12.
(b) Rule 13.
(c) This does not apply to affidavits required to be filed in a District Registry
(d) R. S. C., 1883, O. xxxviii., Rule 10.
(e) Rule 14.
(f) Rule 15.
(g) Rule 18.

Formerly where an affidavit of execution made by the solicitor attesting a bill of sale was sworn by him before a commissioner, who was in partnership with him as a solicitor, it was held the affidavit was duly sworn ; [a] but now no affidavit shall be sufficient if sworn before the solicitor acting for the party on whose behalf the affidavit is to be used, or before any agent or correspondent of such solicitor, or before the party himself ; [b] and an affidavit which would be insufficient if sworn before the solicitor himself, shall be insufficient if sworn before his clerk or partner. [c]

A false statement in an affidavit in non-judicial proceedings was a misdemeanour at Common Law. [d] Perjury is punishable by penal servitude not exceeding seven years, or by imprisonment.

18. (1878.) There shall be paid and received in common law stamps the following fees, viz. :—

On filing a bill of sale...　　...　　...　2s.

On filing the affidavit of execution of a bill of sale ...　　...　　...　　...　2s.

On the affidavit used for the purpose of re-registering a bill of sale (to include the fee for filing) ...　　...　5s.

By order as to Supreme Court Fees, 1884, the following fees for searches and inspection are payable :—

114. On a request for a search and certificate, pursuant to Order LXI., Rule 23　5s.

115. If more than one name included in the same request, for each additional name　　...　　...　　...　　...　　...　2s.

116. On a duplicate certificate, if not more than three folios　　...　　...　　...　1s.

117. For every additional folio　　...　　...　6d.

118. On every continuation search, if requested within 14 days of any former search (the result to be endorsed on such certificate) ...　　...　　...　　...　1s.

(a) Vernon v. Cooke, 49 L. J. C. P. 767.
(b) R. S. C., 1883, O. xxxviii., Rule 16.
(c) Rule 17.
(d) R. v. Hodgkiss, L. R. 1 C. C. R. 212; 39 L. J. M. C. 14; 11 Cox, 365 ; 18 W. R. 150　21 L. T. 564.

By the order as to Supreme Court Fees, 1884, the
following are prescribed :—

		£	s.	d.
36. On filing a bill of sale and affidavit therewith where the consideration (including further advances) does not exceed £100...		0	5	0
37. Above £100 and not exceeding £200 ...		0	10	0
38. Above £200		1	0	0
39. On filing under the Bills of Sale Acts, 1878 and 1882, any other document to which the fees Nos. 36, 37 and 38 do not apply		0	10	0
40. On filing an affidavit of re-registration of a bill of sale or any such other document as in No. 39 mentioned		0	10	0
41. On filing a list of satisfaction ...		0	5	0

By order as to fees and percentages, 4th July, 1884, it is
provided that the above fees shall be paid by impressed
stamps.

The following duties are imposed on bills of sale by the Stamp duties.
Stamp Act, 1891, and should be denoted by impressed
stamps, except in cases within sec. 7, Stamp Act, 1891, where
the duty not exceeding 2s. 6d., adhesive stamps may be used,
calculated according to the amount or value of the consideration appearing on the face of the deed. By sec. 41 of the
Act a bill of sale is not to be registered under any Act for
the time being in force relating to the registration of bills of
sale unless the original duly stamped is produced to the
proper officer. But a bill of sale though not duly stamped at
the time of filing the copy, was admitted in evidence on the
duty and penalty being paid.[a]

An absolute bill of sale is a conveyance within the Stamp
Act, and is subject to a stamp duty upon the amount or
value of the consideration for the sale as follows :—

Not exceeding £25 a duty of 6d. for every £5 or part of £5.				£	s.	d.
Exceeding	25 and not exceeding £50	...		£0	5	0
,,	50 ,, ,,	75	...	0	7	6
,,	75 ,, ,,	100	...	0	10	0
,,	100 ,, ,,	125	...	0	12	6
,,	125 ,, ,,	150	...	0	15	0
,,	150 ,, ,,	175	...	0	17	6

(a) Bellamy v. Saull, 4 B. & S. 265; 32 L. J. Q. B. 366; 3 W. R. 807; 8 L. T. 534.

Exceeding	£175 and not exceeding 200	... £1	0	0
"	200 " " 225	... 1	2	6
"	225 " " 250	... 1	5	0
"	275 " " 300	... 1	10	0
"	300, for every £50, and also for any fractional part of £50 of such amount or value	... 0	5	0

Stamp duties.

A conditional bill of sale, being the only or principal security, other than an equitable mortgage, for the payment or repayment of money, is to be stamped as a mortgage as follows : —

Not exceeding £25	... £0	0	8
Exceeding	25 and not exceeding £50	... 0	1	3
"	50 " " 100	... 0	2	6
"	100 " " 150	... 0	3	9
"	150 " " 200	... 0	5	0
"	200 " " 250	... 0	6	3
"	250 " " 300	... 0	7	6
"	300, for every £100, and also for any fractional part of £100 of the amount secured	0	2	6

If a collateral, auxiliary, additional, or substituted security, other than an equitable mortgage, or by way of further assurance, where the principal or primary security is duly stamped :—

For every £100, and for any part of £100 secured £0   0   6

Being an equitable mortgage :—for every £100 and any fractional part of £100, of the amount secured   ...   £0   1   0

A re-conveyance or release, or a transfer or assignment of a bill of sale, or of any money thereby secured, is subject to a duty of 6d. for every £100 or part of £100 of the amount transferred or assigned. If any further money is added to the amount already advanced, the instrument should be stamped as a principal security for such further money ; for it would seem that a transfer of a bill of sale accompanied by a further advance is, for the purposes of the Stamp Act, a transfer of a bill of sale of·the amount of the original advance, and a new security to the extent of the additional advance.[a]

(a) Wale v. Commissioners of Inland Revenue, 41 L. T. 166.

A bill of sale to secure future advances, either with or without money previously due, is to be charged, when the total amount secured is in any way limited, with the same duty as a security for the amount so limited; where such total amount is unlimited the security will only be available for the amount which the stamp thereon impressed extends to cover, but where any advance is made in excess of the amount covered by that duty the security shall, for the purpose of stamp duty, be deemed to be a new and separate instrument, bearing date on the day on which the advance or loan is made. [a]

Under the repealed sec. 15, Stamp Act, 1870, corresponding to sec. 15, Stamp Act, 1891, the Commissioners of Inland Revenue might stamp the security, even after its execution, for the proper amount for which it is sought to be made available. [b]

Stamp duties.

It was usual to insert a proviso that the total principal moneys recoverable under the bill of sale should not exceed a specified sum.

The documents defined as bills of sale by sec. 4 of the principal Act will probably require to be so stamped; thus, an inventory with receipt attached, a receipt for the purchase-money of goods not in the ordinary course of business, or an agreement by which a right shall be conferred in equity to any personal chattels, or to any charge or security thereon, should, it would seem, now be stamped as a bill of sale.

Where a bill of sale assigned specified chattels and all others substituted for them, provided their description should be indorsed on the bill of sale, indorsements describing substituted chattels were held to be only for the purposes of identification, and not to require an additional stamp. [c]

On an issue to try the property in goods, a previous bill of sale of the same goods, although cancelled, is not admissible, even to prove good faith, unless duly stamped; [d] but an unstamped bill of sale may be given in evidence for the purpose of proving an act of bankruptcy. [e] Indeed, it appears that whenever a bill of sale is used, not to establish it, or set it

(a) Sec. 84, Stamp Act, 1891.
b) Fitzgerald v. Mollersh, W. N. 1892, 4.
(c) Barker v. Aston, 1 F. & F. 102.
(d) Williams v. Gerry, 10 M. & W. 296; 11 L. J. Ex. 340.
(e) Ponsford v. Walton, L. R. 3 C. P. 167; 37 L. J. C. P. 113; 16 W. R. 383.

up, but to destroy it altogether, it is, although unstamped, admissible in evidence.[a]

An authority to act under a bill of sale, as, for instance, an authority to sell, does not require a stamp.[b]

Stamp duties.   There were formerly duties imposed on every schedule or inventory or document of any kind whatsoever, referred to, in or by, and intended to be used or given in evidence as part of, or as material to, any other instrument charged with any duty, but which is separate and distinct from, and not indorsed on or annexed to such other instrument.

By sec. 15 (2) (a) Stamp Act, 1891, a bill of sale, unless written upon duly stamped material, shall be duly stamped with the proper *ad valorem* duty before the expiration of 30 days after it is first executed, or after it has been first received in the United Kingdom, in case it is first executed elsewhere.

An unstamped or insufficiently stamped bill of sale may be properly stamped after the execution thereof on payment of the unpaid duty, a penalty of £10, and also, by way of further penalty, where the unpaid duty exceeds £10, of interest on such duty at the rate of £5 per cent. per annum from the date of execution of the bill of sale until such interest is equal in amount to the unpaid duty.[c]

By sec. 15 (2) (c), Stamp Act, 1891, the instruments therein mentioned executed after the 16th May, 1888, shall be duly stamped, otherwise the person specified being, in the case of bills of sale, the grantee or transferee, and of settlements the settlor, shall forfeit the sum of £10, and in addition to the penalty payable on stamping the instrument, there shall be a further penalty equivalent to the stamp duty thereon unless a reasonable excuse for the delay in stamping, or the omission to stamp, or the insufficiency of stamp, be afforded to the satisfaction of the Commissioners of Inland Revenue, or of the court, judge, arbitrator or referee before whom the instrument is produced.

Collection of fees.   **19. (1878.)** Section twenty-six of the Supreme Court of Judicature Act, 1875, and any enactments for the time being in force amending or substituted for that section, shall apply to fees under this Act,

(a) Coppock *v.* Bower, 4 M. & W. 361.
(b) Barker *v.* Dale, 1 F. & F. 271.
(c) Stamp Act, 1891, sec. 15.

and an order under that section may, if need be, be
made in relation to such fees accordingly.

The fees directed to be paid under orders made in pursuance of the section will be found noted to sec. 18.

Further regulations as to fees will be found in the Public
Offices Fees Act, 1879, and in the Order as to Supreme Court
Fees, 1884.

20. (1878.) Chattels comprised in a bill of sale *Order and disposition.*
which has been and continues to be duly registered
under this Act shall not be deemed to be in the
possession, order, or disposition of the grantor of the
bill of sale within the meaning of the Bankruptcy
Act, 1869.

This section is repealed by sec. 15 of the amendment Act,
but it has been held that the repeal is, by sec. 3 of that Act,
limited to bills of sale given as security for the payment of
money, and that bills of sale given by way of absolute transfer,
and registered under the principal Act, are still within the
protection of the section. Therefore, when an absolute bill of
sale was given, after the commencement of the amendment
Act, and duly registered under the principal Act, it was held
that the chattels it comprised could not be deemed to be in
the possession, order, or disposition of the grantor, who had
become bankrupt.[a]

As the amendment Act does not apply to any bill of sale
duly registered before the commencement of the Act, unless
the context otherwise requires,[b] the protection afforded by the
section applies to chattels comprised in a bill of sale duly
registered before the 1st of November, 1882, even though after
that time they may, with the consent of the true owner, be in
the reputed ownership of the grantor at the commencement of
his bankruptcy.[c]

The section, however, would not protect a mortgagee whose
bill of sale is unregistered or invalid from any cause where the
doctrine of reputed ownership would otherwise have applied;
but the protection of the section has been extended to cases
where the grantor became bankrupt within the seven days

[a] Swift v. Pannell, 24 Ch. D. 210. —
[b] Sec. 3 (1882).
[c] Exp. Izard, re Chapple, 23 Ch. D. 409.

allowed for registration, although the bill of sale was un-registered.[a]

Under the Bills of Sale Act, 1854, registration of a bill of sale did not take the goods it comprised out of the grantor's reputed ownership;[b] and the effect of the repeal will be to restore the former law, so far as regards bills of sale within the amendment Act.

Order and disposition.

By the Bankruptcy Act, 1883, sec. 149 (2), where by any Act or instrument reference is made to the Bankruptcy Act, 1869, the Act or instrument shall be construed and have effect as if reference were made therein to the corresponding provisions of this Act. By sec. 44 (2), (III.), the property of the bankrupt divisible amongst his creditors comprises all goods being, at the commencement of the bankruptcy, in the possession, order or disposition of the bankrupt, in his trade or business, by the consent and per-mission of the true owner, under such circumstances that he is the reputed owner thereof; provided that things in action, other than debts due or growing due to the bankrupt in the course of his trade or business, shall not be deemed goods within the meaning of this section.[c]

The section is thus limited to goods in the possession order, or disposition of the bankrupt in his trade or business which means for the purposes of, and as connected with his trade or business. The term business is more extensive than the word trade, and there may be a great many businesses which are not trades; but what is or is not a business must, it seems, depend on the circumstances of each particular case.[d]

The section does not apply to fixtures, whether land-lord's, trade, or tenant's, affixed to and passing with the freehold, though separately assigned or charged, even

(a) *Exp.* Kahen, *re* Hewer, 46 L. T. 856.

(b) Stansfield *v.* Cubitt, 27 L. J. Ch. 266; Badger *v.* Shaw, 2 E. & E. 472; 29 L. J. Q. B. 73; 8 W. R. 210; *exp.* Harding, *re* Fairbrother, 15 Eq. 223; 42 L. J. Bank. 30; 28 L. T. 241.

(c) By sec. 15, sub-sec. 5, the corresponding section of the Bankruptcy Act, 1869, the bankrupt's property comprised all goods and chattels being, at the commencement of the bankruptcy, in the possession, order, or disposition of the bankrupt, being a trader, by the consent and permission of the true owner, of which goods and chattels the bankrupt is reputed owner, or of which he has taken upon himself the sale or disposition as owner; provided that things in action, other than debts due to him in the course of his trade or business, shall not be deemed goods and chattels within the meaning of this clause.

(d) Rolls *v.* Miller, 27 Ch. D. 71; 53 L. J. Ch. 682; 50 L. T. 597; 32 W. R. 806; *xp.* Sully, *re* Wallis, 14 Q. B. D. 950; 2 Mor. 79; 52 L. T. 625; 33 W. R. 733.

such as might be sold as goods and chattels under an
execution; for though for the purposes of the Bills of Sale
Acts fixtures are declared personal chattels, they are not
made so for all other purposes.[a] But plant and trade utensils
are within the Act.[b]

The commencement of the bankruptcy is defined by sec. 43
of the Bankruptcy Act, 1883, as the time of the act of bankruptcy being committed, on which a receiving order is made,
or if the bankrupt is proved to have committed more acts of
bankruptcy than one, at the time of the first of the acts of
bankruptcy proved to have been committed by the bankrupt
within three months next preceding the date of the presentation of the bankruptcy petition. Under the Bankruptcy Act,
1869, by sec. 11, the bankruptcy commenced at the time of the
completion of the act of bankruptcy on which the order of adjudication was made, or the time of the first of the acts of bankruptcy proved to have been committed by the bankrupt within
twelve months next preceding the order of adjudication, provided that at the time of committing such prior act the
bankrupt was indebted to some creditor or creditors in a sum
or sums sufficient to support a petition, which debt or debts
still remained due at the time of the adjudication. The title
of a trustee in liquidation, under sec. 125, sub-sec. 5, of the
Bankruptcy Act, 1869, had a similar relation.[c]

Goods coming into the debtor's possession after the com- *Order and disposition*
mencement of the bankruptcy are not within the section.[d]
To bring the case within the section there must be reputed
ownership, with possession, order, or disposition, by the
consent of the true owner; for the section means that if goods
are in a man's possession, order, or disposition, under such
circumstances as to enable him by means of them to obtain
false credit, then the owner of the goods who has permitted
him to obtain that false credit is to suffer the penalty of
losing his goods for the benefit of those who have given the
credit.[e]

The doctrine of reputed ownership does not require any
investigation into the actual state of knowledge or belief.

(a) Meux v. Jacobs, L. R. 7 H. L. 481.
(b) Horn v. Baker, 2 S. L. Cases, 8th ed., 245.
(c) *Exp.* Duignan, *re* Bissell, L. R. 6 Ch. 605; 40 L. J. Bank. 68; 25 L. T. 286;
19 W. R. 1127.
(d) Lyon v. Weldon, 2 Bing. 334; 9 Moo. 62.
(e) *Exp.* Wingfield, *re* Florence, 10 Ch. D. 591; 40 L. T. 15; 27 W. R. 340, per
James, L.J.

either of all creditors, or of particular creditors, and still less of the outside world, who are no creditors at all, as to the position of particular goods. It is enough for the doctrine if the goods are in such a situation as to convey to the minds of those who know their situation the reputation of ownership. that reputation arising by the legitimate exercise of reason and judgment on the knowledge of those facts which are capable of being generally known to those who choose to make inquiry on the subject.[a]

So, on the other hand, it is not at all necessary, in order to exclude the doctrine of reputed ownership, to shew that every creditor, or any particular creditor, or the outside world who are not creditors, knew anything whatever about particular goods one way or the other, and it is enough if the situation of the goods was such as to exclude all legitimate ground from which those who knew anything about that situation could infer the ownership to be in the person having actual possession.[a]

Order and disposition.

The goods must be in the sole possession, order, or disposition of the bankrupt; thus the joint possession of the bankrupt and his partner is not sufficient;[b] and where the agent of a bill of sale holder held possession with the bankrupt the section did not apply.[c]

With respect to goods of which the bankrupt was the original owner, as will usually be the case with chattels comprised in a bill of sale, the presumption is that his ownership continues whilst they remain in his possession, order, or disposition, and the onus is upon the person claiming the goods against the trustee to shew that the bankrupt has ceased to be the reputed owner. When, however, the bankrupt was not the original owner of the goods, reputation of ownership must be proved by other circumstances;[d] but as to goods connected with the bankrupt's business the inference has always been stronger than in the case of other articles.[e]

If a bill of sale holder permits the grantor to retain possession, the chattels will, it seems, be subject to the section, whether

(a) *Exp.* Watkins, *re* Couston, L. R. 8 Ch. 520; 42 L. J. Bank. 50; 21 W. R. 530; 28 L. T. 793.

(b) *Exp.* Dorman, *re* Lake, L. R. 8 Ch. 51; 42 L. J. Bank. 20.

(c) Vicarino *v.* Hollingsworth, 20 L. T. 302; *exp.* Fletcher, 8 Ch. D. 218.

(d) Lingard *v.* Messiter, 1 B. & C. 308.

(e) *Exp.* Lovering, *re* Murrell, 24 Ch. D. 31; 32 W. R. 217; 52 L. J. Ch. 951; 49 L. T. 242.

possession be consistent with the deed or not;[a] although the contrary has been decided in the Irish Courts.[b] The possession may be actual or constructive; thus goods held by the agent or bailee of the bankrupt have been held to be in his reputed ownership.[c] Where the goods are held under a trust,[d] or notoriously as factor or agent,[e] the section will not apply; and the reputation of ownership may be rebutted, by some custom proved to exist, either by reported cases or by evidence, and not of such a nature as necessarily to deceive, which the creditors of the debtor may be reasonably presumed to have known, for persons in the debtor's position to hold possession of the goods of others.[f]

Thus the custom of the hire of pianos, or of hotel keepers hiring furniture, has been so frequently proved, that the Courts will take judicial notice of it; [g] and it applies to everything which is necessary to furnish an hotel for the purpose of carrying it on as such, though in fact the goods are not on hire; [h] but it seems there is no such general custom of letting furniture on hire as to exclude the doctrine of reputed ownership; [i] and where the purchaser of furniture allowed the vendor to remain in possession at a rent, it was held to remain in his reputed ownership,[j] and so where the purchaser of furniture seized by the sheriff left it in the possession of the execution debtor, he agreeing to pay interest on the purchase-money. [k] A custom for persons to have the goods of others in their custody has been proved in the case, among others, of booksellers,[k] barge owners,[l] clockmakers,[m] coachbuilders,[n]

Order and disposition.

(a) Freshney c. Carrick, 1 H. & N. 653 ; 26 L. J. Ex. 129 ; Spackman c. Miller, 12 C. B. N. S. 659 ; 9 Jur. N. S. 50 ; 31 L. J. C. P. 309.

(b) In re Stanley, 17 L. R. Ir. 457.

(c) Knowles c. Horsfall, 5 B. & Ald. 134 ; Hervey c. Liddiard, 1 Stark, 123 ; Hornsby c. Miller, 1 E. & E. 192 ; 5 Jur. N. S. 938.

(d) Bankruptcy Act, 1883, S. 44 (1).

(e) Exp. Bright re Smith, 10 Ch. D. 566 ; 48 L. J. Bank. 81 ; 27 W. R. 385 ; 39 L. T. 649 ; exp. Buck, re Fawcus, 3 Ch. D. 795 ; 34 L. T. 807.

(f) Exp. Powell, re Matthews, 1 Ch. D. 501 ; 45 L. J. Bank. 100 ; 24 W. R. 811 ; 34 L. T. 234 ; exp. Vaux, L. R. 9 Ch. 602 ; 43 L. J. Bank. 113 ; 22 W. R. 811 ; 30 L. T. 739 ; exp. Emerson, 41 L. J. Bank. 20 ; Smith c. Hudson, 34 L. J. Q. B. 145 ; 13 W. R. 683 ; 12 L. T. 377 ; 11 Jur. N. S. 622.

(g) Crawcour c. Salter, 18 Ch. D. 30 ; exp. Hattersley, re Blanshard, 8 Ch. D. 601 ; 47 L. J. Bank. 113 ; 38 L. T. 619 ; 26 W. R. 636.

(h) Exp. Turquand, re Parker, 14 Q. B. D. 636.

(i) Exp. Brooks, re Fowler, 44 L. T. 453 ; 31 W. R. 833 ; 23 Ch. D. 261.

(j) Exp. Lovering, re Jones, L. R. 9 Ch. 621 ; 43 L. J. Bank. 116 ; 30 L. T. 622 ; 22 W. R. 853.

(k) Whitfield c. Brand, 16 M. & W. 282 ; 16 L. J. Ex. 103.

(l) Watson c. Peache, 1 Bing. N. C. 327.

(m) Hamilton c. Bell, 10 Exch. 545 ; 18 Jur. 1169 ; 24 L. J. Ex. 45.

(n) Exp. Wiggins, 2 D. & C. 269 ; M. & B. 168 ; Carruthers c. Payne, 5 Bi g. 270 ; 2 M. & P. 420.

farmers,[a] wine merchants,[b] hop merchants,[c] malting agents,[d] printers as to printing machines,[e] dealers in iron safes,[f] gas engines,[g] and horse dealers,[h] and where, according to the custom of the country, machinery and utensils of trade are included in a lease, as in the case of a colliery, possession by the lessee does not necessarily raise any reputation of ownership.[i]

Consent of the true owner. The true owner's consent is a question of fact to be gathered from all the circumstances of the case:[j] and the onus of proving the consent of the true owner rests with the trustee.[k] A person claiming a legal or equitable interest in the goods, as for instance, a pawnee, mortgagee, or bailee having a lien, is the true owner for the purposes of the section.[l]

If before any act of bankruptcy the true owner demands, or endeavours to obtain possession of the goods, or does some act to determine his consent to the debtor's possession, this will prevent the application of the section.[m] Thus, if he seizes the goods, although the possession is friendly, and does not disturb the grantor's apparent possession, it will be sufficient; [n] and a mere demand of possession, if made in good faith will negative the consent of the true owner.[o] And even without any personal demand, the consent of the true owner was held to be withdrawn, his agents having made every effort, short of a forcible entry, to seize the goods in premises which had been closed.[p]

(a) Priestley v. Pratt, L. R. 2 Ex. 101.

(b) Exp. Watkins, L. R. 8 Ch. 520; exp. Vaux. L. R. 0 Ch. 602.

(c) Exp. Dyer, re Taylor, 2 Mor. 269; 53 L. T. 768; 34 W. R. 108.

(d) Harris v. Truman, 9 Q. B. D. 264; 30 W. R. 533; 51 L. J. Q. B. 338; 46 L. T. 844.

(e) Exp. Hughes, re Thrackrah, 5 Mor. 235.

(f) Exp. Poppleton, re Lock, 8 Mor. 51.

(g) Re Peel [1894], 1 I. R. 235.

(h) Exp. Wingfield, re Florence, 10 Ch. D. 591.

(i) Coombs v. Beaumont, 5 B. & Ad. 72.

(j) Load v. Green, 15 M. & W. 216 ; Prismall v. Lovegrove, 6 L. T. N. S. 229.

(k) Exp. Alexander, re Eslick, 4 Ch. D. 496 ; 46 L. J. Bank. 30 ; 25 W. R. 280; 35 L. T. 912.

(l) Exp. Union Bank of Manchester, re Jackson, 12 Eq. 354 ; 40 L. J. Bank. 57 ; 24 L. T. 951 ; 19 W. R. 872 ; Colonial Bank v. Whinney, 11 App. Cas. 426. 34 W. R. 705.

(m) Exp. Montagu, 1 Ch. D. 556 ; 24 W. R. 309 ; 34 L. T. 197 ; Spackman v. Miller, 12 C. B. N. S. 659.

(n) Exp. National Guardians Assurance Co., re Francis, 10 Ch. D. 408.

(o) Exp. Ward, re Couston, L. R. 8 Ch. 144 ; 42 L. J. Bank. 17 ; 21 W. R. 115 ; 27 L. T. 502 ; Smith v. Topping, 5 B. & Ad. 674 ; exp. Jay, L. R. 9 Ch. 704, per Mellish, L. J.

p) Exp. Cohen, re Sparke, 40 L. J. Bank. 14 ; 19 W. R. 126.

It appears that if the mortgagee, without notice of an available act of bankruptcy committed by the grantor, takes the goods out of his possession before receiving order, or endeavours to obtain them, or signifies his dissent to their remaining longer in the grantor's possession, the section will not apply, even where an act of bankruptcy has been committed; for although at the commencement of the bankruptcy the goods may have been in the bankrupt's reputed ownership, with the consent of the true owner, his taking possession of the goods will be a dealing protected by sec. 49 of the Bankruptcy Act, 1883. A mere intention, however, to demand or take possession of the goods will not be sufficient,[a] nor will an attempt to dispose of them if they afterwards remain in the bankrupt's possession.[b]

A creditor who receives notice of his debtor's intention to commit an act of bankruptcy is not bound to inquire whether the act has been committed, but is entitled to avail himself of his remedies just as if he had received no notice. Thus, where the holder of a bill of sale received notice that the debtor was about to file a liquidation petition, and at once sent to demand payment of the debt and take possession of the property comprised in the bill of sale, obtaining possession one day after the petition was filed, but having no notice that this had been done, it was held that the taking possession was a dealing with the debtor for valuable consideration within the protective clauses of the Bankruptcy Act, and that the section did not apply, notwithstanding the prior act of bankruptcy.[c]

Order and disposition.

Goods and chattels in the custody of the law will not be in the debtor's order or disposition; as where they are seized by the landlord under a distress for rent,[d] or by a receiver,[e] or by the sheriff under a lawful execution,[f] but where the seizure is wrongful it has been decided that the section will still apply.[g]

(a) Brown v. Short, 5 E. & B. 227; 1 Jur. N. S. 793; 24 L. J. Q. B. 297; Graham v. Furber, 14 C. B. 131.
(b) Reynolds v. Hall, 4 H. & N. 519; 28 L. J. Ex. 257.
(c) Exp. Arnold, re Wright, 3 Ch. D. 70.
(d) Sucker v. Chudley, 13 W. R. 890; 11 Jur. 654.
(e) Taylor v. Eckersley, 5 Ch. D. 740.
(f) Fletcher v. Manning, 12 M. & W. 571, exp. Foss, re Baldwin, 2 De G. & J. 230; 27 L. J. Bank. 17; 4 Jur. N. S. 522; exp. Saffery, re Bremner, 16 Ch. D. 668.
(g) Barrow v. Bell, 5 E. & B. 540; 25 L. J. Q. B. 2; 20 Jur. 159; 4 W. R. 16; 26 L. T. O. S. 71; exp. Edoy, re Cuthbertson, 44 L. J. Bank. 55; L. R. 19 Eq. 264; 33 W. R. 519; 31 L. T. 851.

Sec. 20.
[1878.]
Sec. 2.
[1890.]
Sec. 21.
[1878.]

Things in action, other than debts due or growing due to the bankrupt in the course of his trade or business are exempted from the operation of the reputed ownership clause of the Bankruptcy Act, but it is prudent at once to give notice to the debtor, trustee, or other person from whom such thing in action is claimed; and so where goods are in the custody or warehouse of a third person notice should be given, in order to complete the bill of sale holder's title.

The doctrine of reputed ownership has been here considered only in its application to bills of sale, and its principles will be found more fully discussed in treatises on bankruptcy law.

Saving of 46 & 47 Vict. c. 52 s. 44.

2. (1890.) Nothing in this Act shall affect the operation of section forty-four of the Bankruptcy Act, 1883, in respect of any goods comprised in any such instrument as is hereinbefore described, if such goods would but for this Act be goods within the meaning of sub-section three of that section.

By sec. 1, Bills of Sale Act, 1890, as amended by sec. 1. Bills of Sale Act, 1891, an instrument charging or creating any security on or declaring trusts of imported goods given or executed at any time prior to their deposit in a warehouse, factory, or store, or to their being reshipped for export, or delivered to a purchaser not being the person giving or executing such instrument, shall not be deemed a bill of sale within the meaning of the Bills of Sale Acts, 1878 and 1882.

Rules.

21. (1878) Rules for the purposes of this Act may be made and altered from time to time by the like persons and in the like manner in which rules and regulations may be made under and for the purposes of the Supreme Court of Judicature Acts, 1873 and 1875.

Power to make rules was given by sec. 68 of the Judicature Act, 1873, since repealed, and provisions for making rules are now contained in the Supreme Court of Judicature Act, 1875; the Appellate Jurisdiction Act, 1876 ; and the Supreme

Court of Judicature Acts, 1881 and 1884. All rules made under the Acts are to be laid before each House of Parliament, and are subject to be annulled as by the Acts provided.

Certain rules have been issued in pursuance of these powers, and will be found in the Appendix, Part I.

22. (1878.) When the time for registering a bill of sale expires on a Sunday, or other day on which the registrar's office is closed, the registration shall be valid if made on the next following day on which the office is open.

By R. S. C., 1883, Order lxiii., Rule 6, the several offices of the Supreme Court shall be open on every day of the year except Sundays, Good Friday, Easter Eve, Monday and Tuesday in Easter Week, Whit Monday, Christmas Day, and the next following working day, and all days appointed by proclamation to be observed as days of general fast, humiliation or thanksgiving.

23. (1878.) From and after the commencement of this Act, the Bills of Sale Act, 1854, and the Bills of Sale Act, 1866, shall be repealed : Provided that (except as is herein expressly mentioned with respect to construction and with respect to renewal of registration) nothing in this Act shall affect any bill of sale executed before the commencement of this Act, and as regards bills of sale so executed, the Acts hereby repealed shall continue in force.

Any renewal after the commencement of this Act of the registration of a bill of sale executed before the commencement of this Act, and registered under the Acts hereby repealed, shall be made under this Act in the same manner as the renewal of a registration made under this Act.

The section does not authorize renewal of a bill of sale, the registration of which was void for want of renewal at the commencement of the principal Act.[a]

(a) Re Emery, 21 Q. B. D. 405 ; 37 W. R. 21.

Sec. 18.
[1882.]

Sec. 24.
[1878.]

Mxteut of Act.

18. (1882.) This Act shall not extend to Scotland or Ireland.

Extent of Act.

24. (1878.) This Act shall not extend to Scotland or to Ireland.

Bills of sale given and registered in Ireland are regulated by the Bills of Sale (Ireland) Act, 1879 (42 & 43 Vic. c. 50), and the Bills of Sale (Ireland) Act (1879) Amendment Act, 1883 (46 Vic. c. 7); cited together as the Bills of Sale (Ireland) Acts, 1879 and 1883.

Under the law of Scotland it is necessary, in order to give a charge on corporeal moveables, that they should be delivered to and placed in the possession of the creditor; but if a domiciled Scotchman, resident in London, gave a duly registered bill of sale of the furniture of his house, that would be a complete and effectual transfer of the property without delivery.[b]

(b) *Re* Queensland Mercantile, &c., Co. [1891], 1 Ch. 545; 60 L. J. Ch. 579; 64 L. T. 555; 39 W. R. 447.

SCHEDULES.

SCHEDULE A.

[Affidavit on renewing Registration, see p. 255.]

[1878.]
Section 11.

SCHEDULE B.

[Form of Register, see p. 255.]

[1878.]
Section 12.

SCHEDULE.

[Form of Bill of Sale, see p. 260.]

[1882.]
Section 9.

APPENDIX.

APPENDIX.

PART I.

THE BILLS OF SALE ACT, 1878.

(41 & 42 Vict. c. 31.)

—

AN ACT

TO

CONSOLIDATE AND AMEND THE LAW FOR PREVENTING FRAUDS UPON CREDITORS BY SECRET BILLS OF SALE OF PERSONAL CHATTELS.

[22nd July, 1878.

WHEREAS it is expedient to consolidate and amend the law relating to bills of sale of personal chattels:

BE it enacted by the Queen's Most Excellent Majesty, by and with the advice and consent of the Lords Spiritual and Temporal, and Commons, in this present Parliament assembled, and by the authority of the same, as follows:

1. This Act may be cited for all purposes as the Bills of Sale Act, 1878. *(30)* Short Title.*

2. This Act shall come into operation on the first day of January one thousand eight hundred and seventy nine, which day is in this Act referred to as the commencement of this Act. *(31) Commencement.*

3. This Act shall apply to every bill of sale executed on or after the first day of January one thousand eight hundred and seventy-nine (whether the same be absolute, or subject or not subject to any trust) whereby the holder or grantee has power, either with or *(31) Application of Act.*

---

* The marginal figures refer to the pages where the section is printed in the text.

without notice, and either immediately or at any future time, to seize or take possession of any personal chattels comprised in or made subject to such bill of sale.

[40]   4. In this Act the following words and expressions shall have the meanings in this section assigned to them respectively, unless there be something in the subject or context repugnant to such construction; (that is to say),

Interpretation of terms.

The expression "bill of sale" shall include bills of sale, assignments, transfers, declarations of trust without transfer, inventories of goods with receipt thereto attached, or receipts for purchase-moneys of goods, and other assurances of personal chattels, and also powers of attorney, authorities, or licences to take possession of personal chattels as security for any debt, and also any agreement, whether intended or not to be followed by the execution of any other instrument, by which a right in equity to any personal chattels, or to any charge or security thereon, shall be conferred, but shall not include the following documents; that is to say, assignments for the benefit of the creditors of the person making or giving the same, marriage settlements, transfers or assignments of any ship or vessel or any share thereof, transfers of goods in the ordinary course of business of any trade or calling, bills of sale of goods in foreign parts or at sea, bills of lading, India warrants, warehouse-keepers' certificates, warrants or orders for the delivery of goods, or any other documents used in the ordinary course of business as proof of the possession or control of goods, or authorising or purporting to authorise, either by indorsement or by delivery, the possessor of such document to transfer or receive goods thereby represented:

[67]   The expression "personal chattels" shall mean goods, furniture and other articles capable of complete transfer by delivery, and (when separately assigned or charged) fixtures and growing crops, but shall not include chattel interests in real estate, nor fixtures (except trade machinery as hereinafter defined), when assigned together with a freehold or leasehold interest in any land or building to which they are affixed, nor growing crops when assigned together with any interest in the land on which they grow, nor shares or interests in the stock, funds, or securities of any government, or in the capital or property of incorporated or joint stock companies, nor choses in action, nor any stock or produce upon any farm or lands which by virtue of any covenant or agreement or of the custom of the country

ought not to be removed from any farm where the same are at the time of making or giving of such bill of sale:

Personal chattels shall be deemed to be in the " apparent possession" of the person making or giving a bill of sale, so long as they remain or are in or upon any house, mill, warehouse, building, works, yard, land, or other premises occupied by him, or are used and enjoyed by him in any place whatsoever, notwithstanding that formal possession thereof may have been taken by or given to any other person:

[72.

"Prescribed" means prescribed by rules made under the provisions of this Act.

[89]

5. From and after the commencement of this Act trade machinery shall, for the purposes of this Act, be deemed to be personal chattels, and any mode of disposition of trade machinery by the owner thereof which would be a bill of sale as to any other personal chattels shall be deemed to be a bill of sale within the meaning of this Act.

Application of Act to trade machinery.

For the purposes of this Act—

"Trade machinery" means the machinery used in or attached to any factory or workshop;

1st. Exclusive of the fixed motive-powers, such as the water-wheels and steam engines, and the steam-boilers, donkey engines, and other fixed appurtenances of the said motive-powers; and,

2nd. Exclusive of the fixed power machinery, such as the shafts, wheels, drums, and their fixed appurtenances, which transmit the action of the motive-powers to the other machinery, fixed and loose; and,

3rd. Exclusive of the pipes for steam, gas, and water in the factory or workshop.

The machinery or effects excluded by this section from the definition of trade machinery shall not be deemed to be personal chattels within the meaning of this Act.

"Factory or workshop" means any premises on which any manual labour is exercised by way of trade, or for purposes of gain, in or incidental to the following purposes or any of them; that is to say,

(a.) In or incidental to the making any article or part of an article; or

(b.) In or incidental to the altering, repairing, ornamenting, finishing, of any article; or

(c.) In or incidental to the adapting for sale any article.

[94]
Certain instruments giving powers of distress to be subject to this Act.

6. Every attornment, instrument, or agreement, not being a mining lease, whereby a power of distress is given or agreed to be given by any person to any other person by way of security for any present, future, or contingent debt or advance, and whereby any rent is reserved or made payable as a mode of providing for the payment of interest on such debt or advance, or otherwise for the purpose of such security only, shall be deemed to be a bill of sale, within the meaning of this Act, of any personal chattels which may be seized or taken under such power of distress.

Provided that nothing in this section shall extend to any mortgage of any estate or interest in any land, tenement, or hereditament which the mortgagee, being in possession, shall have demised to the mortgagor as his tenant at a fair and reasonable rent.

[99]
Fixtures or growing crops not to be deemed separately assigned when the land passes by the same instrument.

7. No fixtures or growing crops shall be deemed, under this Act, to be separately assigned or charged by reason only that they are assigned by separate words, or that power is given to sever them from the land or building to which they are affixed, or from the land on which they grow, without otherwise taking possession of or dealing with such land or building, or land, if by the same instrument any freehold or leasehold interest in the land or building to which such fixtures are affixed, or in the land on which such crops grow, is also conveyed or assigned to the same persons or person.

The same rule of construction shall be applied to all deeds or instruments, including fixtures or growing crops, executed before the commencement of this Act and then subsisting and in force, in all questions arising under any bankruptcy, liquidation, assignment for the benefit of creditors, or execution of any process of any court, which shall take place or be issued after the commencement of this Act.

[119]
Avoidance of unregistered bills of sale in certain cases.

8. Every bill of sale to which this Act applies shall be duly attested and shall be registered under this Act, within seven days after the making or giving thereof, and shall set forth the consideration for which such bill of sale was given, otherwise such bill of sale, as against all trustees or assignees of the estate of the person whose chattels, or any of them, are comprised in such bill of sale under the law relating to bankruptcy or liquidation, or under any assignment for the benefit of the creditors of such person, and also as against all sheriffs' officers and other persons seizing any chattels comprised in such bill of sale, in the execution of any process of any court authorizing the seizure of the chattels of the person by whom or of whose chattels such bill has been made, and also as against every person on whose behalf such process shall have been issued, shall be deemed fraudulent and void so far as regards the property in or right to the possession of any chattels comprised in such bill of sale

which, at or after the time of filing the petition for bankruptcy or
liquidation, or of the execution of such assignment, or of executing
such process (as the case may be), and after the expiration of such
seven days are in the possession or apparent possession of the person
making such bill of sale (or of any person against whom the process
has issued under or in the execution of which such bill has been
made or given, as the case may be). [a]

[155]

9. Where a subsequent bill of sale is executed within or on the
expiration of seven days after the execution of a prior unregistered
bill of sale, and comprises all or any part of the personal chattels
comprised in such prior bill of sale, then, if such subsequent bill of
sale is given as a security for the same debt as is secured by the
prior bill of sale, or for any part of such debt, it shall, to the extent
to which it is a security for the same debt or part thereof, and so
far as respects the personal chattels or part thereof comprised in the
prior bill, be absolutely void, unless it is proved to the satisfaction of
the Court having cognizance of the case that the subsequent bill of
sale was *bonâ fide* given for the purpose of correcting some material
error in the prior bill of sale, and not for the purpose of evading
this Act.

Avoidance of certain duplicate bills of sale

[176]

10. A bill of sale shall be attested and registered under this Act
in the following manner :—

Mode of registering bills of sale.

(1.) The execution of every bill of sale shall be attested by a
solicitor of the Supreme Court, and the attestation shall
state that before the execution of the bill of sale the
effect thereof has been explained to the grantor by the
attesting solicitor : [b]

(2.) Such bill, with every schedule or inventory thereto annexed
or therein referred to, and also a true copy of such bill
and of every such schedule or inventory, and of every
attestation of the execution of such bill of sale, together
with an affidavit of the time of such bill of sale being
made or given, and of its due execution and attestation,
and a description of the residence and occupation of the
person making or giving the same (or in case the same is
made or given by any person under or in the execution
of any process, then a description of the residence and
occupation of the person against whom such process
issued), and of every attesting witness to such bill of sale,
shall be presented to and the said copy and affidavit shall
be filed with the registrar within seven clear days after
the making or giving of such bill of sale, in like manner

[178]

(a) Repealed, Bills of Sale Act (1878) Amendment Act, 1882, sec. 15.
(b) Ib., sec. 10.

as a warrant of attorney in any personal action given by a trader is now by law required to be filed:

[192]

(3.) If the bill of sale is made or given subject to any defeasance or condition, or declaration of trust not contained in the body thereof, such defeasance, condition, or declaration shall be deemed to be part of the bill, and shall be written on the same paper or parchment therewith before the registration, and shall be truly set forth in the copy filed under this Act therewith and as part thereof, otherwise the registration shall be void.

[197]

In case two or more bills of sale are given, comprising in whole or in part any of the same chattels, they shall have priority in the order of the date of their registration respectively as regards such chattels.

[203]

A transfer or assignment of a registered bill of sale need not be registered.

|205]
Renewal of
registration.

11. The registration of a bill of sale, whether executed before or after the commencement of this Act, must be renewed once at least every five years, and if a period of five years elapses from the registration or renewed registration of a bill of sale without a renewal or further renewal (as the case may be), the registration shall become void.

The renewal of a registration shall be effected by filing with the registrar an affidavit stating the date of the bill of sale and of the last registration thereof, and the names, residences, and occupations of the parties thereto as stated therein, and that the bill of sale is still a subsisting security.

Every such affidavit may be in the form set forth in the Schedule (A) to this Act annexed.

A renewal of registration shall not become necessary by reason only of a transfer or assignment of a bill of sale.

[209]
Form of
register.

12. The registrar shall keep a book (in this Act called "the register") for the purposes of this Act, and shall, upon the filing of any bill of sale or copy under this Act, enter therein in the form set forth in the Second Schedule (B) to this Act annexed, or in any other prescribed form, the name, residence, and occupation of the person by whom the bill was made or given (or in case the same was made or given by any person under or in the execution of process, then the name, residence, and occupation of the person against whom such process was issued, and also the name of the person or persons to whom or in whose favour the bill was given), and the other particulars shown in the said schedule or to be prescribed under this Act, and shall number all such bills registered in each year consecutively, according to the respective dates of their registration.

Upon the registration of any affidavit of renewal the like entry shall be made, with the addition of the date and number of the last previous entry relating to the same bill, and the bill of sale or copy originally filed shall be thereupon marked with the number affixed to such affidavit of renewal.

The registrar shall also keep an index of the names of the grantors of registered bills of sale with reference to entries in the register of the bills of sale given by each such grantor.

Such index shall be arranged in divisions corresponding with the letters of the alphabet, so that all grantors whose surnames begin with the same letter (and no others) shall be comprised in one division, but the arrangement within each such division need not be strictly alphabetical.

[212]

13. The masters of the Supreme Court of Judicature attached to The Registrar. the Queen's Bench Division of the High Court of Justice, or such other officers as may for the time being be assigned for this purpose under the provisions of the Supreme Court of Judicature Acts, 1873 36 & 37 Vic. and 1875, shall be the registrar for the purposes of this Act, and c. 66; 38 & 39 V c. any one of the said masters may perform all or any of the duties of c. 77. the registrar.

[213]

14. Any Judge of the High Court of Justice on being satisfied Rectification of that the omission to register a bill of sale or an affidavit of renewal register. thereof within the time prescribed by this Act, or the omission or mis-statement of the name, residence, or occupation of any person was accidental or due to inadvertence, may in his discretion order such omission or mis-statement to be rectified by the insertion in the register of the true name, residence, or occupation, or by extending the time for such registration on such terms and conditions (if any) as to security, notice by advertisement or otherwise, or as to any other matter, as he thinks fit to direct.

[215]

15. Subject to and in accordance with any rules to be made Entry of satisfaction. under and for the purposes of this Act, the registrar may order a memorandum of satisfaction to be written upon any registered copy of a bill of sale, upon the prescribed evidence being given that the debt (if any) for which such bill of sale was made or given has been satisfied or discharged.

[218]

16. Any person shall be entitled to have an office copy or extract Copies may be taken, &c. of any registered bill of sale, and affidavit of execution filed therewith, or copy thereof, and of any affidavit filed therewith, if any, or registered affidavit of renewal, upon paying for the same at the like rate as for office copies of judgments of the High Court of Justice, and any copy of a registered bill of sale, and affidavit purporting to be an office copy thereof, shall in all courts and before all arbitrators or other persons, be admitted as *prima facie* evidence thereof, and of

P

the fact and date of registration as shown thereon. Any person shall be entitled at all reasonable times to search the register and every registered bill of sale, upon payment of one shilling for every copy of a bill of sale inspected;[a] such payment shall be made by a judicature stamp.

[225]
Affidavits.

17. Every affidavit required by or for the purposes of this Act may be sworn before a master of any division of the High Court of Justice, or before any commissioner empowered to take affidavits in the Supreme Court of Judicature.

Whoever wilfully makes or uses any false affidavit for the purposes of this Act shall be deemed guilty of wilful and corrupt perjury.

[228]
Fees.

18. There shall be paid and received in common law stamps the following fees, viz. :

On filing a bill of sale	2s.
On filing the affidavit of execution of a bill of sale	2s.
On the affidavit used for the purpose of re-registering a bill of sale (to include the fee for filing)	5s.

[232]
Collection of fees under 38 & 39 Vic. c. 77, s. 26.

19. Section twenty-six of the Supreme Court of Judicature Act, 1875, and any enactments for the time being in force amending or substituted for that section, shall apply to fees under this Act, and an order under that section may, if need be, be made in relation to such fees accordingly.

[233]
Order and disposition.

32 & 33 Vic. c. 71.

20. Chattels comprised in a bill of sale which has been and continues to be duly registered under this Act shall not be deemed to be in the possession, order, or disposition of the grantor of the bill of sale within the meaning of the Bankruptcy Act, 1869.[b]

[240]
Rules.

36 & 37 Vic. c. 66.
38 & 39 Vic. c. 77.

21. Rules for the purposes of this Act may be made and altered from time to time by the like persons and in the like manner in which rules and regulations may be made under and for the purposes of the Supreme Court of Judicature Acts, 1873 and 1875.

241]
Time for registration.

22. When the time for registering a bill of sale expires on a Sunday, or other day on which the registrar's office is closed, the registration shall be valid if made on the next following day on which the office is open.

241]
Repeal of Acts.
17 & 18 Vic. c. 36.
29 & 30 Vic. c. 96.

23. From and after the commencement of this Act, the Bills of Sale Act, 1854, and the Bills of Sale Act, 1866, shall be repealed : Provided that (except as is herein expressly mentioned with respect to construction and with respect to renewal of registration) nothing

(a) Repealed in part, Bills of Sale Act (1878) Amendment Act, 1882, sec. 16.
(b) Repealed, Bills of Sale Act (1878) Amendment Act, 1882, sec. 15.

in this Act shall affect any bill of sale executed before the commencement of this Act, and as regards bills of sale so executed the Acts hereby repealed shall continue in force.

Any renewal after the commencement of this Act of the registration of a bill of sale executed before the commencement of this Act, and registered under the Acts hereby repealed, shall be made under this Act in the same manner as the renewal of a registration made under this Act.

24. This Act shall not extend to Scotland or to Ireland.

[242]
Extent of Act.

SCHEDULES.

SCHEDULE A.

Section 11.

I [*A. B.*]   of   do swear that a bill of sale, bearing date the   day of   18 [*insert the date of the bill*], and made between [*insert the names and descriptions of the parties in the original bill of sale*], and which said bill of sale [*or, and a copy of which said bill of sale, as the case may be*] was registered on the   day   18   [*insert date of registration*], is still a subsisting security.

Sworn, &c.

SCHEDULE B.

Section 12.

Satis-faction entered.	No.	By whom given (or against whom process issued).			To whom given.	Nature of instrument.	Date.	Date of regis-tration.	Date of registration of affidavit of renewal
		Name.	Resi-dence.	Occu-pation.					

THE BILLS OF SALE ACT (1878) AMENDMENT ACT, 1882.

(45 & 46 Vict. c. 43.)

AN ACT

TO

AMEND THE BILLS OF SALE ACT, 1878.

[*18th August*, 1882.

41 & 42 Vic. c. 31.

WHEREAS it is expedient to amend the Bills of Sale Act, 1878:

BE it enacted by the Queen's Most Excellent Majesty, by and with the advice and consent of the Lords Spiritual and Temporal, and Commons, in this present Parliament assembled, and by the authority of the same, as follows:

[30]
Short title.

1. This Act may be cited for all purposes as the Bills of Sale Act (1878) Amendment Act, 1882; and this Act and the Bills of Sale Act, 1878, may be cited together as the Bills of Sale Acts, 1878 and 1882.

[31]
Commencement of Act.

2. This Act shall come into operation on the first day of November one thousand eight hundred and eighty-two, which date is hereinafter referred to as the commencement of this Act.

[37]
Construction of Act.
41 & 42 Vic. c. 31.

3. The Bills of Sale Act, 1878, is hereinafter referred to as "the principal Act," and this Act shall, so far as is consistent with the tenor thereof, be construed as one with the principal Act; but unless the context otherwise requires shall not apply to any bill of sale duly registered before the commencement of this Act, so long as the registration thereof is not avoided by non-renewal or otherwise.

The expression "bill of sale," and other expressions in this Act. have the same meaning as in the principal Act, except as to bills of sale or other documents mentioned in section four of the principal Act, which may be given otherwise than by way of security for the payment of money, to which last-mentioned bills of sale and other documents this Act shall not apply.

[77]
Bill of sale to have schedule of property attached thereto.

4. Every bill of sale shall have annexed thereto or written thereon a schedule containing an inventory of the personal chattels comprised in the bill of sale; and such bill of sale, save as

hereinafter mentioned, shall have effect only in respect of the personal chattels specifically described in the said schedule; and shall be void, except as against the grantor, in respect of any personal chattels not so specifically described.

5. Save as hereinafter mentioned, a bill of sale shall be void, except as against the grantor, in respect of any personal chattels specifically described in the schedule thereto of which the grantor was not the true owner at the time of the execution of the bill of sale.

[83] Bill of sale not to affect after-acquired property

6. Nothing contained in the foregoing sections of this Act shall render a bill of sale void in respect of any of the following things (that is to say),

[92] Exception as to certain things.

(1.) Any growing crops separately assigned or charged where such crops were actually growing at the time when the bill of sale was executed.

(2.) Any fixtures separately assigned or charged, and any plant or trade machinery where such fixtures, plant, or trade machinery are used in, attached to, or brought upon any land, farm, factory, workshop, shop, house, warehouse, or other place in substitution for any of the like fixtures, plant, or trade machinery specifically described in the schedule to such bill of sale.

7. Personal chattels assigned under a bill of sale shall not be liable to be seized or taken possession of by the grantee for any other than the following causes :—

[104] Bill of sale with power to seize except in certain events to be void.

(1.) If the grantor shall make default in payment of the sum or sums of money thereby secured at the time therein provided for payment, or in the performance of any covenant or agreement contained in the bill of sale and necessary for maintaining the security ;

[104]

(2.) If the grantor shall become a bankrupt, or suffer the said goods or any of them to be distrained for rent, rates, or taxes ;

[110]

(3.) If the grantor shall fraudulently either remove or suffer the said goods, or any of them, to be removed from the premises ;

[114]

(4.) If the grantor shall not, without reasonable excuse, upon demand in writing by the grantee, produce to him his last receipts for rent, rates, and taxes ;

[115]

(5.) If execution shall have been levied against the goods of the grantor under any judgment at law :

[115]

Provided that the grantor may within five days from the seizure or taking possession of any chattels on account of any of the above-

116

mentioned causes, apply to the High Court, or to a Judge thereof in chambers, and such Court or Judge, if satisfied that by payment of money or otherwise the said cause of seizure no longer exists, may restrain the grantee from removing or selling the said chattels, or may make such other order as may seem just.

[123]
Bill of sale to
be void unless
attested and
registered.

8. Every bill of sale shall be duly attested, and shall be registered under the principal Act within seven clear days after the execution thereof, or if it is executed in any place out of England then within seven clear days after the time at which it would in the ordinary course of post arrive in England if posted immediately after the execution thereof; and shall truly set forth the consideration for which it was given; otherwise such bill of sale shall be void in respect of the personal chattels comprised therein.

[156]
Form of bill of
sale.

9. A bill of sale made or given by way of security for the payment of money by the grantor thereof shall be void unless made in accordance with the form in the schedule to this Act annexed.

[175]
Attestation.

10. The execution of every bill of sale by the grantor shall be attested by one or more credible witness or witnesses, not being a party or parties thereto. So much of section ten of the principal Act as requires that the execution of every bill of sale shall be attested by a solicitor of the Supreme Court, and that the attestation shall state that before the execution of the bill of sale the effect thereof has been explained to the grantor by the attesting witness, is hereby repealed.

[207]
Local regis-
tration of con-
tents of bills of
sale.

32 & 33 Vic.
c. 71, s. 60.

11. Where the affidavit (which under section ten of the principal Act is required to accompany a bill of sale when presented for registration) describes the residence of the person making or giving the same or of the person against whom the process is issued to be in some place outside the London bankruptcy district as defined by the Bankruptcy Act, 1869, or where the bill of sale describes the chattels enumerated therein as being in some place outside the said London bankruptcy district, the registrar under the principal Act shall forthwith and within three clear days after registration in the principal registry, and in accordance with the prescribed directions, transmit an abstract in the prescribed form of the contents of such bill of sale to the county court registrar in whose district such places are situate, and if such places are in the districts of different registrars, to each such registrar.

Every abstract so transmitted shall be filed, kept, and indexed by the registrar of the county court in the prescribed manner, and any person may search, inspect, make extracts from, and obtain copies of the abstract so registered in the like manner and upon the like terms as to payment or otherwise as near as may be as in the case of bills of sale registered by the registrar under the principal Act

12. Every bill of sale made or given in consideration of any sum under thirty pounds shall be void.

[211]
Bill of sale
under £30, to be
void

13. All personal chattels seized or of which possession is taken after the commencement of this Act, under or by virtue of any bill of sale (whether registered before or after the commencement of this Act), shall remain on the premises where they were so seized or so taken possession of, and shall not be removed or sold until after the expiration of five clear days from the day they were so seized or so taken possession of.

[211]
Chattels not to
be removed
or sold.

14. A bill of sale to which this Act applies shall be no protection in respect of personal chattels included in such bill of sale which but for such bill of sale would have been liable to distress under a warrant for the recovery of taxes and poor and other parochial rates.

[215]
Bill of sale
not to protect
chattels against
poor and
parochial rates.

15. The eighth and the twentieth sections of the principal Act, and also all other enactments contained in the principal Act which are inconsistent with this Act are repealed, but this repeal shall not affect the validity of anything done or suffered under the principal Act before the commencement of this Act.

[217]
Repeal of part
of Bills of Sale
Act, 1878

16. So much of the sixteenth section of the principal Act as enacts that any person shall be entitled at all reasonable times to search the register and every registered bill of sale upon payment of one shilling for every copy of a bill of sale inspected is hereby repealed, and from and after the commencement of this Act any person shall be entitled at all reasonable times to search the register, on payment of a fee of one shilling, or such other fee as may be prescribed, and subject to such regulations as may be prescribed, and shall be entitled at all reasonable times to inspect, examine, and make extracts from any and every registered bill of sale without being required to make a written application, or to specify any particulars in reference thereto, upon payment of one shilling for each bill of sale inspected, and such payment shall be made by a judicature stamp: Provided that the said extracts shall be limited to the dates of execution, registration renewal of registration, and satisfaction, to the names, addresses, and occupations of the parties, to the amount of the consideration, and to any further prescribed particulars.

[221]
Inspection of
registered bills
of sale.

17. Nothing in this Act shall apply to any debentures issued by any mortgage, loan, or other incorporated company, and secured upon the capital stock or goods, chattels, and effects of such company.

[222]
Debentures to
which Act not
to apply.

18. This Act shall not extend to Scotland or Ireland.

[242]
Extent of Act.

SCHEDULE.

---

[156]

FORM OF BILL OF SALE.

This Indenture made the   day of   between
A. B. of   of the one part, and C. D. of
of the other part, witnesseth that
in consideration of the sum of £   now paid to A. B. by
C. D., the receipt of which the said A. B. hereby acknowledges [*or whatever else the consideration may be*], he the said A. B. doth hereby assign unto C. D., his executors, administrators, and assigns, all and singular the several chattels and things specifically described in the schedule hereto annexed by way of security for the payment of the sum of £   , and interest thereon at the rate of
per cent. per annum [*or whatever else may be the rate*]. And the said A. B. doth further agree and declare that he will duly pay to the said C. D. the principal sum aforesaid, together with the interest then due, by equal   payments of £   on the
day of   [*or whatever else may be the stipulated times or time of payment*]. And the said A. B. doth also agree with the said C. D. that he will [*here insert terms as to insurance, payment of rent, or otherwise, which the parties may agree to for the maintenance or defeasance of the security*].

Provided always, that the chattels hereby assigned shall not be liable to seizure or to be taken possession of by the said C. D. for any cause other than those specified in section seven of the Bills of Sale Act (1878) Amendment Act, 1882.

In witness, &c.,

Signed and sealed by the said A. B. in the presence of me E. F.
[*add witness's name, address, and description*].

THE BILLS OF SALE ACT, 1890.

(53 & 54 Vict., c. 53.)

AN ACT

To

EXEMPT CERTAIN LETTERS OF HYPOTHECATION FROM THE OPERATION OF THE BILLS OF SALE ACT, 1882.

[18th August, 1890.

BE it enacted by the Queen's most Excellent Majesty, by and with the advice and consent of the Lords Spiritual and Temporal, and Commons, in this present Parliament assembled, and by the authority of the same, as follows :

1. An instrument given or executed at any time prior to such deposit, reshipment, or delivery as hereinafter mentioned, hypothecating or declaring trusts of imported goods during the interval between the discharge of the goods from the ship in which they are imported and their deposit in a warehouse, factory, or store, or their being reshipped for export or delivered to a purchaser not being the purchaser giving or executing such instrument, shall not be deemed a bill of sale within the meaning of section nine of the Bills of Sale Act, 1882.(a)

[174]
Exemption of letters of hypothecation of imported goods from 45 & 46 Vic. c. 43, s. 9.

2. Nothing in this Act shall affect the operation of section forty-four of the Bankruptcy Act, 1883, in respect of any goods comprised in any such instrument as is hereinbefore described, if such goods would but for this Act be goods within the meaning of sub-section three of that section.

[240]
Saving of 46 & 47 Vic. c. 52, s. 44.

3. This Act may be cited as the Bills of Sale Act, 1890.

[30]
Short title.

(a) Amended, sec. 1, Bills of Sale Act, 1891.

THE BILLS OF SALE ACT, 1891.

(54 & 55 Vict. c. 35.)

AN ACT

TO

AMEND THE BILLS OF SALE ACT, 1890.

[21st *July*, 1891

Exemption of
securities on
imported goods
from 41 & 42
Vic. c. 31, and
45 & 46 Vic. c.
43.

BE it enacted by the Queen's most Excellent Majesty, by and with the advice and consent of the Lords Spiritual and Temporal, and Commons, in this present Parliament assembled, and by the authority of the same, as follows:

[174]

1. Section one of the Bills of Sale Act, 1890, shall be amended so as to read as follows: An instrument charging or creating any security on or declaring trusts of imported goods given or executed at any time prior to their deposit in a warehouse, factory, or store, or to their being reshipped for export, or delivered to a purchaser not being the person giving or executing such instrument, shall not be deemed a bill of sale within the meaning of the Bills of Sale Acts, 1878 and 1882.

[30]
Short title.

2. This Act may be cited as the Bills of Sale Act, 1891.

RULES OF THE SUPREME COURT, 1883.

The following Orders and Rules may be cited as "The Rules of the Supreme Court, 1883." They shall come into operation on the Twenty-fourth day of October, 1883, and shall also apply, so far as may be practicable (unless otherwise expressly provided), to all proceedings taken on or after that day in all causes and matters then pending.

ORDER LXI.

CENTRAL OFFICE.[a]

1. The Central Office shall, for the convenient despatch of business, be divided into the departments specified in the first column of the following scheme, and the business of the Office shall be distributed among the departments in accordance with that scheme, and shall be performed by the several officers and clerks in the said office who are now charged with the same or similar duties, and by such others as may from time to time be appointed by lawful authority for that purpose.

Scheme.

Name of Department.	Business.
* * * * * * * * *	
7. Bills of sale ..	The registry of bills of sale, and other duties connected therewith.
* * * * * * * * *	

7. All copies, certificates, and other documents appearing to be sealed with a seal of the Central Office shall be presumed to be office copies or certificates or other documents issued from the Central Office, and if duly stamped may be received in evidence, and no signature or other formality, except the sealing with a seal of the Central Office, shall be required for the authentication of any such copy, certificate, or other document.

17. Proper indexes or calendars to the files or bundles of all documents filed at the Central Office shall be kept, so that the same

(a) The Central Office was established by sec. 4, Judicature (Offices) Act, 1879. By sec. 5, the Offices of the Masters of the Queen's Bench, Common Pleas, and Exchequer Divisions, including the Bills of Sale Office, are concentrated in and amalgamated with the Central Office.

may be conveniently referred to when required ; and such indexes or calendars and documents, shall, at all times during office hours, be accessible to the public on payment of the usual fee.

18. There shall also be entered in proper books kept for the purpose the time when any certificate is delivered at the Central Office to be filed, with the name of the cause and the date of the certificate ; and the like entry shall be made of the time of delivery of every other document filed at the Central Office ; and such books shall, at all times during office hours, be accessible to the public on payment of the usual fee.

19. Every judgment, order, certificate, petition or document made, presented or used in any cause or matter, shall be distinguished by having plainly written or stamped on the first page thereof the year, the letter, and the number by which the cause or matter is distinguished in the books kept at the Central Office.

23. The clerk of enrolments and each of the following registrars, namely the registrar of bills of sale, the registrar of certificates of acknowledgments of deeds by married women, and the registrar of judgments shall, on a request in writing giving sufficient particulars, and on payment of the prescribed fee, cause a search to be made in the registers or indexes under his custody, and issue a certificate of the result of the search.[a]

24. For the purpose of enabling all persons to obtain precise information as to the state of any cause or matter, and to take the means of preventing improper delay in the progress thereof, the proper officer shall, at the request of any person, whether a party or not to the cause or matter inquired after, but on payment of the usual fee, give a certificate specifying therein the dates and general description of the several proceedings which have been taken in such cause or matter in the Central Office.

25. The masters shall execute the office of the registrar for the purposes of the Bills of Sale Act, 1878, and the Bills of Sale Act (1878) Amendment Act, 1882, and any one of the masters may perform all or any of the duties of the registrar.

26. A memorandum of satisfaction may be ordered to be written upon a registered copy of a bill of sale, on a consent to the satisfaction, signed by the person entitled to the benefit of the bill of sale and verified by affidavit, being produced to the registrar, and filed in the Central Office.[b]

27. Where the consent in the last preceding Rule mentioned cannot be obtained, the registrar may, on application by summons

(a) Form of Search, p. 273.
(b) Form of Consent and Affidavit, pp. 273, 274.

and on hearing the person entitled to the benefit of the bill of sale,
or on affidavit of service of the summons on that person, and in
either case on proof to the satisfaction of the registrar that the debt
(if any) for which the bill of sale was made has been satisfied or
discharged, order a memorandum of satisfaction to be written upon
a registered copy thereof.[a]

28. No affidavit or record of the Court shall be taken out of the
Central Office without the order of a Judge or master, and no subpœna for the production of any such document shall be issued.

29. Any officer of the Central Office, being required to attend
with any record or document at any assizes or at any court or place
out of the Royal Courts of Justice, shall be entitled to require that
the solicitor or party desiring his attendance shall deposit with him
a sufficient sum of money to answer his just fees, charges and
expenses in respect of such attendance, and undertake to pay any
further just fees, charges and expenses which may not be fully
answered by such deposit.

RULES OF THE SUPREME COURT.

Bills of Sale Acts, 1878 *and* 1882.

1. These Rules may be cited as " The Rules of the Supreme
Court Bills of Sale Act, 1878 and 1882," and shall stand in lieu of
" The Rules of the Supreme Court, December, 1882," which shall be
and are hereby annulled.

2. These Rules shall come into operation on the 1st January,
1884.

ORDER LXb.

LOCAL REGISTRATION OF BILLS OF SALE.

3. *Abstract.* The abstract of the contents of a bill of sale,
required by the Bills of Sale Act (1878) Amendment Act, 1882, to
be transmitted to the registrar of a County Court, shall be in the
form given in the Appendix hereto.

4. *Abstract to be sealed and dated.* The abstract shall be sealed
with the seal of the Bills of Sale Department of the Central Office
of the Supreme Court of Judicature, and dated on the day on which
it is transmitted by post to the registrar of the County Court
named therein.

5. *Abstract of re-registered Bills of Sale.* Where a bill of sale
has been re-registered since the 31st October, 1882, or shall be
re-registered hereafter under sec. 11 of the Bills of Sale Act,
1878, an abstract of the re-registration, sealed and dated, shall be
transmitted by post to the registrar of the County Court to which
such abstract should have been transmitted had the bill of sale

(a) Form of Summons, p. 274.

been registered under the Bills of Sale Act (1878) Amendment
Act, 1882.

6. *Notice of a satisfaction of a Bill of Sale to be transmitted to
local registry.*—Where a memorandum of satisfaction has been or
shall be written under sec. 15 of the Bills of Sale Act, 1878,
upon any registered or re-registered copy of a bill of sale, an
abstract of which has been transmitted to any Registrar of a County
Court, a notice of such satisfaction, in the form in the Appendix
hereto, duly sealed and dated, shall be transmitted to each of the
registrars to whom an abstract of such bill of sale shall have been
transmitted.

7. *Abstracts to be numbered and filed.*—The registrar shall
number the abstracts and notices of satisfaction in the order in
which they shall respectively be received by him, and shall file and
keep them in his office.

8. *Index, how to be kept.*—The registrar shall keep an index,
alphabetically arranged, in which he shall enter under the first
letters of the surname of the mortgagor or assignor such surname,
with his Christian name or names, address, and description, and the
number which has been affixed to the abstract.

9. *Satisfaction to be noted in index.*—Upon the receipt of a notice
of satisfaction, the registrar shall enter the notice of satisfaction
on the abstract of the Bill to which it relates, and shall note in the
index against the name of the mortgagor or assignor the fact of the
satisfaction having been entered.

10. *Search and inspection of abstract.* The registrar shall allow
any person to search the index at any time during which he is
required by the County Court Rules for the time being to keep his
office open, upon payment by such person of one shilling; and to
make extracts from the abstract or notice of satisfaction upon
payment of one shilling for each abstract or notice of satisfaction
inspected.

11. *Office copy of abstract.*—The registrar shall also, if required,
cause an office copy to be made of any abstract or notice of satisfaction, and shall be entitled for making, marking, and sealing the
same to the same fee as is payable in the Bills of Sale Department
of the Central Office of the Supreme Court of Judicature, viz.,
sixpence per folio.

12. *Authority to take oaths.*—Every first and second class clerk in
the Bills of Sale Department of the Central Office of the Supreme
Court of Judicature shall, by virtue of his office, have authority to
take oaths and affidavits in matters relating to that department.

28th December, 1883.

APPENDIX.

No. 1.

[*Abstract. Local Registration of Bills of Sale, see p. 276.*

No. 2.

[*Notice of Satisfaction, see p. 277.*]

CENTRAL OFFICE PRACTICE RULES.

Settled by the Practice Masters, March, 1884.

As to Satisfaction of Bills of Sale.

If the attesting witness and deponent is a solicitor, and described as such, the entry of the satisfaction will be directed by the master (the papers being otherwise correct) as of course; but under special circumstances the master may accept any other deponent, if satisfied that he is a proper person to attest and verify the signature and consent.

RULES UNDER SECTION 2 OF THE CON-VEYANCING ACT, 1882.[a]

---

1. Every requisition for an official search shall state the name and address of the person requiring the search to be made. Every requisition and certificate shall be filed in the office where the search was made.

(*a.*) Section 2 of the Conveyancing Act, 1882 (45 & 46 Vic. c. 39), so far as it is applicable to bills of sale, is as follows: (1.) Where any person requires, for purposes of this section, search to be made in the central office for entries of judgments, deeds, or other matters or documents, whereof entries are required or allowed to be made in that office by any Act, he may deliver in the office a requisition in that behalf, referring to this section. (2.) Thereupon the proper officer shall diligently make the search required, and shall make and file in the office a certificate setting forth the result thereof, and office copies of that certificate shall be issued on requisition, and an office copy shall be evidence of the certificate. (3.) In favour of a purchaser, as against persons interested under or in respect of judgments, deeds, or other matters or documents whereof entries are required or allowed as aforesaid, the certificate, according to the tenor thereof, shall be conclusive, affirmatively or negatively, as the case may be. (4.) Every requisition under this section shall be in writing, signed by the person making the same, specifying the name against which he desires search to be made, or in relation to which he requires an office copy certificate or result of search, and other sufficient particulars; and the person making any such requisition shall not be entitled to a search, or an office copy certificate, until he has satisfied the proper officer that the same is required for the purposes of this section. (5.) General rules shall be made for the purposes of this section, prescribing forms and contents of requisitions and certificates, and regulating the practice of the office, and prescribing, with the concurrence of the Commissioners of Her Majesty's Treasury, the fees to be taken therein . . . . (6.) If any officer, clerk, or person employed in the office commits, or is party or privy to, any act of fraud or collusion, or is wilfully negligent in the making of or otherwise in relation to any certificate or office copy under this section, he shall be guilty of a misdemeanour. (7.) Nothing in this section or

2. Every person requiring an official search to be made pursuant to sec. 2 of the Conveyancing Act, 1882, shall deliver to the officer a declaration according to the Forms 1 and 2 in the Appendix,[b] purporting to be signed by the person requiring the search to be made, or by a solicitor, which declaration may be accepted by the officer as sufficient evidence that the search is required for the purposes of the said section. The declaration may be made in the requisition, or in a separate document.

3. Requisitions for searches under sec. 2 of the Conveyancing Act, 1882, shall be in the Forms 3 to 4 in the Appendix,[b] and the certificates of the results of such searches shall be in the Forms 7 to 10,[b] with such modifications as the circumstances may require.

4. Where a certificate setting forth the result of a search in any name has been issued, and it is desired that the search be continued in that name, to a date not more than one calendar month subsequent to the date of the certificate, a requisition in writing in the Form 11 in the Appendix[b] may be left with the proper officer, who shall cause the search to be continued, and the result of the continued search shall be endorsed on the original certificate and upon any office copy thereof which may have been issued, if produced to the officer for that purpose. The endorsement shall be in the Form 12 in the Appendix,[b] with such modifications as circumstances require.

5. Every person shall upon payment of the prescribed fee be entitled to have a copy of the whole or any part of any deed or document enrolled in the Enrolment Department of the Central Office.

in any rule made thereunder shall take away, abridge, or prejudicially affect any right which any person may have independently of this section to make any search in the office ; and every such search may be made as if this section or any such rule had not been enacted or made. (8.) Where a solicitor obtains an office copy certificate of result of search under this section, he shall not be answerable in respect of any loss that may arise from error in the certificate. (9.) Where a solicitor is acting for trustees, executors, agents, or other persons in a fiduciary position, those persons also shall not be so answerable. (10.) Where such persons obtain such an office copy without a solicitor, they shall also be protected in like manner.

(b) Forms, pp. 277-279.

APPENDIX.

Part II.

No. 1.

Affidavit on Registration of Bill of Sale. [a]

(Rules of Supreme Court, 1883, *Appendix B.* 24.)

18   .— .—No.

In the High Court of Justice.

DIVISION.

I,   of

make oath and say as follows :—

1. The paper writing hereto annexed and marked " A " is a true copy of a bill of sale, and of every schedule or inventory thereto, annexed or therein referred to, and of every attestation of the execution thereof, as made and given and executed by

2. The said bill of sale was made and given by the said on the   day of   18 .

3. I was present and saw the said   duly execute the said bill on the said   day of   18 .

4. The said   resides at [*state residence at time of swearing affidavit*] and is [*state occupation*].

5. The name   subscribed to the said bill of sale as that of the witness attesting the due execution thereof is in the proper handwriting of me this deponent.

6. I am a Solicitor of the Supreme Court, and reside at

7. Before the execution of the said bill of sale by the said   I fully explained to   the nature and effect thereof.

Sworn at

the   day of
                18 .

Before me,

This Affidavit is filed on behalf of

(a) Bills of sale given otherwise than as security appear still to be regulated by the principal Act, and to require attestation by a solicitor. The above form is given in the Appendix to R. S. C., 1883, as an affidavit on registration of bill of sale, but applies to bills of sale under the principal Act.

Q

No. 2.

Affidavit on Registration of Bill of Sale, given otherwise than to secure payment of money, with two Attesting Witnesses, one not being a Solicitor.

18   —.   .—No.   .

In the High Court of Justice.

DIVISION.

I,   of

make oath and say as follows :—

1. The paper writing hereto annexed, marked " A," is a true copy of a bill of sale, and of every schedule or inventory thereto annexed or therein referred to, and of every attestation of the execution thereof, as made and given and executed by

2. The said bill of sale was made and given by the said on the day it bears date, being the   day of   18   .

3. I was present and saw the said duly execute the said bill of sale on the said   day of   18   .

4. The said   resides at [*state residence at time of swearing affidavit*] and is [*state occupation*].

5. The said bill of sale was executed in the presence of the attesting Solicitor, and was by him duly attested, and the said   did, before its execution by the said , explain to him the effect thereof.

6. The names   and   subscribed to the said bill of sale as that of the witnesses attesting the due execution thereof, are respectively of the proper handwriting of me this deponent, and of the said

7. I reside at   and am a and the said   resides at and is a Solicitor of the Supreme Court of Judicature.

8. The said   and I, this deponent, are the only attesting witnesses to the said bill of sale.

Sworn at

the   day of }
          18   .

Before me,

A Commissioner to administer oaths in the Supreme Court of Judicature in England.

This affidavit is filed on behalf of

No. 3.

Affidavit of Execution of an absolute Bill of Sale, by way of Inventory and Receipt, under Process.

18   No.

In the High Court of Justice.
Division.

I,

make oath and say as follows :

1.   The paper writing marked "A," hereto annexed, is a true copy of an inventory of goods, with a receipt thereto attached, and of every attestation of the execution thereof, being a bill of sale made and given and executed by   the bailiff of (a)   to

of

2.   The said bill of sale was made and given and executed by the said bailiff on the   day of   , 18   , under and by virtue of a writ of fieri facias issued out of the said (a)

on the   day of   directed to the said bailiff   to levy a sum of   upon the goods and chattels of

and under and by virtue of an order of   Division dated   18 .

3.   The said   resides at

and is

4.   I was present and saw the said   duly execute the said bill of sale, on the said   day of

18   , and I duly attested his execution thereof.

5.   The name   ·   , subscribed to the said bill of sale, as the witness attesting the due execution thereof, is in the proper handwriting of me this deponent.

6.   I am a Solicitor of the Supreme Court, and reside at

7.   Before the execution of the said bill of sale by the said   , I explained to   the nature and effect thereof.

Sworn at

    the   day of

              18   ,

    Before me,

A Commissioner to administer oaths in the
 Supreme Court of Judicature in England.

        This affidavit is filed on behalf of

              (a) Court from which process issued.

No. 4.

Declaration by Grantor against Incumbrances.

I,   of
do solemnly and sincerely declare that no receiving order has been
made against me, and that I am not a bankrupt or liquidating debtor,
and have not done or committed any act, matter, or thing, whereby
or whereupon I am liable to have a receiving order made against me,
or to be adjudicated a bankrupt, nor have I assigned my estate for
the benefit of my creditors, nor have I conveyed, assigned, or charged
the dwelling-house and premises aforesaid or any part thereof, and
there are no judgments, executions, or incumbrances of any kind
affecting the chattels and things specifically described in the schedule
or inventory now produced to me marked " A," which said chattels
and things I have this day by a deed or bill of sale bearing even
date herewith, assigned to   for securing to him the
repayment of   and interest thereon. And I further declare
that at the time of the execution of the said bill of sale I was the
true owner of all and every the said chattels and things, and that
the same then were my own and absolute property, and that I then
had in myself good right, full power, and lawful and absolute
authority to assign the same to the said
his executors, administrators and assigns in manner aforesaid, free
from incumbrances. And further that all rent, rates and taxes in
respect of the dwelling-house and premises aforesaid have been fully
paid to the   day of   now last past. And I
make this solemn declaration, conscientiously believing the same to
be true, and by virtue of the provisions of the Statutory Declarations
Act, 1835.

Declared and subscribed at
in the   of   this
day of   , in the year of our
Lord 18   ,

Before me,

A Commissioner to administer oaths in the
Supreme Court of Judicature in England.

No. 5.

Form of Register.

(Schedule B, Bills of Sale Act, 1878, see p. 255.)

———

No. 6.

Search. [a]

18   .—   .—No.

In the High Court of Justice.

QUEEN'S BENCH DIVISION.

———

e.

Search for

Dated the   day of   18   .

(Signed)

(Address)

Agent for   Solicitor for

———

No. 7.

Affidavit on renewing Registration.

(Schedule A, Bills of Sale Act, 1878, see p. 255.)

———

No. 8.

Affidavit for Order to enter Memorandum of Satisfaction.

18   .   .—No.

In the High Court of Justice.

QUEEN'S BENCH DIVISION.

———

I,   of   make oath
and say as follows :—

1. On the   day of   18   , I was present
and saw   of   sign the consent
hereunto annexed marked "A" to an order that a Memorandum
of Satisfaction should be written upon the registered copy of a bill
of sale dated the   day of   18   , and made
between   of   and
of   the debt for which such bill of sale was made
or given having been satisfied or discharged.

2. The name signed to the said consent is in the proper handwriting of the said   who is the same person as
mentioned in the said bill of sale.

3. The name   set and subscribed as witness

(a) R. S. C., 1883, App. G, No. 27.

to the signature of the said   is in the proper
handwriting of me this deponent.

     4. I am a   and reside at

Sworn at

the   day of

               18   ,

     Before me,

A Commissioner to administer oaths in the
Supreme Court of Judicature in England.

     Filed on behalf of

No. 9.
Consent to Memorandum of Satisfaction.

     I,   of   being the
person entitled to the benefit of a bill of sale bearing date the
     day of   18   , and made between
of the one part, and   of the other part, and given
for securing the sum of £   a copy of which said bill of sale
was registered on the   day of   do hereby
certify and declare that all moneys secured by or due and owing in
respect of the said bill of sale are fully paid and satisfied, and I
hereby consent to an order that a memorandum of satisfaction be
written upon such registered copy of the said bill of sale.

     Dated the   day of
     Signed in the presence of

No. 10.
Summons for Entry of Satisfaction on a Registered Bill of Sale.[a]

In the High Court of Justice.

     In the matter of a bill of sale by
to   dated the   day of
18   , and registered on the   day of   18   .
     Let all parties concerned attend the Registrar of Bills of Sale at
the Central Office, Royal Courts of Justice, London, on the
day of   18   , at   o'clock in the   noon,
on the hearing of an application on the part of
that satisfaction be entered on the above-mentioned bill of sale.

         Dated the   day of   18
     This summons was taken out by
of
     To

               (a) R. S. C., 1883, Appendix K, No. 5s.

No. 101.

Order for entry of Satisfaction on a Registered Bill of Sale.

In the High Court of Justice.

Division.

In the matter of a bill of sale by

to   dated the   day of
                          Upon hearing   and upon
reading

It is ordered that satisfaction be entered on the above-mentioned
bill of sale.

Dated the   day of

No. 11.

Abstract. Local Registration of Bills of Sale.[a]

Satisfaction entered.	No.	Mortgagor or Assignor.	Residence and Occupation.	Mortgagee or Assignee.	Nature of Instrument and Consideration.	Nature of Property assigned.	Amount secured and how repayable.	Rate of Interest.	Date of Instrument.	Date of Registration.	Date of filing Affidavit of Renewal.
									18 .	18	18 .

To the Registrar of the County Court of

holden at   Sent on the   day of   18 ,

(L.S.)

(a) App. L, R. S. C. Bills of Sale Acts, 1878 & 1882.

No. 12.

Notice of Satisfaction.[a]

Bills of Sale Registry,
Royal Courts of Justice,
London.

to

Registered , or re-registered	18
Abstract transmitted	18
Satisfaction entered	18

TAKE NOTICE THAT

A memorandum of satisfaction to the above Bill of Sale was entered on the register on the above date.

(Signed)

To the Registrar of the County Court of
holden at   .

Sent on the   *day of*

───────

No. 12A.

Order under Sec. 14 (1878).

In the matter of a bill of sale made between   and
, dated   , and registered the   day
of   18   .
Upon the application of   and reading the
affidavit of   filed   day of   18   ,
It is ordered that the time for registering [or re-registering ,
the said bill of sale be extended until   next
inclusive, but this order to be without prejudice to the rights of
parties acquired prior to the time when such bill of sale shall be
actually registered ' or re-registered'.
Dated   18

───────

No. 13.

FORM 11.[b]

Declaration as to Purposes of Search contained in the Requisition.

I declare that the above-mentioned search is required for the
purposes of a sale [*or mortgage, or lease, or as the case may be*], by
A. B. to C. D.

(a) App. No. 2, R.S.C., Bills of Sale Acts, 1876 & 1882.
(b) App. to Rules under sec. 2 Conveyancing Act, 1882.

No. 14.

FORM IV.[a]

Requisition for Search in the Bills of Sale Department under the Conveyancing Act, 1882, sec. 2.

Supreme Court of Judicature.

CENTRAL OFFICE.

REQUISITION FOR SEARCH.

To the Registrar of Bills of Sale,
  Royal Courts of Justice, London.
In the matter of *A. B.* and *C. D.*

Pursuant to sec. 2 of the Conveyancing Act, 1882, search for instruments registered or re-registered as bills of sale during the period from   18   to   18   both inclusive, in the following name [*or* names].

Surname.	Christian Name or Names.	Usual or last known place of abode.	Title, Trade, or Profession.

[*Add declaration, Form II.*]
[*State if an office copy of the certificate is desired, and whether it is to be sent by post or called for.*]

Signature, address, and ⎫
  description of person ⎬
  requiring the search ⎭
Dated

No. 15.

FORM VIII.[a]

Certificate of Search by the Registrar of Bills of Sale, under the Conveyancing Act, 1882.

Supreme Court of Judicature.

CENTRAL OFFICE,
  Bills of Sale Department.

CERTIFICATE OF SEARCH PURSUANT TO SEC. 2 OF THE CONVEYANCING ACT, 1882.

In the matter of *A. B.* and *C. D.*

This is to certify that a search has been diligently made in the Register of Bills of Sale in the name [*or* names] of

(a) App. to Rules under sec. 2, Conveyancing Act, 1882.

for the period from 18 18 both inclusive,
and that no instrument has been registered or re-registered as a bill
of sale in that name [or in any one or more of those names during
that period,
or, and that except the described in the schedule hereto,
no instrument has been registered or re-registered as a bill of sale
in that name [or in any one or more of those names] during the
period aforesaid.

THE SCHEDULE.

Dated .

No. 16.

FORM XI.(a)

Requisition for Continuation of Search under the Conveyancing Act, 1882.

Supreme Court of Judicature.

CENTRAL OFFICE.

Requisition for continuation of Search.

To the Clerk of Enrolments
or The Registrar of Royal Courts of Justice,
London, W.C.

In the matter of A. B. and C.D.

Pursuant to sec. 2 of the Conveyancing Act, 1882, continue
the search for [ ], made pursuant to the requisition dated
the day of 18 , in the name [or names] of
from the day of to the day of 18
both inclusive.

Signature, address, and
description of person
requiring the search

Dated .

No. 17.

FORM XII.(a)

Certificate of result of Continued Search under the Conveyancing Act, 1882, s. 2, to be endorsed on original Certificate.

This is to certify that the search [or searches] mentioned in the
within written certificate has [or have] been diligently continued to
the day of 18 , and that up to and including that
date [except the mentioned in the schedule hereto (these
words to be omitted where nothing is found) , no deed or other document has been enrolled, or no instrument has been registered, or
re-registered, as a bill of sale, or no certificate has been filed, or no
judgment, revival, decree, order, rule, lis pendens, judgment at the
suit of the crown, statute, recognizance, Crown bond, inquisition,
acceptance of office, execution or annuity, has been registered or
re-registered in the within-mentioned name [or in any one or more
of the within-mentioned names .

Dated

APPENDIX.

Part III.

No. 1.

Statutory Form of Bill of Sale.

See Schedule, Bills of Sale Act (1878) Amendment A t, 1882, p. 26o

---

No. 2.

Bill of Sale—Concise Form.

𝕿𝖍𝖎𝖘 𝕴𝖓𝖉𝖊𝖓𝖙𝖚𝖗𝖊 made the   day of
One thousand eight hundred and   Between
of
of the one part and   of
of the other part Witnesseth that in consideration of the sum of
£   now paid to   by
the receipt of which the said   hereby
acknowledges he the said   doth hereby
assign unto   his executors administrators and assigns
all and singular the several chattels and things specifically
described in the schedule hereto annexed by way of security for the
payment of the sum of £   and interest thereon
at the rate of   per cent. per annum And the said
                    doth further agree and declare that he will duly pay
to the said   the principal sum aforesaid
together with the interest then due by equal   payments
of £   on the   day of   and the   day of
                    And the said   doth also agree with the said
that he will at all times during the continuance of this security
insure and keep the said chattels and things insured against loss
or damage by fire in the sum of   pounds at the least
And will pay all rent to become due and payable by him in respect
of the premises on which the said chattels and things or any of them
now are   Provided always that the chattels hereby assigned shall
not be liable to seizure or to be taken possession of by the said
                    for any cause other than those specified in section seven of
the Bills of Sale Act (1878) Amendment Act 1882 In witness
whereof the parties to these presents have hereunto set their hands
and seals the day and year first above written.   ·

Signed and sealed by the said
in the presence of me

    "*Add witness's
    name, address
    and description.*]

THE SCHEDULE.

No. 3.

Bill of Sale—Concise Form, with power of Sale.

This Indenture made the   day of
One thousand eight hundred and   Between
                              of
of the one part and   of
of the other part Witnesseth that in consideration of the sum of
£   now paid to
by   the receipt of which the said   hereby
acknowledges he the said   doth hereby
assign unto   his executors administrators and assigns
all and singular the several chattels and things specifically
described in the schedule hereto annexed by way of security for the
payment of the sum of £   and interest thereon
at the rate of   per cent. per annum And the said
                    doth further agree and declare that he will duly pay
to the said   the principal sum aforesaid
together with the interest then due on the   day of
And the said   doth also agree with the said
that he will at all times during the continuance of this security
insure and keep the said chattels and things insured against loss
or damage by fire in the sum of £   at the least in
the joint names of the said   and the said[a]
And will punctually pay all rent to become due and payable by
him in respect of the premises on which the said chattels and
things or any of them are. And also that in any of the events
specified as causes of seizure in section seven of the Bills of
Sale Act (1878) Amendment Act. 1882, it shall be lawful for
the said   his servants or agents to enter
into and upon the premises on which the said chattels and things
or any of them are and to seize or take possession of the said
chattels and things and after the expiration of five clear days from
the day of so seizing or taking possession to remove and sell the
same Provided always that the chattels hereby assigned shall
not be liable to seizure or to be taken possession of by the
said   for any cause other than those specified
in section seven of the Bills of Sale Act (1878) Amendment Act

(a) Where a bill of sale contained a covenant to insure, but no provision for
application of the policy moneys in case of fire, the mortgagees were held to have no
claim to the benefit of the policy. (Lees *v.* Whiteley, 2 Eq. 143; 35 L. J. Ch. 412; 14 W.
R. 534; 14 L. T. N. S. 472.) By the Conveyancing Act, 1881, sec. 23 (4) all money
received on an insurance effected under the mortgage deed or under the Act shall, if
the mortgagee so requires, be applied by the mortgagor in making good the loss or
damage in respect of which the money is received; (b) without prejudice to any obligation to the contrary imposed by law, or by special contract, a mortgagee may require
that all money received on an insurance be applied in or towards discharge of the
money due under his mortgage.

1882 In witness whereof the parties to these presents have hereunto set their hands and seals the day and year first above written

Add witness's name, address and description.

Signed and sealed by the said

in the presence of me

THE SCHEDULE.

No. 4.

Absolute Bill of Sale.—Concise Form.[a]

This Indenture made the   day of

One thousand eight hundred and

Between

of the one part and

of the other part   Whereas the said

has agreed with the said

for the absolute sale to him of the

                 and effects specified in the

schedule hereunder written for the sum of

Now this indenture witnesseth that in pursuance of the said

agreement and in consideration of the sum of

                 to the

said   paid by the said

                 (the receipt of which

the said   hereby

acknowledges) he the said

as beneficial owner doth hereby convey and assign unto the said

            all and singular the said   and effects

                 To hold

the said   and effects

unto the said

            his executors administrators and assigns absolutely

In witness whereof the said parties to these presents have hereunto set their hands and seals the day and year first above written·

Signed sealed and delivered by

the said

in my presence the effect of the

above-written bill of sale having

been explained to the said

            before his execution

thereof by me the attesting soli-

citor.

THE SCHEDULE.

(a) Absolute bills of sale are still governed by the principal Act, and would appear to require attestation and registration. If given to secure the payment of money, though absolute in form, they would be void, as an infringement of sec. 9 of the Amendment Act.

No. 5.

Bill of Sale, from the Sheriff, of Goods taken in Execution. (a)

This Indenture made the   day of
One thousand eight hundred and   Between
                              of   Esquire, High
Sheriff of the county of   (hereinafter called the said
sheriff) of the one part and   of
(hereinafter called the purchaser) of the other part   Whereas a
writ of fieri facias issuing out of the   Division of Her
Majesty's High Court of Justice directed to the sheriff was
received at the office of the under-sheriff of the said county com-
manding the sheriff that he should cause to be levied of the
goods and chattels of   within his bailiwick a
certain debt of   which   had recovered
against him in the said division together with the sum of
for interest damages costs and charges which the said
had sustained and expended by reason of his suit   And whereas
the sheriff hath by virtue of the said writ seized and taken in
execution certain goods and chattels of the said
being in and upon the messuage buildings and premises now in the
occupation of the said   situate and being
in the county aforesaid and hath caused the same goods and
chattels to be appraised by   a person of
competent skill who hath valued the same at the sum of
And whereas [*recite order for private sale*]

Now this indenture witnesseth
that in consideration of the sum of   upon the execution of

(a) By sec. 145, B. A., 1883, where the sheriff sells the goods of a debtor under an
execution for a sum exceeding £20 (including legal incidental expenses), the sale shall,
unless the Court from which the process issued otherwise orders, be made by public
auction, and not by bill of sale or private contract, and shall be publicly advertised by
the sheriff on and during three days next preceding the day of sale. By sec. 12,
B. A. 1890, where the sheriff has notice of another execution or other executions, the
Court shall not consider an application for leave to sell privately until the notice
required by rules of Court has been given to the other execution creditor or creditors,
who may appear before the Court and be heard upon the application. R. S. C. Order 44.
Rules 8–14 prescribe the practice on applying for leave, and the notices required to
be given. A sale to which the debtor consents, without any order of the Court, is
until set aside valid against a subsequent execution (Crawshaw v. Harrison   1894 , 1
Q. B. 79 ; 63 L. J. Q. B. 94 ; 69 L. T. 880). A sheriff might sell the goods to the execution creditor ; and if they were valued and delivered to a purchaser in good faith, the
sale was valid without a bill of sale. (Herrnman v. Bowker, 11 Ex. 760 ; *ex parte*
Villars, *re* Rogers, L. R. 9 Ch. 432 ; 42 L. J. Bank. 76 ; 22 W. R. 663 ; 30 L. T. 348 .
A sale by the sheriff confers a valid title on the purchaser, which will not be affected
although the writ of execution be afterwards set aside (Manning's Case s Co., 91 &
Doe. v. Thorn, 1 M. & S. 425) ; unless, it seems, the warrant is illegal on the face of it
(Lock v. Sellwood, 1 Q. B. 736 ; but it was otherwise on a sale under an elegit, which
writ formerly applied to goods, where if the judgment was reversed restitution was
ordered (Goodyere v. Ince, Cro. Jac., 246), nor can a sheriff make a valid e xtract for
sale of the goods of a judgment debtor against whom he holds a writ of *fi. fa.*
until he has actually seized the goods (*exp.* Hall, *v.* Townsend, 14 Ch. D. 132 ; 28
W. R. 556 ; 42 L. T. 1021). A bill of sale from the sheriff, coupled with evidence of a
seizure, and acquiescence by the judgment debtor, is *prima facie* evidence of the
title of the bill of sale holder, though it would seem the judgment and writ of
execution should be produced (Hornidge v. Cooper, 27 L. J., Ex. 311 .

these presents by the purchaser paid to the sheriff the receipt
whereof is hereby acknowledged   He the sheriff as far as he
lawfully can or may by virtue of his said office of sheriff but no
further or otherwise doth hereby assign unto the purchaser his
executors administrators and assigns   All and singular the goods
chattels effects and things which have been taken in execution by
the sheriff by virtue of the said writ of fieri facias and which are
specifically described in the schedule or inventory hereunder
written or hereunto annexed   To hold the said goods chattels
effects and things unto the purchaser his executors administrators
and assigns absolutely   In witness whereof the said parties to
these presents have hereunto set their hands and seals the day
and year first above written.

THE SCHEDULE ABOVE REFERRED TO.

Signed with the name of
             sheriff of the county
of   , sealed with his seal
of office and delivered as his act
and deed by   under-
sheriff[a] of the said county in my
presence the effect of the above
written bill of sale having been
explained to the said
before his execution thereof by me
the attesting solicitor.

No. 6.

Assignment of Bill of Sale.

This Indenture made the   day of
One thousand eight hundred and   **Between**
                    of   of the one part
and   of   of the other
part Whereas   of   by an
indenture bearing date the   day of   did for
the consideration therein set forth assign unto the said
                    his executors administrators and assigns all and
singular the several chattels and things specifically described

----

(a) The bill of sale is sufficiently executed by either the under-sheriff or his
deputy (Cookson *v.* Fryer, 1 F. & F. 328); and where a bill of sale of goods taken
under a fieri facias is made by an officer of the sheriff, the Court will presume that he
was duly authorized to make it (Robinson *v.* Collingwood, 17 C. B. N. S. 777).

in the schedule thereto annexed by way of security for the payment of the sum of pounds and interest thereon at the rate of per cent. per annum And whereas there is now due to the said on the security of the said indenture the sum of but all interest thereon has been duly paid up to the day of last And whereas the said has agreed to pay to the said the said sum of upon having such assignment as is hereinafter contained of the said sum of and the securities for the same Now this indenture witnesseth that in pursuance of the said agreement and in consideration of nt or upon the execution of these presents by the said paid to the said the receipt whereof is hereby acknowledged He the said doth hereby assign unto the said his executors administrators and assigns All that the said principal sum of now remaining due and owing to the said as aforesaid on the security of the said indenture and the interest now due or to become due for the same And also all and singular the said several chattels and things assigned by the said recited indenture And all the estate right title interest claim and demand of him the said in to or upon the said premises or any part thereof To hold the same respectively unto the said his executors administrators and assigns Subject nevertheless to the proviso or right of redemption of the said several premises on payment by the said his executors or administrators of the said sum of with interest as aforesaid And the said doth hereby for himself his heirs executors and administrators covenant with the said his executors administrators and assigns that the said debt or sum of is still due and owing on the security of the said recited indenture And that he the said hath not done or suffered or been knowingly party or privy to any act deed matter or thing whereby the said several chattels and things hereinbefore expressed to be hereby assigned are is or may be impeached incumbered or affected in title or otherwise howsoever or whereby the said his executors administrators or assigns might or could be prevented from recovering the said sum of hereby assigned or any part thereof And the said doth hereby for himself his executors administrators and assigns covenant with the said his executors and administrators that he the said his executors administrators and assigns will at all times hereafter save harmless

and keep indemnified the said   his executors
and administrators of from and against all costs charges damages
and expenses whatsoever which shall or may become payable by
the said   his executors or administrators for
or by reason of any action or other proceeding which shall or
may be brought or prosecuted in respect of any act matter or
thing done or to be done committed or suffered in respect of the
said recited indenture or these presents In witness whereof the
said parties to these presents have hereunto set their hands and
seals the day and year first above written.

Signed sealed and delivered by ⎫
the said   in the ⎬
presence of   ⎭

Received the day and year first ⎫
above written of and from the   ⎪
above-named   ⎬ £
the sum of   being the   ⎪
consideration money above ex-   ⎪
pressed to be paid by him to me ⎭

Witness

No. 7.

CONTESTED CLAUSES.

Clauses in accordance with the Form.

Payment.

Assignment of chattels . . . to hold the same by way of security
for payment in the manner hereinafter appearing of the sum of £500 and
interest thereon at the rate of 60 per cent. per annum. And the mortgagor doth further agree and declare that he will duly pay to the
mortgagee the principal sum aforesaid, with the interest then due, by
twelve equal monthly payments of £41 13s. 4d. on the . . . . now
next, and on the . . . . of each and every succeeding month until
the whole of the said sum and interest shall be fully paid. And in
default of payment of any instalment then that the mortgagor will pay
interest thereon at the rate aforesaid from the date when such instalment
shall become due until full payment thereof.[a]

(a) Goldstrom v. Tallerman, 18 Q. B. D. 1. A covenant to this effect is necessary
where the rate of interest exceeds five per cent., for in the absence of a covenant to
pay interest on the principal sum, or any part of it remaining unpaid after the day
named for repayment, interest is recoverable only as damages, and will be limited to five
per cent. (Goodchap v. Roberts, 14 Ch. D. 49; 42 L. T. 666; 28 W. R. 870.) Formerly
there might have been added a covenant that interest in arrear might be capitalized
at half-yearly rests, the bill of sale thus becoming a security for compound interest
for the period for which interest was in arrear. (Clarkson v. Henderson, 28 W. R. 907
49 L. J. Ch. 289; 43 L. T. 20.)

Agreement to pay principal sum, with interest, at the rate of 1s. in the £ per month, by equal monthly payments, and that if default shall be made in any payment when it becomes due the whole of the principal (or so much thereof as shall then remain unpaid) together with the interest then due shall at once become payable . . . . [a]

Bill of sale by way of security for the payment of £500 and interest thereon at the rate of 9d. in the £ per month. Agreement to pay the principal sum aforesaid, together with the interest then due by monthly payments of £30 on the 18th day of every month, the first payment to be made on the 18th day of July next. [b]

Agreement to pay principal sum by monthly instalments, and the Payment. balance with interest at a day named and . . . . will so long as the principal sum aforesaid or any part thereof shall remain unpaid at the time hereinbefore appointed for payment of the said instalments pay interest after the rate aforesaid upon the said debt, or upon so much thereof as shall for the time being remain unpaid. [c]

Bill of sale, dated 6th March, 1889, by mortgagors to mortgagees, in consideration of £30 then paid . . . by way of security for the payment of the sum of £30, and interest thereon, at the rate of £60 per cent. per annum. . . . . Agreement by mortgagors that they or one of them will duly pay to the mortgagees the principal sum aforesaid by the instalments following, that is to say, the sum of £5 on the 9th day of March instant, £2 on the 6th day of April, 1889, and the sum of £2 on the 6th day of every succeeding month until the 6th day of February, 1890, and the balance of the said principal sum on the 6th day of March, 1890. And will on the 6th day of March, 1890, also pay the interest which shall have accrued, at the rate aforesaid, upon the said principal sum. And in case default shall be made in payment of any of the said instalments of the principal sum the same shall, until payment, continue to bear interest at the rate aforesaid. . . . . [*Power of seizure on default in payment of the money thereby secured or for other causes in sec. 7.* . . . . . *Stat for proviso*]. [d]

Bill of sale, dated 26th September, 1887, to secure £50 and interest at £5 per cent. per month. . . . Agreement by grantor . . . that he will pay to the grantee the principal sum aforesaid, together with the interest then due as follows: the sum of £2 10s. on the 26th October, 1887, and the like sum of £2 10s. on the 26th of each and every succeeding month until the 26th September, 1889, when the balance and interest as aforesaid is to be paid. [e]

(a) Lumley v. Simmons, 34 Ch. D. 698. A clause making the whole debt due on failure to pay an instalment does not operate as a penalty. (Wallingford v. Mutual Society, 5 App. Cases, 685.)

(b) Simmons v. Woodward [1892], A. C. 100.

(c) Exp. Rawlings, re Cleaver, 18 Q. B. D. 489.

(d) Hazlewood v. Consolidated Credit Co., 64 L. T. 71; 25 Q. B. D. 575.

(e) Edwards v. Marston [1891], 1 Q. B. 225.

Bill of sale, dated 13th January, 1892, to secure the repayment of £200 and interest thereon at the rate of 6d. in the £ per month. . . . Agreement by grantor that . . . he will pay the principal sum aforesaid, together with the interest then due by weekly payments of £2 6s. 2d., the first of such payments to be made on January 25th instant, and the like payment to be made on the Monday of each and every succeeding week until the whole be paid.[a]

Bill of sale by way of security for the payment in manner thereinafter appearing of the sum of £150 and interest thereon at the rate of £4 per cent. per annum. . . . Agreement by grantor . . . that he will duly pay to the grantee the principal sum aforesaid by equal yearly payments of £30 on May 20th, 1893, and on May 20th in each succeeding year until the whole of the principal and interest is fully paid, and will also pay to the grantee interest on the said sum of £150 at the rate of £4 per cent. per annum, such interest being payable by quarterly instalments on August 20th, November 20th, February 20th, and May 20th in each year, the first being payable on August 20th, 1892. . . . . . [b]

Agreement to pay principal sum together with the interest then due on the . . . . provided always that if the grantor shall not break any of the covenants herein contained and shall not become bankrupt and shall pay the principal sum and interest by equal monthly instalments on the . . day of each month, the grantee shall accept payment by such instalments.[c]

Agreement to pay principal sum, together with the interest then due, by equal payments on the 5th July and 5th January. [*Not stating year*].[d]

Agreement by grantor . . . . . that he will at all times during the continuance of the security duly pay all rent, rates and taxes payable in respect of the said premises, and also all premiums and other sums necessary for insuring and keeping insured the said chattels against loss or damage by fire in . . . . . and forthwith after every payment in respect of such insurance produce, and, if required, deliver to the grantee the receipt or voucher for the same. . . . . Agreement that, subject to the provisions of the Act, the chattels may be seized . . . . . if the grantor shall make default in the performance of any covenant or agreement on his part herein contained [*statutory proviso*].[e]

Agreement by grantor to insure. . . . . And that if he shall not, without reasonable excuse, upon demand in writing by the mortgagee, produce to him the last receipts of the grantor for rent, rates and taxes, or the said policy of insurance, or the receipt for the current premiums thereon, it shall be lawful for the mortgagee to seize [*statutory proviso*].[f]

(a) *Exp.* Hasluck, *re* Bargen [1894], 1 Q. B. 444.
(b) Weardale Coal and Iron Co., *v.* Hodson [1894], 1 Q. B. 598.
(c) *Exp.* Payne, *re* Coton, 4 Mor. 90.
(d) Grannell *v.* Monck, 24 L. R. Ir. 241.
(e) Hammond *v.* Hocking, 12 Q. B. D. 291.
(f) Duff *v.* Valentine, W. N. 1883, 225.

Agreement by grantor . . . . that he will pay all rent, rates, taxes, assessments or outgoings, and will take receipts therefor, and will on demand in writing, produce to the grantee or his authorized agent the said receipts . . . . [*statutory proviso* .*]

Agreement by grantor . . . . to pay rent, rates and taxes of any message or premises whereon the assigned chattels may be. And also to keep the chattels insured . . . . And that on default it shall be lawful for the grantee to keep on foot the said insurance and charge the cost thereof and interest at the rate of   per annum to the grantor, and the same shall be considered as included in this security. And that the grantee may pay all rent, rates, taxes, charges, assessments and outgoings at any time due and payable in respect of the premises in which the goods may be, and thereupon all such payments, together with interest at   per cent. per annum, shall be a charge upon the chattels assigned, which shall not be redeemed until full payment of all such sums and interest . . . . And that the grantor will on demand repay all such premiums and payments and all costs, charges and expenses incurred by the grantee in manner aforesaid, with interest thereon at the rate last aforesaid. [b]

Mortgage's payments

Agreement by the grantor that he will at all times during the continuance of the security keep the chattels assigned insured . . . . and will pay all premiums necessary for effecting and keeping up the said insurance, and will on demand produce to the grantee the policy or policies of such insurance, and the receipt for every such payment, and that if default shall at any time be made by the grantor in effecting or keeping up such insurance, it shall be lawful for the grantee to insure and keep insured the chattels in . . . . . and that all moneys expended by him for that purpose, together with interest thereon, at the rate of 5 per cent. per annum, from the time of the same having been expended, shall on demand be repaid to him by the grantor, and until such repayment shall be a charge upon all the premises hereby mortgaged.   Provided always, &c. [*statutory proviso*]. [c]

Agreement by grantor that he will insure the said chattels and things in the sum of £1,000, and will pay the premiums on such insurance, and that in case of default the grantee shall be at liberty to keep the said chattels and things insured, and that all moneys expended by the grantee for such purpose, together with interest thereon at £5 per cent., shall be repaid by the grantor upon demand, and until such payment shall be a charge upon the chattels and things hereby assigned . . . .   Power of seizure . . . . on default of payment of the sum or sums of money hereby secured at the time hereinbefore appointed for payment . . . . . [*statutory proviso*]. [d]

(a) Turner v. Culpan, 36 W. R. 278.
(b) Goldstrom v. Tallerman, 18 Q. B. D. 1 . ; f. Real, &c., Advance C . . Comrs. 18 Q. B. D. 304.
(c) *Exp.* Stanford, *re* Barber, 17 Q. B. D. 259.
(d) Briggs v. Pike, 66 L. T. 637; 61 L. J. Q. B. 418.

Maintenance of security.

Agreement by grantor from time to time during continuance of the security to replace such of the said chattels and things as shall be worn out by other articles of equal value so as to keep up the total value of the said chattels and things to the present value.[a]

And will not permit or suffer the said chattels and things or any part thereof to be destroyed or injured, or to deteriorate subsequently to the execution of these presents in a greater degree than they would deteriorate by reasonable use and wear thereof, and will whenever any of the said chattels and things are destroyed, injured or deteriorated, forthwith replace, repair and make good the same . . . . [*Power of seizure on default, inter alia, of performance of any of the covenants.*][b]

And so long as any money shall remain owing on this security, will not remove any of the said chattels and things from the said dwelling-house in the schedule mentioned, without the previous consent of the grantee, except for necessary repairs, and will replace any articles damaged or worn out with others of equal value, to be included in this security.[c]

. . . . And will keep the said chattels in good and substantial repair, and in perfect working order, and insured . . . . and will duly and punctually pay all premiums or moneys necessary for effecting and keeping up the insurance on the first day on which the same ought to be paid, and will, on demand, produce to the grantee the policy or policies of insurance and the receipt for every payment, and that if default shall at any time be made by the grantor in effecting or keeping up such insurance, or in keeping the chattels or any part thereof in good and substantial repair, it shall be lawful for the grantee to insure and keep insured the chattels or any part thereof in any sum not exceeding . . . . . and to repair and keep in repair the same, and to put the same in perfect working order, and to enter upon the premises on which the chattels may be for the time being for that purpose, and that all moneys expended by the grantee for such purpose, together with interest at £5 per cent. per annum, from the time of the same having been expended, shall, on demand, be repaid to the grantee by the grantor, and until such repayment shall be a charge upon the chattels. And [*power to seize on events mentioned in sec. 7 and proviso*].[d]

And will not without consent remove or suffer to be removed any of the said chattels and things, or do any act whereby they may be prejudicially affected. And that the grantee may at reasonable times enter on the premises, to view, inspect, and take inventories of the chattels.

. . . . And will not do anything whereby he . . . . may have execution levied, but will preserve and keep the said chattels and things

(a) Consolidated Credit and Mortgage Corporation v. Gosney, 16 Q. B. D. 24.
(b) Furber v. Cobb, 18 Q. B. D. 494.
(c) Seed v. Bradley [1894], 1 Q. B. 319.
(d) Topley v. Corsbie, 20 Q. B. D. 350.

safe and uninjured [*power to seize for statutory causes*]. Provided that the chattels and things shall be held and possessed by the grantor without any let or hindrance from the grantee, until taken possession of in consequence of the breach of any of the covenants herein contained, and that the same shall not be liable [*statutory proviso*].[a]

Power of seizure . . . . . . in case the grantor shall do or suffer any matter or thing whereby he shall become a bankrupt. . . . .[b]

Agreement for further assurance by the grantor, and every other person or persons claiming by or through him any interest in the said chattels and things or any of them. . . . .[c]

Agreement for further assurance by the grantor for himself and every other person claiming any interest in the chattels assigned or any of them.[d]

Provided always that it shall be lawful for the mortgagees at any time or times hereafter for any of the causes specified in the seventh section of the . . . Act, but for no other causes whatever, without giving any previous notice to the mortgagor of their intention in that behalf to take possession of all or any of the fixtures, chattels and things for the time being subject to this security, and for that purpose, or for any other purpose connected therewith, to have at all reasonable times full liberty of ingress, egress and regress into and from any of the premises wherein the same may be, and every part thereof, and, if necessary, to break open any outer or inner doors and windows thereof, in order to obtain admittance for that purpose, and to retain possession of all or any of the said fixtures, chattels or things, either there or in any other place to which they may think fit to remove them, so long as they may think fit, or at any time to give up and retake and resume such possession without being responsible for any loss or damage which may arise thereby to the mortgagor, but until possession shall be so taken or retaken, the said fixtures, chattels and things shall remain in the possession of the mortgagor or his assigns.[e]

Power of seizure.

. . . . And . . . that the power of sale conferred upon the mortgagees by the Conveyancing and Law of Property Act, 1881, shall be exercisable by them in every respect as if the twentieth section of the said Act had not been enacted, and the mortgagees shall stand possessed of the proceeds of any sale made by them upon trust to retain thereout the said principal sum, or so much thereof as may for the time being

Power of sale.

(a) *Exp.* Pope *re* Paxton, 60 L. T. 428.

(b) *Exp.* Allam, *re* Munday, 14 Q. B. D. 43 ; *exp.* Pope *re* Paxton, 60 L. T. 428 ; cf. *exp.* Pearce, 25 Ch. D. 656.

(c) *Exp.* Rawlings, *re* Cleaver, 18 Q. B. D. 489.

(d) Setwick *v.* Hillier, 31 S. J. 601 ; Tillett *v.* Goshee, Ril. 1887, Mart. w A Ca. e, JJ. (MS. note) ; cf. Liverpool, &c., Co. *v.* Richardson, 2 T. L. R. 692.

(e) *Exp.* Official Receiver, *re* Morritt, 18 Q. B. D. 222.

remain unpaid, and the interest then due, together with all costs, charges, payments and expenses incurred, made or sustained by the mortgagees in or about entering upon the said premises, and in discharging any distress, execution or other incumbrance on the said fixtures, chattels or things, or any of them, and seizing, taking, retaining and keeping possession thereof, and in or about the carriage, removal, warehousing or sale (including the cost of inventories, catalogues, or advertising) thereof, or any part thereof, and to pay over the surplus (if any) of such proceeds to the mortgagor.[a]

Power of seizure and sale.

And that . . . . it shall be lawful for the mortgagees, their servants or agents, to enter into or upon the premises in which the said chattels and things or any of them are or shall be, and to seize or take possession of the whole or any part thereof, and after the expiration of five clear days from the day of seizing or taking possession, to remove, sell and dispose of the same, or any part thereof, for such price or prices as can reasonably be obtained, either by public auction or private contract, and out of the sale-moneys to retain the principal sum aforesaid, or so much thereof as for the time being may remain unpaid, and the interest then due, together with all costs, charges, payments and expenses incurred, made or sustained in and about entering upon the said premises, and in discharging any distress, execution or other incumbrance on the said chattels or things or any of them, and seizing, taking, retaining and maintaining possession of the same or any part thereof, and in and about the carriage, removal, warehousing, valuing or sale (including the cost of inventories, catalogues or advertising) of the said chattels and things, or any part thereof, and to pay over the surplus, if any, to the mortgagor . . . . And that this assignment shall be void if the principal sum aforesaid, together with the interest thereon, shall be paid to the mortgagees as herein provided.[b]

And with power for the grantee to sell the said chattels and things by private treaty or public auction on or off the premises . . . .[c]

Agreement that upon payment of the principal sum and interest and any expenses which the grantee may incur in lawfully seizing and removing the chattels assigned, and any cost which he may properly incur in defending and maintaining his rights hereunder, this security shall be void. And further, that if the grantee shall become entitled to seize the chattels he and his agents may enter and remain upon any premises where the chattels may be, and if necessary break open doors and windows in order to obtain admission, and after the expiration of five clear days from the day of seizure, may remove the chattels and sell them by public auction or private contract, and retain out of the proceeds so much of the principal sum as may then remain unpaid, and the interest then due, and all costs

Power of forcible entry.

(a) *Exp.* Official Receiver, *re* Morritt, 18 Q. B. D. 222.
(b) *Exp.* Rawlings, *re* Cleaver, 16 Q. B. D. 489.
(c) Bourne *v.* Wall, 39 W. R. 510.

and expenses which he may incur as aforesaid, and also any rent, rates and taxes which he may pay in respect of the premises where the said chattels may be.[a]

Agreements by grantor . . . that he will during the continuance of the security duly and regularly pay the rent, rates and taxes payable by him in respect of the premises, and produce to the grantee upon demand in writing the last receipts for such rent, rates and taxes. Provided *statutory proviso*] that is to say [*statutory causes of seizure set out*] Provided further that if the chattels and things hereby assigned shall be seized or taken possession of by the grantee in consequence of the breach of any of the covenants herein contained, the grantee shall be at liberty to remove or sell the same or any part thereof by public auction or private contract, at the expiration of five clear days from the day of such seizure or taking possession.[b]

Clauses not in accordance with the Form.

Assignment of all and singular the chattels and things specifically described in the schedule hereto annexed, together with all other chattels and things the property of the mortgagor now in and about the premises . . . . aforesaid. And also all chattels and things which may at any time during the continuance of this security be in or about the same or any other premises of the mortgagor (to which the said chattels and things or any part thereof may have been removed) whether brought there in substitution for or renewal of or in addition to the chattels and things hereby assigned . . . . [c]

Assignment not specific.

Assignment of all and singular the chattels and things specifically described in the schedule hereto annexed, and also all other chattels and things which may at any time during the continuance of this security be substituted for them or any of them pursuant to the covenant hereinafter contained. [No covenant for substitution inserted. Power to seize, &c., for causes specified in sec. 7. [d]

Assignment of all and singular the several chattels and things specifically described in the schedule hereto annexed, now in and about the said farm and premises, together with all the tenant-right valuation, goodwill, tillages and interest of the mortgagor in and to the said farm and premises. . . . [e]

Assignment by way of security for payment in manner hereinafter appearing of £115, together with the sum of £15 for agreed amount of interest and bonus, making together the sum of £130 . . . . Agreement

Bonus.

(a) Lumley v. Simmons, 34 Ch. D. 698.
(b) Weardale Coal and Iron Co. v. Hodson [1894], 1 Q. B. 598.
(c) Thomas v. Kelly, 13 App. Cases 506.
(d) Hadden v. Oppenheim, 60 L. T. 962.
(e) Cochrane v. Entwistle, 25 Q. B. D. 116.

to pay £130 by twelve equal monthly instalments of £10 16s. 8d., at specified dates. Provided always [*statutory proviso*]. Also that if the said chattels and things or any of them shall be seized or taken possession of in consequence of a breach of any of the covenants herein contained, the grantee shall be at liberty to remove or sell the same or any part thereof at the expiration of five clear days from the day of seizure. . . . . . [a]

Assignment by way of security for the payment of the sum of £50 and interest thereon at the rate of £17 10s. for three years. . . Agreement to pay the principal sum aforesaid, together with the interest then due by 36 equal monthly instalments of £1 17s. 6d. . . . . [b]

Interest.

Agreement for payment of the principal sum and . . . . . of the capitalized interest thereon by instalments as therein mentioned, being at the rate of sixty per cent. per annum. . . . . . Declaration that on breach of any of the covenants, all moneys secured by the bill of sale shall immediately become due and be forthwith paid. Provided, &c. [c]

Assignment by way of security for payment of £350 and interest thereon at the rate of £15 per cent. per annum payable weekly. Agreement that the grantor will duly pay to the grantee the principal sum aforesaid including the interest then due by equal weekly payments of £5 on the Tuesday of each and every week commencing September 4th, 1888, and from and after the before-mentioned date so long as any of the principal sum shall remain unpaid will pay interest thereon at the rate aforesaid on the 4th day of each and every month as the said principal moneys become due. [d]

Bill of sale between grantor and four sets of grantees to secure different debts owing to each at different times, with agreements with each set of grantees to pay their respective debts . . . . . declaration that in case of default in payment of any sum thereby secured, or of any other default, it shall be lawful for the grantees to seize and sell the goods assigned. [e]

Assignment as "beneficial owner." [f]

Time of payment.

Agreement to pay the principal sum and interest then due within 24 hours after demand in writing. . . . . . [g]

Similar agreement to pay 48 hours after demand. [h]

Similar agreement to pay upon demand in writing . . . [i]

(a) Myers v. Elliott, 16 Q. B. D. 526.

(b) Blankenstein v. Robertson, 24 Q. B. D. 543.

(c) Davis v. Burton, 10 Q. B. D. 414; 11 Q. B. D. 537; Roe v. Mutual Loan Association, 56 L. T. 631.

(d) Curtis v. National Bank of Wales, 5 T. L. R. 338.

(e) Melville v. Stringer, 13 Q. B. D. 392.

(f) Exp. Stanford, re Barber, 17 Q. B. D. 259.

(g) Clemson v. Townsend, 1 Cababé & Ellis, 418.

(h) Bishop v. Beale, 1 T. L. R. 140.

(i) Hetherington v. Groome, 13 Q. B. D. 789; Mackay v. Merritt, 34 W. R. 433.

Bill of sale by way of indemnity, grantor agreeing that if the grantee
shall be obliged to pay the debt, the grantor will repay the amount to
the grantee within seven days after demand in writing . . . . . with
power in default to seize and sell the goods.[a]

In consideration of the grantee having at the grantor's request become
guarantee . . . . . and of £40 money owing by the grantor to the
grantee, the grantor assigned chattels, &c., by way of security for the
payment of the sum of £40, and for any moneys the grantee might be
called upon to pay in respect of the said guarantee . . . . . and
interest thereon at the rate of 5 per cent. per annum. And the grantor
agreed to pay to the grantee the principal sum aforesaid, and any further
sums as aforesaid, together with the interest then due, by monthly payments of £2 on the first of every month. . . . .[b]

Agreement that grantor will on demand produce to the grantee his
last receipts for rent, rates and taxes, and will keep the assigned premises
insured, and on demand produce to the grantee the receipt for the current
premium for such insurance, and that in case he shall make default in
performance of any of the covenants or shall become bankrupt or enter
into liquidation or compound with his creditors, the principal sum aforesaid, together with the interest then due, shall become immediately
payable without the necessity for any demand of payment [statutory
proviso].[c]

Agreement by grantor to pay rent, rates, taxes, or other impositions
. . . . and forthwith after every payment to produce and deliver to
the mortgagee the receipts for the same . . . . Power of seizure .
or if the grantor shall make default in the performance of any of the
covenants therein contained, or commit any breach thereof. .
[statutory proviso].[d]

Agreement by mortgagor . . . . to deliver to the mortgagee the
receipts for rent, rates, and other impositions, payable in respect of
the premises, when demanded, in writing or otherwise . . . And
further that all the foregoing agreements are necessary for maintaining
the security [statutory proviso].[e]

Covenant to pay principal and interest by monthly instalments, until
the principal and interest shall be fully paid, and also so long as the
principal sum shall remain unpaid to pay interest upon the said debt [

(a) Sibley v. Higgs, 15 Q. B. D. 619.
(b) Hughes v. Little, 18 Q. B. D. 32; 17 Q. B. D. 204.
(c) Barr v. Kingsford, 56 L. T. 861.
(d) Exp. Pearce, re Williams, 35 Ch. D. 656.
(e) Davis v. Burton, 10 Q. B. D. 414; 11 Q. B. D. 537, cf. Furber v. Cobb, 18 Q. B. D. 404.
(f) Dresser v. Townsend, 81 L. T. J. 230, cf. exp. Rawlings, re Cleaver, 18 Q. B. D. 489.

Payments.

Agreement to pay rent, rates, taxes and outgoings of the premises where the chattels or things are or shall be within seven days after the same respectively become payable . . . . . and that if the grantor shall neglect or refuse to pay the said rent, rates, taxes and outgoings, within the said seven days or on the expiration thereof, or to produce to the mortgagee the respective receipts for such payments, it shall be lawful for the grantee, if he shall think fit, to pay any rent, rates, taxes, and outgoings which may then be due and owing, and all sums of money so paid by the grantee, together with interest thereon at the rate aforesaid, computed from the day of payment up to the actual day of repayment shall be charged on the chattels and things, and shall be recoverable in the same manner as the principal moneys and interest thereby secured. And further, that the chattels and things shall be liable to seizure for any of the causes specified in section seven of the Bills of Sale Act (1878) Amendment Act, 1882. Provided [*statutory proviso*].[a]

Agreement for further assurance by the grantor for himself and every other person claiming any interest in the chattels assigned or any of them. . . . . .[b]

After reciting a certain indenture, agreement by grantor to perform the covenants and stipulations contained in the said recited indenture. . . . . [*not appearing in Bill of Sale*].[c]

Agreement to pay all . . . . . interest on mortgages, if any, payable in respect of the premises where the goods assigned now are or may be removed to with the grantor's consent . . . . Declaration that on the moneys secured being paid or satisfied the indenture and any document signed by the grantor relating to the loan shall remain in the custody of and be the property of the mortgagee.[d]

. . . . . Power of seizure if the grantor shall remove, or suffer the said chattels, and things, or any of them, to be removed from the premises. . . . . [*statutory proviso*].[e]

. . . . . Power of seizure if the grantor shall do or suffer any matter or thing whereby he shall render himself liable to become a bankrupt. . . . .[f]

Power of seizure.

Power of seizure if the grantor shall take the benefit of any Bankruptcy Act. . . . .[g]

(a) Real and Personal Advance Co. v. Clears, 20 Q. B. D. 304; Bianchi v. Offord, 17 Q. B. D. 484.
(b) Liverpool Commercial Investment Society v. Richardson, 55 L. J. Q. B. 455 n.; not followed, Sedwick v. Hillier, 31 S. J. 661.
(c) Lee v. Barnes, 17 Q. B. D. 77.
(d) Watson v. Strickland, 19 Q. B. D. 391.
(e) Exp. Pearce, re Williams, 25 Ch. D. 656; cf. Furber v. Cobb, 18 Q. B. D. 404.
(f) Exp. Pearce, re Williams, 25 Ch. D. 656; cf. exp. Allam re Munday, 14 Q. B. D. 43.
(g) Gilroy v. Bowey, 59 L. T. 223.

Power of sale in events specified as causes of seizure in section seven Power of sale.
of Act . . . . . proviso that upon any such sale the purchaser shall
not be bound to see or inquire whether any such default has been made as
aforesaid. . . . .[a]

Agreement that upon a sale by the mortgagee the receipt or receipts
of the mortgagee for the purchase-money shall be sufficient discharge to
all and every purchaser or purchasers, who shall not be bound to see to the
application thereof by the mortgagee.[b]

Power to mortgagee to sell the goods assigned, or to have them valued
and to purchase them at such valuation, and receive the moneys to arise
from such sale or valuation. . . . . .[c]

. . . . . . That the mortgagee may for the purpose of any such sale,
or for preserving the security, or for any other purpose, at any time during
the subsistence of the security, affix such bills or placards having reference
to the said chattels and things as he may think fit on any premises for the
time being in the occupation of the grantor.[d]

Power out of sale-moneys to reimburse the mortgagees the costs,
charges and expenses of and attending such sale, including therein the full
charges and commission of the mortgagees as auctioneers, as if they were
selling on behalf of the grantor.[e]

Agreement that on sale the grantee should be at liberty to retain the
principal sum and interest, together with all expenses attending the
sale or otherwise incurred in relation to the security. . . .[f]

Agreement for payment of all rates, taxes, and outgoings whatsoever
in respect of the house and premises on which the said chattels and things
now are. And that in default of payment the grantee may pay the
same, and charge the amount to the grantor, and all expenses to which he
may be put, which said sums shall be added to and form part of the
security. . . . Power to seize for statutory causes. . .[g]

And also that it shall be lawful for the mortgagee to enter the premises
where the chattels may be, and to seize and take possession thereof, and
to sell the same or any part thereof, if the mortgagor shall make default
. . . . Provided, &c. [statutory proviso.][h]

(a) Bhaiberg v. Beckett, 18 Q. B. D. 96 ; Bhaiberg v. Parsons, 17 Q. B. D. 156.
(b) Gibbs v. Parsons, L. J. N. 1887, 96.
(c) Lyon c. Morris, 19 Q. B. D. 139.
(d) Bardell v. Daykin, 3 T. L. R. 526.
(e) Furber v. Cobb, 18 Q. B. D. 494.
(f) Calvert v. Thomas, 19 Q. B. D. 204.
(g) Macey v. Gilbert, 57 L. J. B. Q. 901.
(h) Hetherington v. Groome, 13 Q. B. D. 789.

INDEX.

— o —

320 INDEX.

PAGE

INDEX 335

v

U 2

www.ingramcontent.com/pod-product-compliance
Lightning Source LLC
Chambersburg PA
CBHW021115270326
41929CB00009B/889